The Haig Book of Village Cricket

The Haig Book of Village Cricket

JOHN FOGG

With a Foreword by
AIDAN CRAWLEY, M.B.E.
President, M.C.C.

PELHAM BOOKS

First published in Great Britain by PELHAM BOOKS LTD
52 Bedford Square, London, W.C.1
1972

© 1972 by John Fogg

All Rights Reserved. No part of this publication
may be reproduced, stored in a retrieval system,
or transmitted, in any form or by any means,
electronic, mechanical, photocopying, recording
or otherwise, without the prior permission
of the Copyright owner

7207 0467 7

*Set and printed in Great Britain by
Tonbridge Printers Ltd, Peach Hall Works, Tonbridge, Kent
in Baskerville eleven on twelve point on paper supplied by
P. F. Bingham Ltd, and bound by James Burn
at Esher, Surrey*

To
the hard-working, tea-making cricketing wives of Britain and to the nursing staff of King George V Ward, Middlesex Hospital, this volume is most humbly dedicated

Acknowledgements

Innumerable debts of gratitude are due to those unsung heroes of Club Cricket – the Honorary Historians, Secretaries, Treasurers, etc. for much of the information provided. Unfortunately they must still remain anonymous as they are much too numerous to list. I am also most grateful to my wife and Miss Janet Simpson for all their help in preparing the manuscript, and I owe a special vote of thanks to A. A. Thomas, my colleague on *The Daily Telegraph* for his research into the origins of cricket and also for his invaluable help with this book at a time when I was stricken by sickness. I am also indebted to Mrs Biddy Hiscox for her help in providing details which might otherwise not have been available.

Contents

	Foreword	13
1.	Troon take the title to Cornwall	15
2.	'The Haig' and the Villages	30
3.	The Enduring Village	87
4.	Village Cricket Tales – For After Dinner Speakers	103
5.	The Battle for the Group titles	112
6.	The Road to Lord's	167
7.	The Lord's Taverners, and the Village Clubs	194
8.	Results of the County Group matches	205
	Appendix – The Rules of The Haig National Village Cricket Championship	229

Illustrations

facing page

1. The solid silver Haig Trophy — 32
2. Announcing the birth of the Haig competition — 32
3. Meigle become Scotland's first village cricket champions — 33
4. Mr Walter Rustage mows the outfield of near Knutsford — 33
5. Brooksbottom C.C.'s ground at Summerseatt, Lancs. — 64
6. Cuckney, group champions of Notts. and Lincs. — 65
7. The Shamley Green team who won the Surrey group title — 65
8. Action at Greenmount's ground, outside Bury, Lancs. — 96
9. Birlingham consider their ground one of the prettiest in England — 97
10. Gowerton are justly proud of their ground — 97
11. The magnificent pavilion at Shrivenham's ground in Wiltshire — 128
12. P. Forty is presented with a Haig tie by Shrivenham's treasurer — 128
13. A match in progress at Littlewick Green, Berkshire — 129
14. Contrasts in light and shade at Stanway C.C.'s ground — 129
15. The bat swings mightily in the game between Kimbolton and Bradfield — 160
16. Mr Irvine presents one-gallon bottles of Haig to the captains of Warenford and Collingham — 160
17. Warenford's opening batsmen, brothers Ian and Alan Patterson — 161

Between pages 192 and 193

18. The Collingham team which played Astwood Bank in the semi-finals
19. Ian Redpath makes the presentation to John Yoxall, after Astwood Bank's semi-final victory
20. A catch 'behind' in the semi-final between Astwood Bank and Collingham
21. The Kent champions Linton Park
22. Grandstand village style at the semi-final at Troon
23. Linton Park's captain, J. Thirkell, signs autographs
24. Troon's J. Spry chaired from the field after his team's victory over Linton Park in the semi-final

facing page

25. Astwood Bank, losing finalists in the 1972 Haig	200
26. Champions Troon at cricket's 'headquarters'	200
27. Terry Carter hooks Morrall in his 79 not out in the final at Lord's	201
28. John Yoxall off-drives in the final	201
29. Troon triumphant! Terry Carter displays the Haig Trophy to happy Cornish supporters	201

Acknowledgements

The author's grateful thanks are due to the following whose pictures are reproduced in this book:
Manchester Evening News: 4, 5, 8;
Peter R. Morell: 6;
British Tourist Authority: 13, 14;
Photo-Centre: 16, 17;
Layland Ross Ltd 18, 19, 20, 25;
Grindley Studios Ltd: 21, 22, 23, 24;
Sport & General: 26, 27, 28, 29.
Also to Captain Jack Broome D.S.C., R.N. (Rtd) for his delightful drawings reproduced in Chapters Three and Seven

Foreword

by

Aidan Crawley M.B.E.

PRESIDENT, M.C.C.

The first national village cricket competition is certainly an occasion for reviewing the origins of the great game as well as reporting its present state of health; Mr Fogg has made the most of his opportunity. This book is full of fascinating historical detail and shows that cricket was played much earlier than is generally assumed. It has been part of the life of rural England since the Middle Ages.

Mr Fogg's researches into the state of many of the village clubs which entered the competition show the remarkable resilience of cricketers who refuse to allow the game to die even when the character of village life changes. One can only hope that the publication of this book will help satisfy the 'dearest wish' of that village which longs for a ground of its own. The good work done by the Lord's Taverners and The National Playing Fields Association gives one ground for hope.

The Haig National Village Cricket Championship, which Mr Fogg so faithfully records, is a landmark. It has shown that the grass roots of cricket are strong and that the spirit in which village cricket is played is every bit as keen as that of the Leagues or the first class game. Tens of thousands of families find it worth watching and supporting. My only regret is that no television cameras were available to catch the four-year-old boy being coached by his father and brothers in front of the pavilion at Lord's while we were waiting for the Final to begin.

I commend this book to every player and lover of the game.

CHAPTER ONE

Troon take Title to Cornwall

Troon, from Cornwall, emerged at the head of the 795 clubs who entered the first Haig National Village Championship. On September 9th the 5–2 on favourites defeated Astwood Bank, the Worcestershire side whose ground is a quarter-of-a-mile down the road in Warwickshire, by seven wickets in a lively high-scoring match at Lord's. In congratulating the sides, the President of M.C.C., Freddie Brown, the former England captain, spoke of 'this unique tournament which has captured the interest of all in the game', adding that he felt sure that in 1973 the number of entries would be much higher even than in this first highly successful venture.

Michael Henderson, Managing Director of John Haig & Co, Ltd., who presented the £1,000 silver trophy to Troon's captain, Terry Carter for a year's safe-keeping said that the competition had been far more successful than they had initially hoped and that already more than 750 clubs had applied to play for the 1973 title. Certainly the crowd (approaching 3,000) were well pleased with the match and the only sad note of the day was the train derailment 250 miles away at Dawlish which prevented some 600 Troon supporters from reaching London, causing some sharp words of protest to British Rail. When I spoke to Terry Carter the following night in Troon's crowded and jubilant bar he was in no doubt that his 600 Cornishmen would want 'to know the reason why'.

Troon's faithful, however, gained no little consolation from their splendid victory and from the fact that Terry Carter was chosen by Ian Redpath, the former Australian batsman, as the Cornishmen's outstanding player. Redpath named all-rounder Brian Spittle as the cricketer who had made the greatest contribution for Astwood Bank. The latter seemed, soon after tea, to be gaining a firm hold on the match until a fierce counter-assault by the Troon captain, aided by opening batsman Tommy Edwards and the 45-year-old Jimmy Vincent, snatched the trophy from the Midlanders.

Carter, however, put things more in perspective when he said after the game that people had overlooked the splendid straight bowling by Troon's Peter Johns who came back for his second spell with the score at 139-4. Johns took four wickets for 12 runs before the innings was closed, Astwood Bank scoring only 26 in the final eight overs. 'If they'd managed to cut loose then,' said Carter, 'we might have been pushed to get the runs.'

With plenty of firm driving by both sides the game had a freer flavour than many one-day affairs engaged in by the first-class counties. The wicket, pitched towards the Tavern side, carried enough pace to bring the ball on to the bat. The bowling generally contained some inevitable medium-paced sameness about it and the fielding, though handicapped for a long time by a damp ball and greasy outfield, was always willing and brave, and there were many fine stops. Alas, both sides seem to have adopted the bad habits of their seniors in the game, for they got through no more than 17 overs an hour on average – even Astwood Bank, who employed two slow bowlers. Television has indeed, done much to put cricket back on the map as a spectator sport, but someone, somewhere, just has to get the over-rate back to something like 20 in the hour, without restricting the bowlers' run-ups.

The ground had been soaked by almost continuous rain on the Friday, so that although play was due to begin at noon a start could not be made until 1.30 p.m. With greying skies and a chilly northerly wind blowing, conditions were anything but cheerful. The crowd on the other hand were bursting with good humour. Armed with rattles, hunting horns and handbells they noisily acclaimed every run, every ball that beat the bat and every good stop in the field.

Troon, winning the toss, sent in their opponents, gambling that nerves and the tension of the occasion might bring them early wickets with the new ball, although clearly the shine would be unlikely to last long with the very damp outfield. The pitch, which had been covered, looked bare of grass and proved amiable from the first ball.

Terry Carter led off with his two medium-paced left-handers, Johns (from the Pavilion End) and Edwards. Both began with maidens, so that the first runs did not come until the third over, when John Yoxall, the Astwood Bank captain, thumped Johns up the hill to the Grandstand boundary with a pedigree cover drive, a superb shot and one that probably gave him more pleasure than any other in his career. To produce a stroke of that quality on such an occasion is a memory for him to treasure, and intensely pleasured the Press Box pundits.

Yoxall immediately settled in; Robinson, more apprehensive, played and missed at Edwards, bowling from the Nursery End, several times before he began middling the ball, and picking up runs with tickles round the corner. Troon for several overs persisted with two slips, a gully and a short square-leg, to which both batsmen replied by stealing singles with short pushes into the covers. Yoxall, in addition, drove well on both sides of the wicket, and by the tenth over all but one slip of the close field had disappeared.

By then the score was 37–0, and Robinson was gaining in confidence and runs. He, too, began forcing into the covers and struck his first four that way off Edwards. The 50 came up in the thirteenth over, excellent going at any stage of the Haig and particularly in so august a final. Troon's gamble began to look a losing one as the runs flowed. Only the soaked outfield kept the total within bounds. Then at 69, in the seventeenth over, Troon broke through. Robinson, who had been cross-batting successfully to mid-wicket, played across the line once too often and was bowled. Yoxall followed him in the next over, caught by his fellow captain at mid-off.

So the innings had to be rebuilt and Spittle, quick and compact, and Davies, a free-swinging left-hander, set about the job sensibly. Troon at last withdrew their remaining slip and began concentrating on saving runs. For a while they succeeded, but Davies greeted Dunstan coming on at the Nursery End with a straight drive to the boundary, cover-drove Thomas for four, and off-drove Dunstan soon after to bring up the 100 in the 26th over.

Four runs later the band of the Royal Green Jackets, who were secreted under the Tavern Stand, struck up a march, probably in honour of the three figures being reached. This put everyone on the field somewhat out of humour, for while the band played the cricketers refused to, and for a minute or two there were as, *Hansard* would put it, cheers and counter-cheers from the rival bands of supporters. With the help of the Astwood Bank captain the over-eager musicians were finally muzzled, although if George Gunn, the great Notts opener, had been concerned he would have protested. He loved to hear the band while he was at the wicket and once scored a century against Australia to the accompaniment of Gilbert and Sullivan airs.

This musical interruption was, in one way, a fitting reply to a hitherto unreported remark by Mike Henderson at a summer lunch at Distillers' House. 'There is no truth at all,' Mr Henderson said, 'that we have engaged a lone piper from the Green Jackets to march the ramparts of Lord's playing *'The Amazing W. G. Grace.'* ... sic transit.

Spittle, completely unperturbed by the break in concentration, soon after swung Moyle into the Mound Stand and hit the next ball right over the top of it. The ball was lost for some minutes and umpire Robinson, hoping to hurry things up, went off to fetch another. However, in his absence, the ball was found, so that, for a while, it became a case of 'lost umpire'. The third-wicket stand reached 70 before Troon could break it. Spittle, going for another big hit, was bowled and, as was the case with the opening pair, his partner left in the following over, deftly stumped by Rashleigh, who kept wicket well, although he removed the bails more often than appeared decently necessary.

Worse followed for Astwood Bank. Altogether in six overs they lost five wickets for nine runs, the main destroyer being the left-handed Johns who had returned to the Pavilion End. Among his victims was Colin Robinson, the

Midlanders' big hitter, who was bowled before he could get a sighter. There remained only some lively sprinting by the tail before the innings closed at 165–8, Johns returning the magnificent figures of five for 27 in his nine overs.

Troon, as usual, batted cautiously when they set out on their task. They have always believed that most sides have only two good bowlers and that if the opening pair can be seen off, run-getting becomes progressively easier. In this case their openers had plenty of uncomfortable moments against Morrall from the Pavilion End and the decidedly quick Crumpton from the Nursery. Crumpton, in this spell by far the quickest bowler in the match, got far more lift, bounce and movement out of the pitch than anyone else and beat both batsmen frequently, yet the break came at the other end, Spry holing out at mid-wicket.

The blond left-handed Edwards, living dangerously at times, took a while getting used to the light which, never good at any time in the game, could not have been pleasant to bat in as the afternoon wore on. The score moved slowly, only 23 coming in the first twelve overs, though Troon's rate brightened when Yoxall came on. Brian Carter twice drove him to the cover boundary and joined Edwards in taking a number of quick singles. Edwards was particularly fast between wickets, time and again turning singles into twos.

Thus the Troon innings soon began to right itself and the 50 came up in the 16th over; almost immediately, however, Colin Robinson, who had replaced Morrall, trapped Carter leg-before.

The arrival of Terry Carter was the signal for the score to accelerate very sharply. In seven more overs he and Edwards rushed the total to the 100 with splendid carefree driving, and daring, sometimes almost too daring, fast, short singles, Carter nearly matching Edwards for speed. Carter's timing at first was a shade out, but very soon he was middling the ball perfectly and runs seemed to come from almost every delivery.

Yoxall now had quite a problem on his hands and at 93 he brought back Crumpton. Carter promptly pulled him to the mid-wicket boundary, thumped him into the Mound

Stand for six, drove him past extra-cover and finally cracked him straight – 18 off the over and the Troon supporters shouted themselves hoarse. This was glorious full-blooded attacking cricket. Carter had almost overhauled Edwards when the opener, who was trying to match his captain drive for drive, played round a ball from Morrall, who had been brought back to the Pavilion end. That was 117–3 in the 25th over. Astwood Bank had already seemed unsure about their line of attack at the two left-handers, so they must have watched the arrival of Vincent, another left-hander, with dismay.

Carter reached his 50 out of 78 in 42 minutes and there was scarcely a stroke in which his bat did not meet the ball dead centre. The 150 arrived in the 31st over and soon after Carter was dropped at mid-off, a difficult running chance, low down to the left, off Yoxall. But by then it scarcely seemed to matter.

The end came in the 34th over with Carter hitting Colin Robinson for four to the square-leg boundary and then a six into the laps of the unhappy Astwood Bank supporters outside the Tavern. A fitting ending to a superb innings and to a thoroughly enjoyable, hard-fought game.

THE TWO TEAMS

Allowing time for the jubilation to die down, I telephoned Maurice Bolitho, Troon's secretary, early on the Tuesday morning. The feeling of his committee was, he told me, to put the £250 prize money towards the rebuilding of their pavilion. The Haig trophy stands in pride of place in the window of one of the village shops and Mr Bolitho then rushed away to his waiting pupils at Treswithian Secondary School.

Time, now, I feel, for a quick look at the Troon heroes:

JOHN SPRY (27) is the 'foreigner' in the side. He comes from North Cornwall and this was his first season at Troon after three years at Redruth. A right-hand bat and occasional bowler, with career best of 126 for North Cornwall, he is married, and works for Lloyds Bank in Camborne.

TOMMY EDWARDS (21) and powerfully built is the

left-hand opening bat. He has played for the club for six years, making his debut for the 1st XI when he was 16. Apart from his batting skills, he is a left-arm fast medium bowler. Unmarried, he works as a builder.

BRIAN CARTER (31), has played for Troon for 13 years, making his debut when 14. The elder of Troon's two well-known cricketing brothers, and a very attractive and aggressive right-hand bat, he has had trials for both Gloucestershire and Hampshire and has appeared for Cornwall between 30 and 40 times. Married with two children he works as an engineer.

TERRY CARTER (26) captain, is a left-hand bat and has been playing for Troon since making his debut at the age of 15. His highest score of 130, was made against Mullion. He has been capped for Cornwall at both cricket and rugby, gained the first of his five rugby caps at the age of 18 and became the youngest scrum-half to play for the county since the war. He is still very keen on the game, was vice-captain for two seasons and intends playing this winter. This is his first season as captain of Troon, having been vice-captain for four years. A machine setter with Holman Bros., he is married with a three-year-old son.

JIMMY VINCENT (45). In his time had captained both the club and Cornwall. He was opening bat for Troon for 18 years, although he now goes in at No. 5. He is a left-handed bat and played regularly for Cornwall between 1951 and 1962, making 122 against Dorset. An engineer with Holman Bros., he is married with two children.

MIKE SWEENEY (29) a former local rugby star, began his cricketing career as a bowler, but now concentrates on batting and fielding. He has played for Troon for nine seasons. A right-hand bat, he is married and employed as an engineer with Holmans.

PETER JOHNS (21). Now back with Troon after a spell as match professional with Mullion, is a hard-hitting right-hand bat and left-arm medium pace bowler. During his seven years with Troon he has taken a hat-trick as well as going one better and taking four wickets in four balls. Unmarried, he is an engineer with Holmans.

BRIAN MOYLE (18) is Cornwall Colts' current opening bat, is in his second season at Troon and has played in all but one of their Haig Cup matches. A right-hand bat, plays in spectacles and is a good gully fielder. He was captain of the Cornwall Under-15 team in 1969 and is Troon's youngest player in their Haig squad. He is a Technical College student.

DAVID RASHLEIGH (33), vice-captain and wicket-keeper, has played for the club for 11 seasons. Married with a baby daughter, he is a Civil Servant.

GERALD DUNSTAN (47) is Troon's senior player but belies his years with highly skilful and effective right-arm medium pace bowling. His best return was 8 for 27 against Redruth and he once did the hat-trick against Penzance. He has been capped 28 times for Cornwall, and his son is the professional with St Just CC.

PETER THOMAS (24) is now in his ninth season with Troon and is one of the side's opening bowlers. Right-arm fast medium, he is 5 ft 9 in. tall and stockily built. He is a Civil Servant and married.

KEITH LEAN (19) was 12th man at Lord's. An all rounder – he has played for Troon for three years and for Cornwall Schools in 1968. He played rugby for Camborne Colts and appeared at fly half for the Cornwall Under 19s but has now given up rugby for soccer. Unmarried, he works as a clerk at the School of Mines.

How Troon got to Lords
1st *Round:* Troon 119 for 4; Bocconoc 115 for 6.
2nd *Round:* Troon 85 for 3; Perranarworthal 84 for 9.
3rd *Round:* Troon 62 for 0; Werrington 128 all out.
Rain stopped play in this game, the decision being taken on 15 overs.
4th *Round:* Troon 205 for 4; Gorran 127 all out.
Country Group Final: Troon 169 for 9; Thorverton (Devon) 158 for 7.
6th *Round:* Troon 145 for 6; Evercreech (Somerset) 142 all out.
7th *Round:* Troon 85 for 1; Shillingstone (Dorset) 83 all out.

Quarter-Final: Troon 205 for 5; Bledlow (Oxfordshire) 204 for 4.
Semi-Final: Troon 171 for 1; Linton Park (Kent) 167 all out.

Astwood Bank Stalwarts:
JOHN YOXALL (28) captain, a position he has held seven times since he was first appointed at the age of 21, is a fine tactician as well as being a stylish opening batsman, and useful change bowler. John has completed his 1,000 runs in each of the past eight seasons. He has also played for the Gentlemen of Worcestershire for many years. Unmarried, he works as an engineer in a Bromsgrove factory.

JOHN ROBINSON (29) no relation to Colin, has also lived practically all his life in Astwood Bank. He was educated at Oldswinford Hospital School in Stourbridge and is now employed as wages supervisor in a Redditch factory.

BRIAN SPITTLE (32) is a truly all-round sportsman having played soccer and being on Aston Villa's books until his career was cut short by a broken jaw, as well as being on the Worcestershire ground staff for three years. He is director and company secretary of a Kidderminster carpet company and has played regularly for Astwood Bank for many years as a forcing batsman and left-arm spin bowler who is also an extremely fine fielder. Brian is married with two children.

ROB DAVIES (29) is Head of the Technical Studies department at Redditch County High School and has been with the club for four seasons. He is a left-hand batsman, going in at number five or six, and a first-rate fielder. Rob married last year after meeting his wife while on cricket tour in Southampton.

MIKE WEDGBURY (39) who has just been appointed Headmaster of Gig Mill School in Stourbridge, was educated at Redditch County High School and has played cricket for Redditch and Studley before moving to Astwood Bank several years ago. He, like many other club members is also often selected for the Gentlemen of Worcestershire. Mike is married with two daughters.

COLIN ROBINSON (26) at 18 stone, 6 ft. $2\frac{1}{2}$ in. tall and wearing size 13 boots is one of the characters of Astwood

Bank. He has lived in the village all his life, went to The Ridgeway School, and is now employed as a bricklayer. Colin played his first game for the club at the age of eight and has developed into a fine all-rounder, bowling very accurately at medium pace and being a forcing bat.

JOHN POOLE (36) has just taken up the post of Schools Liaison Officer in charge of Bristol Science and Technology Centre, and consequently this was his last season with Astwood. He came to the club via Coleshill and Westbury on Trym, Bristol. John is married with two children.

RAY NASH (39) is a truly top class wicket-keeper, showing some fine examples of his art during his long service to the club. Originally from Clevedon in Somerset he is employed as regional manager for a button producing company, his other interest include the Round Table movement; he is married with two children.

JOE CRUMPTON (32) was educated at Bromsgrove and played cricket for both Worcestershire Schoolboys and England Schoolboys. He has been playing for Astwood Bank for three seasons. Joe is a quick left-arm opening bowler who has taken many wickets this season. He has a striking likeness to Australian paceman Dennis Lillee, except for bowling left-handed.

TERRY BIRD (27) during the last two seasons established himself as a regular member of Astwood Bank's first team as a very useful left-arm spin bowler. A self-employed painter and decorator, Terry is married with one son.

FRANK MORRALL (31) opens the bowling with Joe Crumpton, a formidable partnership. He was educated at Alcester Grammar School and previously played for Studley C.C. for a number of years before moving to Astwood Bank. He shows his loyalty to the club by travelling regularly from his home at Harbury Wells near Leamington Spa.

GRAHAM BALDWIN (24) a police constable from Cleobury Mortimer in Shropshire stationed in Redditch, has been playing for the club for only two years but is a competent bat and very useful seam bowler. Graham, who is single was 12th man at Lord's.

Astwood Bank's road to Lord's
1st Round: Astwood Bank 43 for 1; Earlswood 42 all out.
2nd Round: Astwood Bank 48 for 2; Nether Whitacre 47 for 7.
3rd Round: Astwood Bank 68 for 3; Catherine de Barnes 67 for 9.
4th Round: Astwood Bank 110 for 7; Rowington 51 all out.
County Group Final: Astwood Bank 209 for 7; Hockley Heath 136 for 5.
6th Round: Astwood Bank 102 for 4; Swynnerton Park (Staffs) 101 all out.
7th Round: Astwood Bank 93 for 4; Horton House (Northants) 89 all out.
Quarter-Final: Astwwod Bank 86 for 3; Kimbolton (Hunts) 85 all out.
Semi-Final: Astwood Bank 137 for 4; Collingham (Notts) 134 for 9.

WHAT THE PRESS THOUGHT

Almost without exception the Press, radio and TV commentators and writers were in favour of The Haig Championship from its inception, and Final Day drew its expected coverage. John Morgan, Sports Editor of the *Daily Express*, in his weekly 'Morgan on Monday' feature, put things in perhaps the best perspective with a second deck headline: *Village Cricket does Lord's Proud:* 'Not a pair of braces in sight... no one spurning pads or gloves... not a single bat held shoulder high as a warning of the cow shot to come,' Morgan wrote. 'Instead, immaculately flannelled and sweatered *cricketers,* field placing inch-perfect and batsmen attacking off the front foot with near-classic strokes that had the more elderly observers tut-tutting that if this is village cricket what on earth has happened to our Test men.'

Morgan was also in ear-shot when the two skippers were told by M.C.C. President Freddie Brown that band music was quite usual at festival matches. 'This,' Messrs Yoxall and Carter reasoned, 'isn't a festival game – it's a bloody

Cup Final.' Morgan concluded: 'Compton, Evans Trueman, Dexter and me were just left scratching our heads... and hoping that Michael Henderson, Managing Director of John Haig, and motivating force behind this splendid idea, will ensure that the National Village Cricket Championship becomes an annual event. This may not be the village game that Lord's last remembered (more than 100 years ago) but, by golly, it has every right to be back there.'

And in the *Sunday Times*, Robin Marlar commented on the band incident, adding that the rival skippers also told Mr Brown 'what he could do with his piccolo'. Praise, too, from Marlar for Mike Henderson and the sponsors of an event that 'has served the game well this happy (sic) summer'.

In the *Sunday Mirror* Ted Dexter drew attention to the fact that for third time in as many matches at Lord's, the team batting second had had no difficulty in matching the run-rate required – for Troon to be bracketed with the achievements of Australia and Lancashire was a typically generous comment. 'Troon won,' wrote Dexter, 'because they kept their heads and stuck to the country-style cricket which they know best.'

Ian Peebles – never averse, to my knowledge, to a little bucolic batting – seemed a little put out in the *Observer* that the village cricket of his day – featuring sheep, braces, cow pats, long grass and the vicar – had changed somewhat for 'immaculate dress and a high degree of professionalism ... for Troon Edwards and Carter added 67 in just more than eight overs for the third wicket. Both looked like Test match prospects'. Have no fear, sweet I.A.R., elsewhere in this volume are your vicars, sheep and a fine 'Crusoe' cow pat tale.

In the *Guardian*, Frank Keating deplored the band's dismissal but praised what he termed 'the spirited farewell' in the sponsors' box, and referred to 'this whoppingly successful competition'. I trust he reads this volume thoroughly for he will find many more amusing stories of village cricket life than he quoted from my own chapter on this subject.

It had, of course, to be Denis Compton, *Sunday Express*, who felt that it would not have been inappropriate for

Father Time to pop down from the Grand Stand roof to partake of a dram of the Haig 'hard stuff as he viewed the exciting village-green cricket' from his windy perch. 'I hope,' wrote D.C.S., 'that the sponsorship which reaches deep into the very heart of English cricket is continued for many years... the interest and support generated by players and spectators alike can only help to stimulate the game.' Almost exactly, in fact, what Mike Henderson said in early 1971 when we first discussed the Haig National Village Cricket Championship.

Some quote has to come last and in the best family tradition I have left this for Michael Melford of *The Sunday Telegraph*. 'Cornwall,' he wrote, 'has played no great part in the history of cricket in the past, but the men of Troon changed that yesterday.' Of Terry Carter's superb knock Melford said: 'He played an innings of which none of the eminent players who have made runs on this famous ground would have been ashamed.'

But that is not the last quote of all. All writers, commentators, players and officials have completely condemned the failure of British Rail to convey some 600–700 Troon supporters to London. As I write this I am told of the strongest possible complaints going to the Rail Board, who I gather are not, at this time of writing, prepared to do much more than apologise. What about a sizable contribution to the National Playing Fields Association which would help village clubs in dire need of funds? What about the collections those hard-working Lord's Taverners went without?

Michael Richardson, 17, of Belsay in Northumberland, also played his part at Lord's. He won the cricket ball-throwing contest with a distance of 106 yards 2 feet 1 inch – admittedly some distance behind the 1884 record of 140 yards 2 feet set by a Mr R. Percival, but enough to win him a cheque for £15 and a half-a-gallon of Haig. 'If there was a few thick heads at St Cuthbert's Grammar School,' is John Morgan's tailpiece, 'it will be because Michael has kept his promise to share part of his winnings with his fellow students.'

But perhaps Michael might bowl them over with the Haig Googlie. This was invented by Tom Langley of Jules

Bar, one of the country's greatest producers of new drink ideas and a keen follower of cricket.

Take:
- 1 measure of Haig
- 1 measure of Dry Martini
- $\frac{1}{2}$ measure of ordinary orange squash
- 1 dash of Angustura
- Top up for a long drink with lemonade
- Garnish with cucumber and mint

Just the drink to toast The Haig National Village Cricket Championship!

THE SCOREBOARD
Troon won the toss and put Astwood Bank in
ASTWOOD BANK

*J. Yoxall, c T. Carter, b Edwards	36
J. Robinson, b Thomas	30
B. Spittle, b Johns	36
R. Davies, st Rashleigh, b Dunstan	30
M. Wedgbury, lbw b Johns	0
C. Robinson, b Johns	3
J. Crumpton, not out	16
J. Poole, lbw b Johns	0
T. Bird, b Johns	1
†R. Nash, not out	2
Extras (B 5, lb 6)	11
40 overs. Total (8 wkts)	165

Did not bat: F. Morrall.
Fall of wickets: 1–69, 2–69, 3–139, 4–139, 5–141, 6–148, 7–148, 8–162.
Bowling: Johns 9–1–25–5; Edwards 9–2–35–1; Thomas 9–0–35–1; Moyle 4–0–25–0; Dunstan 9–1–34–1.

TROON

J. Spry, c Poole, b Morrall	2
T. Edwards, b Morrall	45
B. Carter, lbw b C. Robinson	19

*T. Carter, not out	79
J. Vincent, not out	14
Extras (Lb 8, nb 2, w 1)	11
33.4 overs. Total (3 wkts)	170

Did not bat: M. Sweeney, P. Johns, B. Moyle, †D. Rashleigh, G. Dunstan, P. Thomas.

Fall of wickets: 1–14, 2–50, 3–117.

Bowling: Morrall 9–2–25–2; Crumpton 9–1–39–0; Yoxall 4–0–26–0; C. Robinson 6.4–1–41–1; Spittle 4–0–23–0; Bird 1–0–5–0.

Umpires: L. H. Gray and H. E. Robinson.
Scorers: R. Pratt and T. Ambrose.
*Captain †Wicket-keeper.
Troon won by seven wickets.

CHAPTER TWO
'The Haig' and the Villages

The origins of what is now the highly successful Haig competition go back to the winter of 1970. Then, following an analysis of their joint survey of English club cricket, *The Cricketer* magazine and the National Cricket Association decided that the village game seemed to have the biggest growth potential and would benefit from the institution of a national competition.

Ben Brocklehurst, former Somerset captain and managing director of *The Cricketer,* and Jim Dunbar, secretary of the N.C.A, held a Press conference and announced their plans for the event, adding the hope that it would be possible to find an acceptable sponsor.

For the subsequent marriage-brokering, consummation and birth I can, with all modesty claim due credit – at least up to the midwifery stage – and regard the first-born Haig season as a very bonny child, certain to grow in stature and vigour. Most 'happy events' seem to stem from an element of chance, and the birth of the Haig was no exception.

Shortly after the story of the proposed Cricketer-N.C.A. competition had appeared in *The Daily Telegraph*, written by John Mason and sub-edited by myself, I was asked to recommend a sporting event suitable for sponsorship. Discarding golf and lawn tennis as being already oversubscribed, and with John Player and Gillette safely looking after 'instant' cricket at top-level, I tentatively suggested virile village cricket as a worthy cause.

At that time the potential sponsor's name was not revealed, for obvious reasons, but very shortly I was delighted to hear that John Haig and Co. Ltd., had looked on my suggestion with considerable interest. It did not take long thereafter to bring together Jim Dunbar, Ben Brocklehurst and Michael B. Henderson, Haig's managing director, plus the public relations firm of Metcalfe International.

General agreement to launch the Haig National Village Cricket Championship in 1972 was quickly reached, although there were a number of financial details to be discussed and decided by both main parties – the sponsor and the joint organisers. By February 1971, the stage was all set, the preliminary meetings were kept to a minimum by general agreement and enthusiasm for 'grass roots' cricket, where we all felt sponsorshop could do nothing but good. I cannot recall, over many years of comparable meetings, such an atmosphere of intended goodwill on all sides.

It was also most convenient to conclude a meeting at Distillers' House in St James's Square with an adjournment for further discussion in Mike Henderson's 'dispensary'.

With all the preliminaries settled, the Haig committee came into action headed by Aidan Crawley, chairman of the N.C.A. and now a most popular President of M.C.C., with Messrs Brocklehurst, Henderson and Dunbar as his members, plus co-opted specialists as seemed from time to time necessary.

After the financial agreement came the formulation of a set of rules for the competition. These are reproduced in full in the Appendix at the end of this book and, in their final form, seemed to cover most cricketing eventualities, although, at that time I doubt if the organisational enthusiasts envisaged the dismal summer to come in 1972 and the consequent need to call so often on the rules for reduced-overs matches and, most unfortunately, for the toss of a coin to decide ties which had been first wrecked by rain and then proved impossible to re-arrange for a variety of reasons.

May the sun shine long and hot in 1973 and every subsequent summer, to give the village clubs every satisfaction from full 40-over a side contests!

Now the prime objective of this championship was to base it at true grass roots level – the village club – but the definition of what actually constituted 'a village' proved rather more tricky than was first envisaged. For my own part I spent hours at my telephone asking the question of Government departments, rural associations, the Women's Institute and the Mother's Union – but apart from general amazement that I didn't know what 'a village' was, and the startled realisation that my alleged informants did not know either, the only gainer was the Telephone Manager.

Luckily the Haig committee are nothing if not resourceful and came up with their own definition of 'a rural community with a population not exceeding 2,500'. Obviously some clubs which had considered themselves as village teams became ineligible by this arbitrary definition, but at least a standard had been set and it was preferable that the qualifying population should be on the low side rather than the higher.

So with that matter settled, a firm promise of the final at Lord's in September, and some necessary stipulations in the rules against obvious 'pot hunting', the Haig in its accepted format was ready for public announcement. Mid-March seemed the right time, and the River Room at the Savoy Hotel the right venue, for the first H.N.V.C.C. Press conference. Invitations went out via Metcalfe's to national newspaper cricket writers, to London representatives of provincial newspapers, to the trade press and, of course, to radio and television.

I would not yield pride of place to anyone in my admiration for the concept of the Haig competition, or in my pleasure that so many village clubs seemed certain to benefit, but I must admit that the massive turnout of journalists at this inaugural Press conference was greater than even I had expected. Quite obviously the idea to give village cricket a much deserved slice of sponsorship cake had appealed to the imagination of all cricket-lovers and writers and they gave Mr Crawley and his committee colleagues every possible encouragement.

The subsequent nationwide publicity which the Haig received in all media was even more encouraging at all levels, and as the Metcalfe International press-cuttings book swelled to overflowing, so also did entries for the 1972 com-

The solid silver Haig Trophy, valued at £1,000, and featuring in its design crossed cricket bats on a Dimple Whisky bottle

Announcing the birth of the Haig competition at the Press conference held in the Savoy Hotel, London, are (right to left) Michael B. Henderson, Managing Director of John Haig & Co. Ltd, Aidan Crawley, Chairman of the National Cricket Association and now President of M.C.C., B. G. Brocklehurst, Managing Director of *The Cricketer* magazine, and J. G. Dunbar, Secretary of the National Cricket Association and an Assistant Secretary of M.C.C.

Play in progress beneath lowering clouds, as Meigle go on their way to becoming Scotland's first village cricket champions by defeating Glendelvine

Mr Walter Rustage mows the outfield of Toft's ground near Knutsford, framed by two of the four trees within the boundary. Four runs goes to a batsman hitting a tree

petition pour into *The Cricketer* office, to add to those already received before the sponsorship was announced. The entries came from far and wide – from Scotland and Somerset, from Cornwall and Cumberland, from Wales and Westmorland, from Devon and Durham, and, of course, from the traditional cricket counties of Kent and Sussex, the Midlands, Lancashire and Yorkshire. Some, unfortunately, were not acceptable, either from the 'population' ruling or from the difficulties of travel which clubs from Northern Ireland, Army units on the Continent and Royal Navy ships at seas would have encountered.

All these were minor setbacks and a further proof of the great interest the event had aroused in cricketers everywhere, so that after the end of the 1971 season some 795 clubs had been accepted and divided into the 32 County Groups, whose localised knock-out competitions would provide the starting point for the first National Championship. A pre-season Press conference gave all the details of the competition and once again the headlines in national and provincial papers proclaimed : 'Village clubs set out for Lord's'.

During the winter months I designed a form of club questionnaire which went to each club accompanied by a personalised letter from Mr Henderson. Despite the 'close' season, the response was staggering and by mid-February I was able to start the task of analysing the answers – plus innumerable anecdotes – in the initial batch of 500 or so replies (many more arrived in each post). The clubs had dug deep into their archives and humour. The omnipresent aroma from the stack proclaimed – if I needed telling – where most of the forms had been completed!

The information supplied has formed the basis of the remainder of this chapter and I must at this stage express my warmest thanks to the many, many club officials who went to so much trouble to help. First some facts and figures; then to the clubs themselves :

Of the Haig clubs 81.25% were formed before 1939 and, in fact, nearly half of this figure claim to have originated in the latter part of the nineteenth century – to say nothing of historic *Hambledon* (1750), *Maresfield*, Sussex (1720), where Joe Hart and 'Peace' Miller battled in friendly rivalry for 40 consecutive seasons, *East Hoathly,* Sussex (1757), *Peper Harow,* Surrey (1727), and *Nostel Priory,* Yorkshire ('time immemorial' *sic*). Due to the 1939-45 war, many clubs re-formed themselves in 1946, when changing social conditions, the disappearance of large estates, re-building and other non-cricket 'progress' forced them to seek new grounds.

Some 71% of the clubs have more than 25 full playing members – although very few can claim more than 30 – yet in many cases manage to field two XIs. Even Hambledon have a mere 25, but the great advantage of 160 non-playing members, including famous vice-presidents and life members at £5 each from most cricketing countries. Only 42.25% clubs charge a playing subscription of £1.50 or more, but 83% levy match fees, the average being 10p per game. Subscriptions vary by locality and the outgoings for the ground; clubs using local authority grounds can often charge subscriptions of as little as 50p per annum.

Fortunate, too, are clubs such as *Belsay,* Northumberland, whose president, Sir Stephen Middleton rents them the ground at 25p a year, *Birlingham,* Worcestershire, who pay a mere 5p to Major H. R. M. Parker, *Little Durnford,* Wilts, to whom Lord Chichester makes the same charge, and *High Halden,* Ashford, Kent, who operate rent-free from Mr W. Carter. Mr Carter, incidentally, was 99 last April, and not only watched every match he could, but also supervised the renovation of the cricket 'table' in the winter months.

Some 41% of the clubs play in a league, either on Saturdays or mid-week, but 85.5% – before the introduction of The Haig, of course – competed in one or more local knock-out competitions. Not unexpectedly, the preponderance of league play is in the northern and midlands areas, knock-outs being somewhat more popular in the south.

Predictably, a mere 11% of clubs can afford to use a new ball at the start of each match although some captains added, with rare honesty, 'only if the opposition bat first'. And Maurice Barnett, secretary of *Nether Whitacre,* Warwickshire, says his club have 'no problems – we have Arthur Luckett, a voluntary ball reconditioning marvel'.

But almost all clubs report adequate playing equipment in good condition.

Cost again limits only 32% of clubs to the employment of a paid groundsman, either full or part-time. Most rely on members turning the roller and pushing the mower. Other lucky clubs enjoy the services of local authority labour, if only for outfield mowing.

I found that 35% of clubs provide a sight-screen at each end, a further 13% enjoy this facility at one end only. The single screen is partly explained by the fact that many grounds slope away, at least at one end, from the table at a considerable gradient. At *Holme,* Carnforth, Lancashire, for example, the secretary states that 'fine leg's head is level with the pitch', while at *Monks Risborough,* Buckinghamshire, D. M. Miller described their ground as having 'the steepest slope I've ever seen', and A. H. D. Constable, captain of *Balcombe,* Haywards Heath, Sussex, says 'deep square leg cannot see deep point'.

Only 27.5% of the clubs boast shower bath facilities and 20.5% a licensed bar in the club house. But many clubs reported current fund-raising plans for new pavilions, and the provision of showers is high on the priority lists. In contrast most clubs still prefer to use their favourite 'local' in the village for post-match 'get-togethers', many in fact, using the pub as their headquarters throughout the year. This includes *Hambledon* who, despite a fine new pavilion, still stick by the New Inn.

Progress and Bad Luck

Cookridge, near Leeds, suffered a great misfortune in November 1971, when a 12-year-old boy, playing truant from school, set fire to the pavilion which was completely destroyed – without compensation. The club are now desperarately seeking to raise funds to rebuild – any benefactors would be most welcome. *Cookridge* bowed out in the first round to *Cawthorne* scoring only 49 to which their opponents replied with 50 for 2. In the same area the *Great Preston* club survives perilously the constant threat of inundation from the spreading city. 'We may not have many more seasons in 'The Haig', says chairman, Martin Baldwin. A great pity this, for *Great Preston* had an excellent first year in the Haig, winning through to the Group II final which they lost to *Tong*. *Fillongley,* near Coventry, found misfortune with a silver lining. In 1970 the members built themselves a new pavilion; in January 1971 it was destroyed by fire. The club raised subscriptions to help provide a brick-built pavilion, opened this June. Help came from all sides and, most importantly, from the local brickworks who have supplied bricks at a nominal price. After a splendid first-round score of 240 for 8 to beat *Bearley* (37 for 9), *Fillongley* fell in the next round to *Dunton Bassett*.

Stewkley Vicarage, Bedfordshire, has been saved from extinction by the choice of Foulness as the site of London's third airport, and work can now go ahead on a new pavilion. Unfortunately, costs have risen sharply during the delay.

Generally, the question of women players brought a strong 'No! No! No!' from clubs who, however, all claim their ladies provide the finest teas in their district! At *Yoxford* in Suffolk, there is a ladies' team which uses the club ground and *Sessay,* Yorkshire, planned to start a ladies' side this season. *Skelton Castle,* near Saltburn have Mrs M. W. Ringrose-Wharton as their president, with 40 years service in the club's cause, while *Hempstead* in Kent boast a 'fully qualified' lady umpire.

A modern 'Cobbett'

As a political pamphleteer William Cobbett made little impact other than nuisance value, but passed into literary history for his *Rural Rides* around eighteenth century England. Since the Haig championship came into being I must confess to a great desire to do a modern 'Cobbett' around the cricketing villages – an ambition I fear, for time reasons, unlikely to be realised. However, I am quite sure that as the Haig grows any number of village clubs will look at the prospects of a cricket tour to clubs outside their own

'THE HAIG' AND THE VILLAGES

county groups, an excellent way of making new friends.

But a 'Haig Cobbett' on paper is *not* an impossibility so, with fullest apologies to clubs whom space restrictions have forced me to omit, off we go. And where better to start than the home of Haig, in Scotland?

The *Kintore* club was founded in 1878 and play their cricket at the Pleasure Park, sharing the ground with a local football club. The first XI were the Aberdeenshire Grade One champions in 1971 and runners-up in the county cup. Although secretary David Low tells me that 'at the moment' they have no club personalities 'of world-shattering importance', they can boast James W. Duncan as their oldest, and youngest, playing member; aged 52, he was born on February 29th. Mr Low also recalls from *Kintore* history between the wars a match against *Kemnay*, a neighbouring village which *Kintore* won by one run – the only one scored, and that was an extra! In their Haig match against *Lennox*, *Kintore* scored 189 for five wickets, holding the visitors to 128 – 8 at the end of their allotted overs. *Kintore* hero was Stuart Martin who hit a splendid 90 runs in near even time and, rounding off the match with two wickets for 19 runs, gained the club award of a Haig tie.

Crosshill, Fife, travelled some 144 miles to and from their first round match with *St Boswells* and although they were dismissed for 50 and lost to *Boswells* 51 for 8, Angus Cameron had a good match, scoring 15 runs and taking three wickets for 11, thus winning the Haig tie. *St Boswells*, a Roxburghshire side who play on their open village green, again did well in their next match, beating *Freuchies'* 141 with a well-judged 142 for 7. However, they ran into trouble in the third round scoring only 44 to lose to *Meigle;* beaten but not disgraced as *Meigle* went on to emerge as Scottish champions, with a victory over *Glendelvine* in the group final.

Meigle, founded in 1876, and with a population of 700, have 26 playing members and their ground, aptly, is at the Victory Park.

Fochabers own their ground, purchased through their fund-raising efforts, and improvements are still being made. Surrounded by trees, one boundary looks down on the

River Spey and incidentally the offer of a bottle of whisky for anyone driving a ball into the Spey is still available.

Rossie Prior, 'one of the oldest clubs in Perthshire', says James Miller, the club secretary, only entered competitive cricket two seasons ago and had previously played 'friendlies' since their formation in 1828. Their president, Lord Kinnaird, played for them before the 1914–18 war. They had a good first-round win over *Luncarty,* M. Cormack making 34 of their 138 for 9, and I. McKenzie taking 3 for 13 in Luncarty's 64.

Scroggie Park, Fifeshire, home ground of *Falkland C.C.,* has a distinct slope on the north side and, George Imrie Brown tells me, is overlooked by Lomond Hill, 1,461 ft above sea level. Founded in 1860, the club had George Gamble, a former Surrey player, as their professional in 1908.

Over the border then to Group 2 territory, made up from village clubs in Northumberland, Durham, Cumberland, and Westmorland. The *Belford* club founded in 1837, has some 30 playing members and an excellent record, but unfortunately departed the Haig in the first round, losing to *Kirkley. Blagdon Park,* though, fared much better, reaching the semi-finals before losing to *Warenford,* the eventual winners. *Blagdon* play in a private park near Seaton Burn, and in 1963 to mark the club's 75th year, an extension to the pavilion was opened by Viscount and Viscountess Ridley, Blagdon's patrons. In early days the club's home was a wooden hut in one corner of the field and teas were taken in the Laundry at the Hall. A massive early hero was Jack Crozier, the only man to hit a ball into the Park lake, but for a left-hander surprisingly vulnerable on his leg-stump. *Blagdon* play an annual Boxing Day match – usually on a snow-covered pitch – then they and their guests adjourn to the Ridley Arms.

Near Kendal in Westmorland, *Burneside* have the advantage of a beautiful ground set in the Lake District National Park; they are also worthy cricketers with a splendid record in local leagues and knock-outs. This served them well in the Haig, taking them to the group final against *Warenford* where they found T. Thompson (5 for

20) in top form and the *Burneside* total of 59 cost them a four-wickets defeat.

From the *Cleator* club's ground in Cumberland one gets a superb Lakeland view to the West. They won both their league and cup competitions in 1970 and 1971, with their captain Alan Wishart as the leading all-rounder and 'Big Joe' Rooney, stumper and six-hit specialist, who scored 77 of a partnership of 102 off 11 overs.

Cowpen Bewley, near Billingham, was formed in 1898 and a feature of their winter activities are regular mole-catching sessions. They went out in the first round but not before a fighting innings of 47 by secretary K. Johnson, who, coming in at 22 for 3, took them to 160 for 9 in reply to *Coxhoe's* 40-over total of 225. Haig tie for Mr Johnson! *Coxhoe* eventually lost in the third round to *Burneside.*

Felton, Morpeth, secretary Jack Hall tells me, have played on numerous grounds around the village since the early 1900s 'and never a laid wicket yet'. Out first round, unfortunately, with 95 to *Stockfield's* 116. The *Lowther* club near Penrith, was formed more than 100 years ago and features of the ground are a lovely ancient oak tree at one corner and magnificent views of the Eden Valley. Club secretary, John Peel no less, has served the club since 1923. *Lowther* lost their first round tie to *Lanercost,* the Cumberland club going on to the semi-final – another *Burneside* victim.

Undeterred by losing by 70 runs to *Newbrough, Mitford* near Morpeth 'look forward to competing in the Haig next year', says George Brown, their secretary. Their Haig tie winner was P. Robson who took 3 for 17 in *Newbrough's* total of 147.

Keith Fairness won the *Stockfield* club's Haig tie for scoring 36 against *Felton* in the first round. The club, whose patron is Viscount Allendale, did not fare quite so well against *Wylam Boy's Brigade Old Boys* in the second round, being dismissed for only 24. *Wylam* then had a tough third-round match with *Blagdon Park,* whose 201 for 5 was successful against the Old Boy's 200 for 8. *Wolviston,* near Billingham, although formed in 1884, have always been handicapped by not having their own ground, but I understand from Albert Roxborough, their secretary, that the club is now actively negotiating for a field of their own, presumably one where overhead electric power cables do not cross part of the 'square'. These caused the death of a homing pigeon in 1970 ... plus several 'ducks'? Club patron is D. C. H. Townsend, ex-England and Oxford batsman and a Varsity match century-maker in 1934.

Yorkshire divided

The response to the Haig from Yorkshire villages was so great that the county was divided into two groups. In the southern group, mainly centred around the large industrial towns, *Tong* outside Bradford, emerged as the finals winners, which for a club founded in only 1957 and adjoining the Greyhound pub, was no mean achievement. But for sheer hard luck the Haig fortunes of *East Bierley* in the second round – they had a bye in the first – deserve a tear or two. They made an admirable 202 against *Cawthorne* only for the rain to start and never finish, and the inevitable toss of a coin put an end to their hopes. Founded before 1850, *East Bierley* have an excellent ground with banking around three-quarters of the field for spectators who can also enjoy splendid views of open countryside for miles. On the nearby village green still stand the ancient punishment stocks; altogether a most picturesque setting and with the New Inn the scene of many after-match post mortems – the *Cawthorne* game being, I understand, no exception.

Great Preston, losing group finalists to *Tong,* is a part-agricultural, and historically, coal mining village but now largely a 'dormitory' for Leeds and Castleford, although Martin Baldwin, the club chairman, says that there is still plenty of rural atmosphere, 'particularly concerning the cricket'.

Bradfield, outside Sheffield, play on the village green set in one of the most beautiful valleys in South Yorkshire and known as Sheffield's 'Lakeland', says F. White who has been the club's secretary for the past 26 years. *Bradfield,* defeated by *Tong* in the semi-final, disposed of *Lascelles Hall* in the second round with 86 for 6 against the Hall's 85 – a sad blow for a proud club which once beat an All-England XI, and then put up an entire family of Thewlises against all-comers.

Bradshaw (94) lost their first-round match to *Everton* (98 for 3), but with the Bradshaw Tavern situated at the edge of the field, presumably found adjacent consolation. The Tavern must also come in fairly handy for their Boxing Day matches – afterwards, according to M. Gavin, 'an attack is made on the world record for egg throwing'.

And *Wheldrake C.C.*, established more than 100 years ago, use the Wenlock Arms in the village as their headquarters. After beating *Thorpe Hesley,* whose ground adjoins the M.1 motorway, *Wheldrake* were beaten by *Great Preston,* surely no disgrace there.

Whitley Hall, near Sheffield, also use their 'local', the Black Bull, as club headquarters. I. H. Baxter, a playing member when the club formed in 1925, has been honorary secretary and voluntary groundsman for 37 years and captained the second team to league promotion in 1970 at the age of 63, having a batting average of 42.

Adwick-on-Dearne, near Mexborough, in the other Yorkshire group, believe in travelling to their cricket and since 1970 have enjoyed long weekends in Holland, playing at Alkmaar and Hilversum. Frank Weaver praises their lady members as 'the best gang ... in any club in the country', but added 'No, they don't go to Holland'. *Adwick* did not have such a good trip in the Haig first round, going down to *Folkton and Flixton,* the eventual group winners.

Altofts, near Normanton, had more success, winning through to the final against *Folkton,* beating *Carlton Towers, Bradley, Bubwith* and *Stamford Bridge* en route by substantial margins, with W. Greatorex their outstanding bowler. *Bradley,* incidentally, were formed 100 years or so ago, and now field a regular junior team from 20 members aged between 10 and 15. On the other side of the scale their president R. L. Fryers was a regular player for nearly 50 years, secretary K. Walker for 35 and treasurer C. R. Fryers for 45.

Carlton Towers, near Goole, with their ground at Fish

Pond Field, enjoy a lovely rural setting – somewhat different from their namesake in London's Sloane Street – awarded their Haig tie to captain and opening batsman Neville Townsend for his innings of 35 in their total of 120 for 7 against Altoft's winning reply of 123 for 5.

Cloughton, third-round losers to *Folkton*, awarded their Haig tie to Mick Readman for his large share in their first-round victory at *New Earswick*. Readman took 4 for 15 in *Earswick's* 86 and then scored 28 of *Cloughton's* first 37 runs; *Cloughton* won with 87 for 5. *New Earswick*, near York, by the way, is a 'model village' administered by the Joseph Rowntree Trust; the first houses were built in 1901 and the cricket club formed in 1923. Mr E. Bryan has served them well for 45 years as player, umpire and groundsman.

Situated in the park grounds, the *Londesborough Park* team was formerly known as Lord Londesborough's XI and cricket has been played on the ground for more than 150 years. In the 1930's matches were played there between eleven Edrich's – then farming in the area – and eleven Featherbys, one of whom, Billy, played for Yorkshire around 1914 and was a *Londesborough* stalwart until he was 67 years of age. After a very good run in the Haig, the club lost to *Folkton* in the semi-finals.

Near Wakefield, *Nostell St Oswalds* have been playing cricket for more years than anyone can remember, on a most pleasant ground belonging to Nostell Priory, a famous National Trust tourist attraction. *Nostell* lost their first round match to *Spofforth*, one of Yorkshire's prettiest villages between Harrogate and Wetherby. The cricket ground lies in a natural basin – quite a hazard in rainy weather. It did not rain for *Spofforth's* home second round match with *Glasshouses* but, commented M. R. Irvine of Haig, there was 'a cold wind that would have done justice to the North Pole'.

Spofforth started badly, losing their first wicket for one run, but then came a sparkling partnership of 123 for the second and the side were all out for 182 in 38 overs *Glasshouses's* middle-order batting did not prosper and they were dismissed for 114. Mr Irvine said he asked what time the match would finish and was told 'opening time'. 'How right they were,' he reported, 'the game ended at 6.45 p.m. and we were at the Castle Inn dead on 7 o'clock.' Chris Young won *Spofforth's* Haig tie for his four wickets for 23 runs in their victory over *Nostell*.

Sessay, near Thirsk, have a small ground and a six-hit must clear the boundary hedges and go out of the ground. Their secretary Mr W. B. Flintoff has opened the innings for 24 seasons, with 35 centuries to his credit. After a bye in the first round, *Sessay* could only muster 112 in the second round in reply to *Folkton's* 166.

Group 5 – Lancashire

Lindal Moor, Ulverston, the Lancashire group champions, combined the occasion of their first-round home Haig match with the opening of their fine new pavilion. The ceremony was carried out by Mr T. K. Postlethwaite, General Manager and Deputy Managing Director of Vickers (Shipbuilders) Ltd, a native of Lindal and a former playing member of the club. *Lindall* held *Caton* to 73 for 6 and then knocked off the runs for the loss of only two wickets, with 20 overs to spare, thanks largely to an unbeaten 37 by E. Shuttleworth.

Lindal knocked out *Salesbury,* a Blackburn club in the second round, winning by seven wickets, and a successful toss of the coin saw them through the third round against *Heyside.* They beat *Delph and Dobcross* by eight wickets in the semi-final and won the county title by defeating *Read.*

Although some quirk of a postal address put them in the Lancashire section of the Haig, *Delph* is a Yorkshire village four miles over the border on the main Oldham-Huddersfield Road, and the cricketers are Yorkshire at heart. And if their wives are having babies there are still Delph cricketers who make sure that they use a Huddersfield maternity hospital – to ensure a Yorkshire birth qualification for the budding county player. The ground is rugged rather than pretty, but the standard of cricket played there in the 100 years of the club's life has always been high... 'none of this swinging stuff wi' bat,' as Bill Schofield, a member of the club for 52 years, puts it.

Delph defeated *Ince Blundell* in the first round, scoring 103 for 9 and bowling out the opposition for 83; they made short work of *Alvanley* in the third only to fall, fighting gallantly, to *Lindal Moor* in the semi-final.

In their first round match *Withnell Fold* ran into *Greenmount* at full strength and could only manage to score 153 against the target figure of 175. Theirs is a charming ground outside Chorley surrounded by trees and with reservoirs on two sides. Between 1965–69 the village twice won the competition for the best-kept village in Lancashire and were runners-up on three occasions.

The *Greenmount* club was founded in 1880, and their ground, near Bury, has been described in the *Manchester Evening News* as one of the most attractive in the North-west. D. J. Hodgson, the club secretary, feels they hold a record which should be in *Wisden* – a player, now dead, once took four wickets with four balls, all to different decisions; bowled, lbw, caught, and stumped! In the Haig they rattled up 174 for 9 against *Withnell Fold* and 134 for 4 to *Mawdesley's* 131, only to lose a thrilling semi-final by 59 to 60 for 9 by *Hoghton*.

Hoghton, only some six miles from Blackburn, is nevertheless a delightful rural spot, practically owned by the de Hoghton family, one of whose ancestors served so delicious a loin of beef to Henry VIII that the masticating monarch immediately knighted it – hence 'sirloin'. I have however, heard this story in many parts of the country and also seen an 'orginal' table sold four times at different country house auctions.

The *Hoghton* cricket ground is in a saucer-shaped field and rises so sharply to the boundary in places that certain fours on the level are reduced to twos and singles. *Hoghton* put *Walshaw* out for 66 in their second-round Haig match in 37 overs and lost only two wickets in scoring the required 67, off 26 overs. They were dismissed for 91 by *Read* in the group semi-final, losing by five wickets. Gerald Dearden won *Walshaw's* Haig tie, the club captain taking 7 wickets for 12 runs in 7 overs against *Arnside;* six of his victims were bowled.

Thornham, near Middleton, Lancashire, do not lack medical support – Mr Oliver Jelly, the Manchester surgeon, is their president and Dr A. J. Crook, a hard-working honorary secretary. Peter Fitton, now second XI captain, recalls matches in which England fast bowlers Brian Statham and Frank Tyson took part in their youth as did Tommy Greenhough, the Lancashire and England leg-spinner. In 1947, Greenhough, then only 15, took 7 for 19 against *Thornham*.... 'I don't think I've ever been made to look such a fool on a cricket field,' Mr Fitton admitted, 'and by a 15-year-old boy at that.' But for all their past glories, *Thornham* went down badly in their first Haig match. For *Alvanley* K. Hinkley scored an unbeaten 144 in a 40-over total of 225 for 3 and then R. Peace's 5 wickets for 44 runs were the main factor of *Thornham's* all-out total of 150.

On a wet and windy Sunday in May, *Heyside* could not start their innings against *Cherry Tree* until 5 p.m., but went all out for quick runs and achieved 214 for 5 off their 40 overs. *Cherry Tree* had reached 94 for 4 in 20 overs when heavy rain finished play for the day, and *Heyside* with the higher run-rate were the winners. However, in their third round *they* were the weather's victims, losing on the toss of a coin to *Lindal Moor*.

Brooksbottom is not a Lancashire village, just the name of the cricket club in the village of Summerseat at the entrance to the Rossendale Valley. The club takes its name from Joshua Hoyle's Brooksbottoms cotton mill. In 1883 they moved up the hill to their present ground next to the school and church. 'And on this ground, something of a hill in itself,' wrote Brian Bearshaw in the *Manchester Evening News,* 'visiting teams do not fare at all well. It is three-and-a-half years since Brooksbottom lost a match at home, and if they can get through their first round Haig tie at *Croston,* their next three matches are all on their home ground.' Jack Bailey the club's secretary says that at home Brooksbottom are capable of sending any team packing – 'with this slope, and a good bowler, a ball can be two feet outside the off stump and still remove the leg peg.'

Alas for Mr Bailey's hopes, *Croston* scored 130 for 9 including 38 from N. Singleton, and with D. Alty taking 3 for 18, *Brooksbottom* were dismissed for 117.

Croston, a village between Preston and Southport, found D. Birch (6 for 20) in top bowling form for *Cartmel* in their second round match and were all out for 122 in reply to *Cartmel's* 140-7. *Cartmel,* 142, had no real answer to *Read's* 261 for 9 in the third round. *Wrea Green* who play on the village green with an adjacent duck pond, known locally as 'The Dub' were *Read's* first-round victims, being all out for 71, and losing by six wickets.

Mawdesley club was founded in the 1890's with, says H. Hinter the secretary, a fine tradition of teams being made up from locally-born players. Building development in the area has brought the village many new residents but so far 'no one of 1st XI standard.' With 164 for 6, including a bright 62 from K. Burton, they disposed of *Winwick* for 67 in their first Haig match, but went down in the second round to *Greenmount* by six wickets.

Group 6 – *Cheshire and North Wales*

Although their postal address is Stockport, Cheshire, *Buxworth C.C.* play in Derbyshire's Peak National Park. They were thus in the Cheshire and North Wales Haig group and drawn at home to *Compstall* in the first round, and did not do too well, being dismissed for 84 (D. Brown 3 for 11) to which *Compstall* replied with 86 for 2. Defeat, though, is not new to *Buxworth* who were once put out for a single run – and that scored by the last man – by neighbouring *Whaley Bridge.*

Apart from the beautiful setting where they play their cricket, the *Buxworth* team have the advantage of the use of the Navigation Inn as their headquarters and a famous licensee – Pat Phoenix, *Coronation Street's* Elsie Tanner. *Buxsworth,* incidentally, was originally called Bugsworth, the sweeter-sounding title being obtained after a pre-war campaign.

Compstall were drawn at home for the next round,

against *Mere* who batted first but could only score 65 with Peter Brown taking five of their wickets for two runs. *Compstall* coasted to 66 for 2 and a third round tie against *Toft*, which they won by 9 wickets – 77 to 78 for 1 – and to an equally convincing win over *Cholmondeley* whom they dismissed for 99, having piled up 198 for 6 in their own innings. In the final, however, they came up against *Northop Hall,* a strong North Wales side, and lost by four wickets in the 38th over.

The *Cholmondeley* club play at the foot of the grassy slope on which stands Cholmondeley Castle, the home of the sixth Marquis whose vast flock of Canadian geese and herd of Highland cattle are among the club's most constant supporters. With the cricket ground in view from the castle, the club have had to design special sightscreens, hinged and painted white to the front, and green to the back so that they can be folded after each match, the green merging with grass and surroundings. Before losing to *Compstall* in the semi-final, *Cholmondeley* had beaten *Ashton Hayes* by 8 wickets, *Elworth* by 2 wickets and *Mellor,* whom they dismissed for 89, going on to make 95 for 1 and victory.

Ron Holland of John Haig & Co. Ltd., who lives nearby, went along to watch the first round match between *Rostherne* and *Pott Shrigley*. *Rostherne,* Mr Holland says, is 'a quaint little hamlet which I had not visited before (no pubs).' *Rostherne* were dismissed for 98 and *Pott Shrigley* knocked off the runs for the loss of five wickets with D. Brooke making 31 not out and receiving his Haig tie from Mr Holland. *Rostherne,* so secretary L. Madeley tells me, originally played in Tatton Park where they used a bell tent as a changing room. They moved to their present ground with the church, 'rather more than a good six hit' down the lane.

A little cluster of cottages, quaintly and charmingly named, a school, a fine 500 year-old church, St Christopher's, and a cricket ground make up the Cheshire village of *Pott Shrigley* which has a population of 360. Situated in a National Park, the cricket ground is set in a dip with outfield slopes which one of their members, Derrick Brooke, described as 'interesting'. Mr Brooke has looked after the pitch for several years and very well, too, for as he says 'we get lots of runs, but we can't bowl the other sides out.'

Pott Shrigley went on to beat *Davenham* at home only to lose to *Charlesworth* in the third round, but from what I hear of the men of *Pott* they will not be unduly worried about a defeat, as long as the game itself was enjoyable.

Davenham, near Northwich, had a comfortable win over *Arley* whom they dismissed for 42 after their own 57 for 4. *Arley's* ground is pretty, but small, and you can only score a six there by hitting the ball clean over the pavilion or full toss into the adjoining woods. The ground, on the Arley Estate of Viscount Ashbrook, is in the depths of the country. A feature is 'The Doctor's Seat' outside the pavilion, in memory of Dr Love, first of three generations of doctors of that name who have been mainstays of the club since 1894.

Jeremy Weston, a typical member of this most friendly club was not optimistic about beating *Davenham*, although he said 'if our more capable batsmen can come off, and we can catch Davenham in the dark, we might just win.' Alas, it was not to be, but I do hope it was not the new batting gloves that caused *Arley's* downfall, for answering my questionnaire about equipment, Mr Weston sadly reported; 'we did have plenty of gloves, but the mice have been at them this winter.'

Menai Bridge C.C. have a new ground encircled by trees and a superb panoramic view of the Menai Straits, the bridges and Snowdonia beyond. New though the club is, they safely negotiated the first round of the Haig, making 195 for 6 and then dismissing *Bersham* for 89. George Lloyd, *Bersham's* secretary, was 'disgusted' with the team's performance and so were the Committee – so much so that they decided to award the Haig tie to John Carlton, the club umpire, as none of the players deserved it and 'umpires in local cricket do not have the opportunity to win medals, do glorious deeds etc.'

Bromborough Pool, a Wirrall side, travelled some 60 miles each way for their second round tie with *Mellor* and although they lost the match, Ron Holland, that intrepid Haig cricket follower, tells me that *Mellor* proved the perfect hosts. Rain delayed the start until after tea and the match had to be limited to 20 overs a side. The *Bromborough* players, wives and sweethearts, however, were entertained to lunch and in the *Mellor* bar, which may, or may not have been why the task of passing *Mellor's* 80 for 9 proved too much for them. Or it may have been the medium pace of Paul Wise, who coming on with *Bromborough* 50 for 1, proceeded to take seven wickets for 20 runs, including the hat-trick, and saw *Mellor* to victory by 13 runs. After the match both sides, supporters, and Mr and Mrs Holland adjourned to the Royal Oak for jugs of beer, drams of Haig and a superb supper of Hot Pot and red cabbage.

Rushton Taverners, a Macclesfield side was formed in 1919, with a ground at Rushton Spencer which has as its special features, according to secretary John Mark Dignam: 'one slope, two small hills, trout stream, watercress bed, one telegraph pole, etc.' – and presumably a wicket. Mr Dignam of the Royal Oak Inn, further commented 'this club is in a strong Methodist farming area (against Sunday cricket), thus it is impossible to rent a permanent field, so we have to move from year to year, and have no chance of preparing a good wicket.'

For all that, the Taverners did well in the Haig, beating *Chelford* by 16 runs in the first round, and only losing to *Toft* by four wickets in the second. And to lose to *Toft,* one of the strongest sides in their group was surely no disgrace. *Toft* have no ground problems for they play their cricket in Booths Park, just outside Knutsford, the land of Mr David Cowburn. 'We were given the land just before the war,' their chairman Bernard Raffo said, 'and the Cowburns generously built the pavilion for us.' Their original 'peppercorn' rent was half-a-crown a year, 'but it's now gone up to 15p,' says John Howard the secretary with mock sadness.

But the main feature of the *Toft* club – apart from the four trees within the boundary – to strike any of which yields four runs – is their magnificent contribution to coaching schoolboy cricketers. Messrs. Howard and Raffo 'saw the light' seven years ago and wrote to five schools in the Knutsford area offering practice and coaching facilities for any boy who cared to come to *Toft*. 'They came out in droves,' says Mr Raffo, who is also the licensee of the Leigh

Arms, 'and we now have some 100 young members aged from eight to 18 who can't wait for each season to start.' Last season two young members of *Toft* won places in the Cheshire Colt's side. With 146 (P. Raffo 50 and B. Manning 47) *Toft* disposed of *Oakmere* for 57 in the first Haig round and beat *Rushton Taverners* in the second before losing by nine wickets to *Compstall.*

Before the start of the Haig competition I would have had a small personal wager that *Marchwiel* would go far in the event, certainly to the final of their group. I would have lost my money for they went out in the first round to *Northop Hall,* admittedly the eventual group champions, but nothing will change my opinion that at *Marchwiel* near Wrexham there is one of the most pleasant and best maintained grounds in the country.

The club play at Marchwiel Hall, at one time the home of Sir Alfred and Lady McAlpine and now occupied by Mr and Mrs Peter Bell. A. J. McAlpine is the club president and his son Bobby and Peter Bell share the expenses of maintaining the ground in tip-top condition, the fortunate groundsman having at his disposal a wide variety of machinery. *Marchwiel* have played host to many county sides and touring teams in the past and their cricket weeks were always matches not to be missed. As I write this they have just tied a two-innings match with an Argentine touring side.

Cricket began at *Northop Hall* in 1908 when the club was brought into being by John Durham, an employee of the Galchog Colliery, and the game has flourished there ever since, the present ground being acquired in 1909. There was no cricket there during World War II, but in 1945 a new Sports Association was formed for the village, some £700 was collected and the money used to provide cricket and football pitches, together with a children's playground. Since 1958 the club has purchased the ground and built a new pavilion and, with a playing strength of around 30 members plus juniors, has established a fine reputation in local cricket circles, having been Flintshire and District League champions seven times.

Against *Marchwiel's* 112 for 7, *Northop* just managed

116 for 9, due mainly to a fighting 34 not out by Haydon Lloyd who was duly awarded the Haig tie. In the second round they dismissed *Hawarden Park* for 47 and knocked off the runs for the loss of four wickets; they beat *Overton* (155 for 9) by nine runs in the third round and moved into the final against *Compstall* by a 44-run semi-final victory over *Charlesworth and Chisworth,* another Derbyshire team allocated to the Cheshire group. In the final *Compstall* struggled to make 105 for 8 and *Northop* got home comfortably by four wickets in the 38th over.

Group 7 – Derbyshire

Shipley Hall's secretary J. K. Fitchen describes their ground at Shipley Heanor as having a 'Lord's slope', but if he intended this as a prophecy for September 9th, Mr Fitchen's crystal ball was shattered in the Derbyshire group final when his club lost, albeit narrowly, to *Holmsfield*.

However, *Shipley,* founded in 1899, started well in the Haig, making 176 in their first round match against *Lullington Park* whom they dismissed for 74. For *Shipley* D. Stott wrote his name in the Haig record book with a splended innings of 115. *Shipley* continued winning by comfortable margins, overcoming *Stainsby* by six wickets in the second round and *Kirk Langley* by a similar margin in the third. In the semi-final, too, although they only made 78 for 9, they dismissed *Openwoodgate* for 58.

Holmsfield had a slightly easier passage to the final with a first round bye and a third round toss-of-the-coin 'victory' over *Willington*. But they were in top form for their semi-final with *Clifton* whom they dismissed for 60 and then proceeded to a nine-wicket win.

Clifton, founded in 1867, awarded their Haig tie to 18-year-old Bill Bailey who is still at Ashbourne Grammar School, for his two wickets for 17 runs and two important catches in their first round victory over *Hilton*. Rain restricted the match to 30 overs a side, but *Clifton* only lasted

23 of theirs, being all out for 92. *Hilton,* faced with tight bowling and keen fielding, finished their 30 overs still four runs short and with one wicket in hand. *Clifton* had things much more to their liking in the second round, making 147 for 6 and then disposing of *Breadsall* for a mere 69. Their third round opponents, *Netherseale St Peter's,* managed a further 10 runs, but *Clifton* had made 156 for nine.

Risley C.C. did not re-form after World War II until 1970, and now play at Risley Hall, an approved school, by permission of the headmaster who also stands as umpire for the club. In pre-war days they played at Risley Park, then the home of Terah Hooley, financier and friend of royalty. The estate was broken up and the Army used the grounds for tank training. The Rev. Douglas Hughes is the club chairman – 'very useful to have the Rector,' says captain Alan Taylor, 'sometimes we need all the "help" we can get.' They didn't expect to do too well in the Haig this year, but enthusiasm is a quality *Risley* have in plenty, the skills and victories will come in due course.

In 1970 *Hathersage* C.C. staged an eight-day Festival of Cricket, not only to celebrate 120 years of cricket in the village, but also to raise funds for ground and pavilion improvements at Baulk Lane. The week was officially opened by the Duke of Devonshire, supported by the Hathersage Silver Band, and a costume match between President's and Captain's XIs. Major David Carr, the Derbyshire secretary and Norman Yardley, former captain of England and Yorkshire, were the principal guests at the dinner dance on the Friday.

Hathersage did not have a successful Haig, losing their first match by five wickets to *Sutton-on-the-Hill* who dismissed them for 123. Nor did *Sutton* survive the next round; they were all out for 37 against *Openwoodgate* who coasted to victory by five wickets.

Youlgrave, near Bakewell, celebrated their centenary in 1971 with the opening of a new pavilion by Ian Buxton, the Derbyshire captain. This season they played in league cricket for the first time.

Group 8 – Nottinghamshire and Lincolnshire

Collingham and District club who play in the Newark area, emerged as champions of the Nottinghamshire and Lincolnshire combined group by beating *Cuckney* in the final. *Collingham,* formed about 1880 play at Dale Field 'an old ground, excellent wicket and beautiful surroundings,' says secretary J. Empsall. The club stage a Notts 2nd XI fixture each season. A high-scoring side they set a club record in 1971, of 336 for 3 wickets in a home match against Sheffield Collegiate. Membership is strong with 46 full playing, 14 juniors and 200 non-playing. *Collingham* had a smooth passage to the final, defeating *Fiskerton* (7 wickets) *Thoresby Park* (8 wickets) and *Blyth* by 3 wickets in a low-scoring semi-final.

Cuckney, near Mansfield was formed in the early 1900's. Secretary D. B. Palmer was an England Schoolboys under-15 player and – shades of this year's first Test – recalls that playing for Midlands Schools against Southern Schools he was out for a distinguished 'duck' – caught A. E. Knott, bowled G. G. Arnold!

Blyth's ground at Old Coates Road has trees on two sides, and a slight slope from the square up to the pavilion. The club is self-supporting, reports B. Ginever, the fixtures secretary, and in the past four years has raised £800 for its pavilion, tractor and gang-mower. *Blyth* have won promotion in the Bassetlaw League for the past three years and Mr Ginever has played a full share in their success. In the first round of the Haig he led them to victory with a fine 119 not out in *Blyth's* 194 for 2, after *Messingham* had made 191 for 7 in their allotted overs.

Family tradition is a feature of *Farndon* C.C. whose playing members including four Heliwell brothers, Keith (44) Ron (40) John (37) and Peter (37), plus Keith's son Neil (18) and three Tindales – John, the club secretary, Geoff the captain, and David (31). They met *Firbeck* in the first Haig round, were all out for 70 and lost by four wickets.

Fiskerton C.C., near Southwell, were *Collingham's* first round victims which must hardly have surprised their captain

Bill Tomlinson who describes their ground as 'formerly, and all too often presently, a paddock.'

However, *Fiskerton* are pursuing a vigorous policy of training boys from the surrounding villages, with coaching one night a week at indoor nets before the start of the season. Their previous ground adjoined the Manor house but, as is so often the case, was ploughed up by the new owner. Now two local benefactors have given the club six acres of land, but some £2,000 is still needed to put the ground in cricketing shape.

The Griffin Inn at Plumtree, some five and a half miles south-east of Nottingham, dates back to 1675 and for years has been the headquarters of *Plumtree* C.C. The club, founded in 1819, celebrated its 150th anniversary in 1969 with a match against Old Notts Cricketers led by Reg Simpson. After a bye in the first round of the Haig, *Plumtree* dismissed *Cuckney* for 123, but could only muster 100 in reply. This was disappointing, but historically interesting as from 1266 to 1330 the village was a Wapentake, or Hundred (an area from which 100 men could be taken for army service).

Group 9 – Staffordshire and Shropshire

One tends to think of Staffordshire in terms of Wolverhampton, Wednesfield and Walsall, the industrial 'Black Country' of the Midlands when that appellation came from reeking factory chimneys, potteries and coal mines, and considerably pre-dated any form of racial description. But, as I found during several happy journalistic years in the area in the late 1950s, there is much more to that part of the country than heavy industry. Small, and very highly independent, villages surround the big towns and the cricket there is as bucolic and rural as it is in Somerset or Suffolk.

The Haig grouping together of Staffordshire and Shropshire village clubs was a particularly happy blending – and the Group 9 table, with *Swynnerton Park*, near Eccleshall, emerging as eventual champions, evokes many personal nostalgic memories. *Abbots Bromley*, for example, home of the age-old Horns Dancers' ritual – unique in England – did not get beyond the second round, but this did not deter secretary John Harrison, top of the club's batting averages for seven consecutive seasons, from referring to his team as 'the best club side in the area ... the best drinking side by far.'

Alveley, near Bridgnorth, describe Roy Newton, their skipper for 17 years, as 'the Fox', but even his shrewdness was not able to take them past the first round; they were all out for 83 and *Forton* beat them by three wickets only to fall in the second round to *Worfield.*

Worfield I know from long experience with the *Wolverhampton Express and Star* Sunday side. Their ground at Davenport Park was always a delight to visit – so was the nearby Davenport Arms – with its four Scotch pines and lime tree all within the boundary. Lieut-General Sir Oliver Leese was their president in those days and is now a vice-president. Keeping village cricket in its true perspective M. Thomas, the club secretary, then reported Sir Oliver's other high positions in cricket '... President of Warwickshire C.C.C. and a past President of M.C.C.' *Worfield* lost in the third round to *Fenns Bank and Iscoyd* and *Fenns Bank* went through only to be beaten in the final. D. R. Gallagher had an excellent match for *Fenns Bank* in their first round against *Shawbury;* he made 61 of their 195 runs and then shattered the opposition with five wickets for 15 runs in his allotted nine overs, to be awarded his club's Haig tie.

Enville, near Stourbridge, also did well at least until they met *Swynnerton* in the semi-final who made 99 without loss against *Enville's* 97 for 5. *Enville's* ground is almost on the lawn of Enville Hall and a venue much sought by local sides, says secretary D. R. Thomas. In 1857, according to the *London Illustrated News,* the playing area at Enville was both larger and more level than Lord's ... and 'therefore take precedence and must be accounted the finest cricket ground in the world.' In 1951 *Enville* staged a festival match between Free Foresters and Flamingoes of Holland and I doubt if anyone who has dined at 'The Cat', the only pub in the village, has ever eaten finer ham and eggs.

Leycett, near Newcastle-under-Lyme in the north of

Staffordshire, had a first-round bye, only to lose by eight wickets to *Milford Hall*. *Leycett* was a mining village until the closure of the pit there some 16 years ago; the village is being slowly demolished and there are now less than 20 houses left. Despite this, says J. H. Hill their secretary; 'our club has grown in stature by contrast and we have just erected a new club room and bar.'

Out towards Burton-on-Trent, *Old Netherseal Colliery*, C.C. founded in 1873 is still very active. They play at Rickman's Corner, Linton Heath, the ground being named after Col. R. B. Rickman who played for Derbyshire.

St George's at Donnington outside Telford New Town, have a most pleasant ground below the main Wellington-Shrewsbury road and did well in the Haig beating *Kings Bromley* and *Milford Hall* before losing their semi-final round to *Fenns Bank*. *Woodville C.C.* particularly welcomed the Haig competition for secretary M. J. Adams reports the lack of a good knock-out event in his part of Staffordshire. *Woodville* beat *Sandyford* in the first round, but perhaps their lack of knock-out experience was responsible for their all-out total of 101 in reply to *Alrewas*' 168 for 5.

Group 10 – Leicestershire, Rutland and Lincolnshire

Empingham, having disposed of Rutland neighbours *Ketton* with four wickets to spare, went on to become champions of the Leicestershire, Rutland and Lincolnshire section, beating *Hathern Old* in the Group 10 final to add to their 1971 victories in their local 20-overs aside knock-outs. In the semi-final of the Haig they triumphed over *Ancaster*.

Apart from that defeat the story of the *Ancaster* club since it was re-formed in 1967 has been one of continual success, particularly in the work done by members to improve the facilities at their attractive ground in Ermine Street. R. D. Carpenter told me last January that on re-formation the club had only £26 in the bank and that this had now risen to about £700 towards the cost of a new pavilion. And that £700 was available after the club had laid a grass pitch (£518) to replace the concrete strip, bought new nets and equipment (£160), sight screens (made by members £65), and made donations to senior citizens of £200. *Ancaster* also have provided three Christmas parties for the village children. Obviously all the village have contributed to the cricket and the club has returned its supporters' loyalty which is, after all, what village cricket is all about.

During the summer I read an article deploring the lack of cricket in Rutland, but G. Cooper captain of the *Braunston* club, past winners of the Oakham League, started off in the Haig competition with considerable optimism – 'we would like to play the Aussies at Lord's,' he wrote. Unfortunately it was not to be, as *Empingham* defeated *Braunston* in the second round. As some consolation for Mr Cooper, I can't recall the flower of England's cricket doing very well in the Lord's Test either!

They have been playing cricket in the tiny north Leicestershire village of *Hathern* since at least 1814, but no one can quite recall how the club came to be known as Hathern 'Old.' The name of the Randon family figures largely in the club's history and no less than five Randons were in the Loughborough side which beat an All-England team in 1868. With Frederick John Randon rests the honour of having bowled out 'W. G.' in both innings at Victoria Park, Leicester, the first time for a 'duck', the second for eight runs, none of which, by the way, was scored off Frederick John.

Group 11 – Worcestershire

Avoncroft C.C., near Bromsgrove, who duly won the Worcestershire county group by defeating *Willersley* in the final, had probably their best victory of the competition when they beat the strong *Stoke Works* side by four wickets in the third round, after dismissing *Stoke* for 72. *Avoncroft's* ground, says John Sketchley, has three trees within the boundary and a local rule that no batsman can be out 'caught' if the ball has been in contact with any part of a tree; what's more he scores four runs for striking a tree, whether the ball has first hit the ground or not.

Stoke Works C.C., also of Bromsgrove, were founded in 1860 and in 1970 had their best recorded season, losing only three matches out of 41 played, with A. Cottrill, the club captain, scoring more than 1,300 runs, including five centuries. *Stoke* only managed 88 in their second round match with *Belbroughton,* but dismissed their opponents for 66.

Cricketers at *Birlingham,* near Pershore, play in idyllic surroundings on a beautiful, compact ground surrounded by many large trees – 'prettiest ground in England' avows R. A. Kibby, their fixtures secretary. *Birlingham's* Haig ambitions, however, did not survive the first round as they lost by the toss of a coin to *Himbleton*. *Himbleton* won through to the third round only to be beaten 98–102 by *Ombersley*. Stan Rogers, the *Himbleton* secretary, names one 'Cocky' Tredwell as the club personality who, whether umpiring or not, will never accept any excuses from anyone. Any relation to the legendary 'Coppy' of old Ned Larkin's reminiscences in the Archers programme, I wonder?

Picturesque grounds abound in Worcestershire and *Knighton-on-Teme* play at Newnham Farm surrounded by hop fields and ornamental trees, while from *Bredon's* ground there is a charming view up Bredon Hill, a well-known beauty spot. *Bredon* have as their president the Rector, the Rev. L. Birch – '*pro ecclesia et cricket*' says John Famey, the secretary – and as vice-president Sir Raymond Priestley, the last survivor of Scott's expedition.

Chaddesley Corbett, too, play in deep country outside Kidderminster and the village draws many town dwellers in the spring for the Harkaway point-to-point. Unfortunately in their first round Haig match they found W. Harrison of *Stoke Works* in top form with an unbeaten 76 in a total of 181 for 4; despite a fighting 58 by A. Gould, *Chaddesley* could only manage 161 for 8 in their reply.

Offenham, near Evesham, time their matches by the clock on the church tower that overlooks the ground, and their captain M. Bell wasted no time in their first-round match, scoring 50 not out in an unbroken sixth-wicket stand of 64.

Offenham reached 163 for 5 in their 40 overs and then dismissed *Cutnall Green* for 56 (P. Cresswell 3 for 9), with Bell being awarded the Haig tie.

Group 12 – Warwickshire

Hockley Heath C.C. losing finalists in the Warwickshire group to *Astwood Bank* are a young – only three members over 30 – and lively side who, according to their chairman Robert A. Davies 'train on Scotch and best bitter and exotic foods, usually after matches.' Mr Dawes early in 1972 valued the club ground near Solihull at £500,000 for development purposes. *Hockley* had a good run in the Haig beating *Flecknoe* by 56 runs, *Leck Wootton* by 81, *Wishaw* by 37 and *Tanworth-in-Arden* in the semi-final by 59.

Also near Solihull, the attractively named *Catherine-de-Barnes* club play on a ground bordered by the Birmingham-Stratford canal. The ground is leased from a local brewery and at one time any batsman hitting a ball full pitch into the canal received a free pint of beer on each occasion – a drive of 100 yards over mid-on or a 'cowshot', somewhat shorter, over square-leg's head. A feat rarely achieved, reports G. H. Bray, the secretary, but 'a great wicket-taker' of thirsty visitors. Despite the withdrawal of this concession, *Catherine-de-Barnes* struggled to the third round of the Haig before losing to *Astwood Bank* by seven wickets.

Berkswell C.C. founded in 1898 play at Meeting House Lane, Balsall Common near Coventry. They lost their first-round match by two wickets to *Rowington* who went on to beat *Offchurch* and *Dunton Bassett,* only to lose by 59 runs in their semi-final with *Astwood Bank.*

Earlswood whose ground is in Watery Lane and whose favourite pub is the 'Reservoir Hotel', sank with all hands to *Astwood Bank* by nine wickets, B. T. Spittle 5 for 13 and C. Robinson 4 for 6, dismissing them for a lowly 41. R. J. Summers is the doyen of *Earlswood* cricket; he played from 1913 until 1966 and now acts as custodian of their equipment, machinery and club records.

Group 13 – Northamptonshire

Although the *Farnborough* club did not survive the second round of the Haig, their membership rules deserve full mention for, says James Nurden, players must live, work or have some family or social connection in the village, with residents having priority of selection. Only 20 village clubs from Northamptonshire entered the Haig competition with *Horton House* emerging as the group champions, beating *Overstone Park* in the final. One would hope for a much greater representation in 1973 from this cricketing county which abounds in villages.

In their first round match *Little Harrowden,* near Wellingborough, scored 147 for 7 and then proceeded to dismiss *Titchmarsh* for only 25 runs. David Tapp, 20, was the terror of Titchmarsh taking six wickets for a mere nine runs and winning his club's Haig tie. *Harrowden* then met *Horton House* in the second round and themselves could only score 87 for 6 to lose by three wickets.

Boddington for whom Eric Southam, 49, is captain, groundsman, opening bowler and batsman, beat *Castle Ashby* in the first round and then dismissed *Hinton-in-the-Hedges* for 52 to win by seven wickets in the second round. However, they suffered a near-similar fate themselves when they lost to *Overstone Park* in the next round.

Hinton-in-the-Hedges were early Haig entrants and the name of this delightful village got its fair measure of publicity. *Hinton C.C.* were formed before 1900, and their history has not been short of incident: Tom Turvey, now a vice-president, was a bowler of some renown having taken all 10 wickets in a match on three occasions. In June 1925 *Hinton* played a two-innings match against Magdalen College School and did not exactly shine; they were dismissed for 7 runs in the first innings but improved this lowly total by one at their second attempt!

Syresham went out in the first round to Rushton, (76–80), but had the man of the match, and Haig tie winner, in J. Neil of Silverstone who scored 19 of *Syresham's* total of 76 and took five *Rushton* wickets for six runs in $4\frac{3}{4}$ overs.

Rushton went on to the semi-final of the Haig, losing to *Horton House,* but theirs is a success story still. P. G. Larking took over as club secretary when he was only 23 and he and D. Kendall, captain at 21, built up a team of young players and a go-ahead committee. Before *Rushton* could enter the Kettering and District League's Premier Division they had to find a new ground and, in fact, played away from home on a council pitch for four years. They concentrated on fund-raising schemes so that when in 1970 they were given a field they were in a position to spend £3,000 on the playing area, fencing and car park. The club, with the help of their bank, the National Playing Fields Association and The Lord's Taverners, started to build a £5,000 pavilion at the start of this season.

Group 14 – Cambridgeshire and Huntingdon

Kimbolton deservedly became group champions for Cambridgeshire and Huntingdon when they beat *Terrington St Clements* in the final. In earlier rounds *Kimbolton* beat *Earith* without many problems. They put *Fenstanton* out in the third round and in the semi-final scored 164 to which *Fordham* could only reply with 63. *Fordham* play on the recreation ground, and being a small village, as their secretary M. J. Arnold reports, 'we have great difficulty in making ends meet, but we do take pride in our wicket and our club.' I would imagine *Fordham* enjoy their cricket immensely, both during and after the games, and when Mr Arnold challenged Mike Henderson of Haig to bring a side to play against them he was most careful to point out that it would be inadvisable to attempt to drive back to London after the *Fordham* hospitality. Unfortunately the match could not be arranged for the 1972 season, but we have it well in mind.

Terrington started off extremely well, beating *Milton* in the first round, with R. Arnold, who took 7 for 14, dismissing them for 45 after he had played a large part in *Terrington's* total of 103. Arnold's 33 runs provided an outstanding all-round performance in the Haig first round.

Terrington dismissed *Haddenham* for only 11 runs in the second round, winning by 8 wickets. In the semi-final *Over* could only muster 46 runs and *Terrington* cruised home with 47 for 1. *Over* scored 129 for 8 in the second round and then dismissed *Isleham* for 101. *Isleham's* man-of-the-match and Haig tie winner was M. Walker with 27 not out and three wickets for 32.

Abington C.C. were founded about 1860, but of recent years the club playing strength has declined quite alarmingly, possibly because the village has now become a commuter area for Cambridge. P. J. Cutmore, their secretary, tells me that in fact *Abington* is really two parishes, Great and Little, but the club, by dropping these titles, has helped to bridge the gap between the parishes. 'What a pity,' says Mr Cutmore, of their decline, 'because our square is reputed to be one of the best playing surfaces in the county, but we still always win our matches... in the pub afterwards.'

Offord C.C. are fortunate in having Mr R. G. Furbank as their president and benefactor. Mr Furbank, a local farmer, provides the cricket field rent-free to the club for as long as he farms the land. A. J. Schearing, the club secretary, told me before the competition started that the entire side would be residents of the village, mostly born and bred there. They were unfortunate to find *Kimbolton* in true championship form for their second round of the match.

Whittlesford, founded in the 1860's came through the first two rounds of the Haig, beating *March St Mary's* by eight wickets and *Horseheath* by six wickets, before bowling to *Terrington* in the third round. P. R. Allcock tells me that his club is 'far from lacking in personalities' and include a greyhound trainer wicket-keeper and an opening bowler who is leader of the London Balaliaka Orchestra.

Group 15 – Norfolk and Suffolk

Bradfield, near North Walsham, came through to win the Norfolk and Suffolk group championship and thus cleared the first few hurdles towards their ambition to play on a London Test Match ground for the second time. Four years ago, G. J. Spinks reminds me, they played a one-day game at the Oval on the day after England had beaten the Australians. *Bradfield* met a team captained by Raman Subba Row, the former England opener, and were hoping to be the first village side to have appeared both at the Oval and Lord's. *Kimbolton,* in the sixth round of the Haig, dashed *Bradfield's* hopes for 1972.

Although *Burrough Green,* near Newmarket, scored 237 for 7 and dismissed *Benhall* for exactly 100 in the third round and then beat *East Bergholt* by a convincing 64 runs in the semi-final, they ran into all sorts of trouble against *Bradfield* being dismissed for only 33; the eventual champions duly knocked off the runs for the loss of three wickets. *Burrough Green,* despite the smallness of the village, and a population of some 300, still manage to field two *XI's* each week. R. Starves, their captain, pays full tribute to the support the club receive from the rest of the village. He tells me that one of their greatest helpers, the late Rev. P. R. K. Wittaker, at one time played for Warwickshire Second XI.

Bealings C.C. have played at Great Bealings House, Woodbridge, since their formation in 1961, but unfortunately their president and patron, Miss E. G. Crane, died early in 1972, and C. C. Stott, secretary, told me that their future was then in some doubt. *Bealings* were all out for 51 and lost to *Bures* in the second round, *Bures* themselves then falling to *East Bergholt*

Benhall, near Saxmundham, claim a unique event in village cricket history – Queen Mother Stopped Play. Ray Woodard, their secretary, said that the main talking point of the 1971 season was when stumps were drawn for the arrival of Her Majesty's helicopter, which landed on the outfield. Shortly afterwards the Queen Mother, who had been paying a short visit to Sternfield House, arrived at the field and was flown to Sandringham. Stumps were re-pitched, and play resumed.

Cricket was first played at *East Bergholt* on July 21, 1756. The club did well in their early Haig fixtures beating *Coddenham* (79–23), *Woolpit* (80–81 for 6) and *Bures* (97 for 5–93), before losing to *Burrough Green* in the semi-final. *Great Whitchingham,* near Norwich, claim to have the largest supporters' club for a village side in Norfolk. Wilf Smith formed this club three years ago and they now have 250 active upporters. Unfortunately, in the Haig, *Whitchingham's* rubber-link matting pitch was not proof against the bowling of R. Bobbin of *Mulbarton* who took nine wickets for 15 out of a total of 42, *Mulbarton* knocking off the runs with nine wickets to spare.

Before the Haig started it became an intriguing Press exercise to speculate how villages with attractive names would fare in the tournament, and *Helions Bumpstead,* near Haverill in Suffolk, attracted many takers, although with a population of only 350 they were one of the smaller clubs in the competition. *Wetherden,* however, held *Helions* to 109 in their allotted overs and then made 112 for 6, to which P. Carr contributed 58 not out.

Mundford, beaten in the semi-final by *Bradfield,* play on an attractive ground in the centre of the village near Thetford, surrounded by a forestry area. After a bye in the first round, they beat *South Walsham* by nine wickets in the second and in the third round dismissed *East Harling* for 48 against their own total 66. *South Walsham,* who used to boast John Edrich as a playing member, have had their problems of recent years, but are now beginning to stablise again, after a dismal 1971 when they failed to win a game. Highlight of the '71 season was the club's match with Bloemfentein Ramblers. 'We lost by five wickets,' reports P. Fisher, their captain, 'but held our own in the pub afterward.'

Group 16 – Hereford and South Wales

Gowerton, near Swansea, who share their ground with the local rugby club and have D. Gwynne Walters, the international Rugby Union referee as their chairman, proved much the strongest side in the Hereford and South Wales group, becoming champions when they beat *Kington* in the final by 72 runs. In the previous round they scored a massive 313 for 8 in their allotted overs against *Crickhowell's* 86 for 5.

Brooksbottom C.C.'s ground at Summerseatt, Lancs. The pronounced slope of the pitch is a notorious wicket-taker

Cuckney, group champions of Notts. and Lincs. with Mrs L. Palmer, their Lady scorer

The Shamley Green team who won the Surrey group title.

Bedwellty formed their cricket club in December 1970, especially to take part in the Haig competition. They had a bye in the first round, and in the second could only muster 38 for nine against *Newton's* 74 for one. *Kington* had a cliff-hanging match in the first round against *Bromyard* who, batting first, scored 223 including a fine 109 by A. Mills. R. Richardson took six Bromyard wickets for 27 and then made 71 out of *Kington's* winning 226 for 6. They went on to beat *Canon Frome* by seven wickets and *Newton* by a similar margin in the semi-final. Probably Tony Mills's century for *Bromyard* came as no surprise to his club for in 1971 he won a national competition for the most scores of over 50 in a season – 17 in all, including five centuries.

Canon Frome play alongside the old Hereford-Gloucester canal, now disused. Excavations for the old canal's tunnel near the ground resulted in large mounds of earth which members used to full advantage by building their pavilion and car park on this natural grandstand.

Jeff Jones, the former Glamorgan and England fast left-arm bowler, whom injury unfortunately caused to retire prematurely from the first-class game, now acts as coach to *Dafen Welfare C.C.*, near Llanelli, where he started his cricket career at the age of 14. *Dafen,* whose first and second teams both won their respective divisions of the South Wales Cricket Association in 1971, had a bye in the first round of the Haig before losing to *Gowerton* by 23 runs.

Pontyberem celebrated their centenary in 1970 with a match against a full Glamorgan side. Their most attractive ground, semi-circled by the river Gwendraeth is situated in the centre of the village and cricket has been played continuously there since the field was donated by Mr T. Seymour, the squire, in 1870. Enterprisingly, in 1962 the club bought an ex-RAF hut, reassembled it and fitted it out as an indoor cricket school. They beat *Rockfield* in the first round of the Haig, but in the second lost to *Nantymoel* on the toss of a coin.

Rockfield proudly claim one of the most attractive settings for cricket in the country, and their ground at Black Meadow attracts many local artists. The club secretary, M. J. Wilding, says 'the club have greatly improved their facilities over the last 10 years, renovating old cow sheds, installing electricity, and toilet and washing amenities.' Next on their list is the building of a club bar.

Group 17 – Gloucestershire

Stephen Hearle, fixture secretary of *Dumbleton C.C.*, who play at Dairy Lane, near Evesham, tells me that despite its Worcestershire postal address, the village is in Gloucestershire, and according to Mr Hearle in the early part of 1932, 'the population of Dumbleton, up until recently was 499 ...' By the end of the 1972 season he had not elaborated on this!

One had great hopes of Dumbleton in the Haig, if only because there they appear to play cricket in the proper village way. Unfortunately this was not reflected in their defeat in the first round by *Frocester,* when they could only manage 58 runs against a total of 113. *Dumbleton,* which derives its title from the Anglo-Saxon 'spur of the bare black hill,' refutes this nomenclature by being a quiet and pretty village – coupled with a new housing estate – which is supported by a farming fraternity and a number of wealthy local landowners. Behind *Dumbleton's* ancient pavilion (now modernised slightly) there is a duck pond where the keen angler can fish, and for after-match festivities Brian Lyes is under great pressure for 'take off' impressions ranging from a love-sick turkey to Harry Secombe.

Frocester were the losing finalists to *Dowdeswell and Foxcote,* accounting for *Stanway* and *Witcombe* in the second and third rounds, and *Speech House,* by 12 runs in the semi-final ... another fascinating name departing from the Haig.

Christopher Legg, who is the secretary of *Barnsley-Beeches C.C.* reports his club's indebtedness to their president Charles Henderson, who provides them with a rent-free ground, so that they only need to charge an annual subscription to members of £1. That is not the only generosity for during 1971 the licensee of 'The Greyhound' in the village provided each member of the team with a free pint of beer, providing they won six matches. 'This we managed three times', says Mr Legg. *Barnsley-Beeches,* with a bye in the first round could only score 37 for 9 against *Dowdeswell's* 105 for 5, and I trust that their supporting landlord provided Haig for victors and vanquished!!

G. Mayo took *Chalford* to 197 for 9 with an unbeaten 38; Mayo, the club captain, had already taken two fine catches and bowled economically to earn *Chalford's* Haig tie in their match against *Lechlade,* but his efforts were in vain as *Lechlade* had scored 235 for 3, with G. Cox 95 not out, and J. Deacon scoring 81.

In the late 1880s G. L. Jessop, the mighty hitter for Gloucestershire and England, played for *Lechlade* when he was a master at Burford Grammar School. On this small circular ground, set in manor parkland, Jessop scored a vast number of runs, particularly in their two-day matches against M.C.C.

Pilning C.C. was founded in 1883 and resumed playing operations in 1946. The club is well known for long-serving members, such as Glyn Williams, who first put bat to ball in 1950 and by the end of the 1971 season had scored more than 10,000 runs for his club; Vernon Humphries reached the same target three weeks into the start of the 1972 season, and Ron Howse, who again played in 1950 for the first time has taken 1,000 wickets. *Pilning* beat *Andoversford* by 82 runs in the second round of the Haig, scored 159 for 8 against *Tormanton's* 135 in the third round, before succumbing to *Dowdeswell* by 56 as against 57 for 2 in the semi-final.

Tormanton, who, says captain C. Orchard, can field eight left-handers on occasions, duly disposed of *South Hill* in the second round, who were all out for 78. In their first-round match *South Hill* scored 77 (J. Houghton 27) and dismissed *Upton St Leonards* for 43; Houghton with four wickets for nine runs in 3.4 overs, was awarded the Haig tie.

As is unfortunately so often the case with village clubs, *Stanway,* near Cheltenham, failed to recapture their pre-war glories, for after a bye in the first round of the Haig they lost to *Frocester,* only making 95 in reply to the losing finalists 205. *Stanway's* very pleasant thatched pavilion was donated by Sir James Barrie, of *Peter Pan* and 'Allahakbarries' fame in 1925 during his many visits to Stanway House. *Stanway* in 1933 staged a superb match; Jardine's successful 'bodyline' touring side in Australia against a Gloucestershire XI, which included Wally Hammond, Barnett, and Parker; the England side turned out Herbert Sutcliffe, C. F. Walters, the Nawab of Pataudi, Maurice Leyland, Bob Wyatt and Gubby Allen.

Group 18 – Buckinghamshire

In the Oxfordshire Group, *Aston Rowant,* after a great start in the first round when they scored 304 for 4 (R. McQueen 77, W. Edwards 61, G. Lindon 67 not out) then proceeded to dismiss *Fleur de Lys* of Dorchester for 74 with P. Lambourne taking four wickets for five runs. *Aston* kept up the pressure, putting out *Ewelme* for 48 in the third round, having themselves scored 157 for 5. They then made 177 for 5, and dismissed *Milton* for 119 to go through to the final against *Bledlow*. *Bledlow* won the title, having previously beaten *Fingest* by five wickets in the second round, and *Hambleden* on the toss of a coin in the third, and *Great and Little Tew* in the semi-final.

Ardley, near Bicester, was formed three years ago from scratch, reports Mrs I. R. Hodges, their secretary, but they went out of the first round of the Haig, scoring 51 against *Charlbury's* 99. *Charlbury,* in fact, have as a member, Bill Fraser, who is chairman of the Commonwealth Cricket Club in Washington D.C. Jessop played on their ground, and they have been hosts to a B.B.C. Sports Forum. In a low-scoring match they were dismissed by *Ewelme* for 32 to lose by eight wickets in the second round.

Combe, founded in 1870, lost in the first round to *Hambleden* for whom C. Vere-Nicholl took 4 for 16, and A. Wilson made 23 in their total of 85 against *Combe's* 82. *Hambleden* came through the second round, scoring 200 for 9 against *Bletchington's* 101. *Forest Hill Sports Club* combine cricket and soccer, although the cricket club, reports Mrs B. G. Spalding, was started in the village in 1887. They lost their match by some considerable distance to *Great and Little Tew,* scoring only 99 in reply to 207 for 9, and decided to award their Haig tie to Roy Smith, a former player who, Mrs Spalding says, 'umpired the game in near-arctic conditions without a controversial decision.'

Greys Green, Henley-on-Thames, were the *Tews* third-round victims, but had seemed an even money bet, because asked for his club's performances in 1971, N. W. Dennis told me; 'Don't know, but we usually end up with about 50%.' He describes their ground as being 'surrounded by hedges, fences, walls, houses, paths, road etc., ... four over the road, six over the far hedge.'

Tetsworth have played on the village green since at least 1850, and the club has supported the Parish Council in developing the green as a playing field. But, says K. Crump, their secretary, all the money had to be raised on a voluntary basis, and so far only £1,000 of an estimated cost of £4,500 had been forthcoming at the start of the 1972 season. Mr Crump also reports, 'in the past five years in the High Wycombe league we have not yet played in the same division ... twice relegated ... twice in succession ... promotion in three years to the first division for the first time ...'

Although *Apsley Guise,* near Leighton Buzzard, have records of a match played against Woburn on June 14, 1858, the club base their date of formation some 13 years later. They play on The Common at West Hill where there is a splendid view from the wicket across 20 miles of countryside. They had a bye in the first round of Group 19 of the Haig and in the second dismissed *Chenies and Latimer* for 107 after running up 150 for 7 themselves. It was a case of third round unlucky for *Apsley* who could only muster 65 runs in reply to *Winchmore Hill's* 130. Another ambition departed here, for Geoffrey White the club secretary had said of their proposed appearance at Lord's ... 'Of course, the main attraction is the whisky, and we shall play like men possessed at the thought of it.'

Brill, near Aylesbury, were founded in 1868 and in their centenary year met a composite side which included many first-class cricketers. Ian Peebles, Oxford, Middlesex and

England leg-spin bowler between the wars played on this attractive ground during his undergraduate days. The ground at Church Close, is some 650 feet above sea level and has a natural grandstand formed by earthworks raised during the Civil War. *Brill* 111 – a neat Nelsonian score – beat *Monk's Risborough* by 10 runs in the second round, but fell to *Brooker* in the next tie.

Eversholt emerged as the Buckinghamshire champions, beating *Brooker* in the semi-final by 29 runs and then overcoming *Winchmore Hill* in the final, *Winchmore* having defeated *Milton Keynes* – a 'rural community?' – in their semi-final by one wicket.

Hyde Heath's 'military' might – they have two members of the Cornish National Army in the club – was insufficient to see them through the first round and in a low-scoring match they lost 45 for 8 to *Maids Moreton's* 46 for 4. Here again we had great hopes of attractively-titled *Maids Moreton* showing up at Lord's, but they did not survive the third round against *Knotty Green*. This Beaconsfield club always aim to combine good cricket with an equal level of hospitality and sportsmanship, reports J. M. Roughley, and certainly they have an attractive ground on which to fulfil this laudable intention. The club, with the aid of the National Playing Fields Association, has recently laid down a high-standard artificial practice wicket. However, in the third round, *Eversholt* rattled up 192 for 6 against them and *Knotty Green* were all out for 88, a sad ending for a club that has actor Stanley Holloway as president.

Group 20 – Bedfordshire and Hertfordshire

Essendon C.C., near Hatfield, was founded in 1810, and got through to the third round of the Bedfordshire and Hertfordshire group where they crashed to the power of *Langleybury* who made 249 for 6 and held *Essendon* to 70 for 9. *Langleybury*, with Orient footballer Gordon Riddick as their captain, were sponsored to the extent of £5 a match by their local Watford newspaper, and got through to the group semi-final only to lose to *Aspenden*. *Aspenden* then met *Blunham,* one of the strongest sides in the southern half of the Haig competition. *Blunham* won this group championship final by four wickets.

Cople, near Cardington, is a village of only 220 houses and club membership is restricted to villagers and their 'next door' village neighbours. They beat a below-strength *Bayford* side in the first round, scoring 148 for 7 of which C. Minney their opening batsman made an unbeaten 80 in the 35 over limit match. *Bayford,* with only three of their 1st XI available due to an old-established match on the same Sunday, could only reach 91.

Audley End, although geographically in Essex, found themselves in the Beds and Herts group and suffered a first-round defeat at the hands of *Langleybury* who made 166 against *Audley's* reply of 134 for 9. Somewhat of a blow to the Essex club, this, who joining the lowest league of the Cambridgeshire C.A. competition in 1959, won promotion to the Senior Division in 1971 – seven steps from bottom rung to top of the ladder in 12 years, and without losing a league match in the latter two years.

Boreham, near Chelmsford, were equally unfortunate in crossing the border, losing their first-round match by eight wickets to *Datchworth* 177-73 for 2. *Datchworth* near Knebworth, Herts, survived until the third round but then bowed out to *Aspenden,* only making 63 against their opponents 134.

Group 21 – Essex

Abberton and District C.C., from near Colchester, who came through to win the Essex group title, make their headquarters the Langenhoe Lion in the village. At one time secretary A. R. Patmore tells me, the club side could include eight members of the Taylor family, but this number is now down to three. They dismissed *Cressing,* a Braintree team for 100 in the first round and knocked off the runs with five wickets to spare. *Cressing* awarded their Haig tie to A. Watson for scoring 29 runs and taking two good catches.

From the ground of *Havering-Atte-Bower* one gets a

splendid view across the Thames, and not surprisingly L. M. T. Gray, their new secretary, says that the ground drainage is 'exceptional.' Havering were too good for *Abridge* in the first round, but went down to *Abberton* in the third round when they could only manage 90 runs in reply to the eventual champions' 142 for 5.

P. Arnold, undefeated with 23, ran out of partners in *High Roding's* first round match with *Little Waltham,* but duly won his Haig tie for his share of the total of 61. *Little Waltham* made light work of their target, winning by nine wickets.

Little Waltham came through the second round by a three-wicket margin, dismissing *Stock* for 80. 'The weather was filthy,' reports K. Power of Haig, 'but both teams were undaunted . . . wind-assisted sixes were a regular feature of the match.' Mr Power went back to the *Stock* clubhouse later in the day where the members were taking their defeat with equanimity and the right spirit – wrong brand, unfortunately!

Pre-season, I had great, if possibly sentimental, hopes of seeing *Great Bentley C.C.* in the Lord's final, for this excellent club celebrated their bi-centenary of cricket on the green in 1971. Graham Aitken, the secretary, tells me that *Great Bentley* has the largest village green in England and that their celebratory match against a strong Essex side led by Gordon Barker, whose benefit year it was, attracted more than 1,000 spectators and helped the beneficiary to the tune of £128; the result was a draw. *Great Bentley* have published two booklets to record their history from 1771–1971 and these are available from Mr Aitken at a nominal price. The club's success, however, in the first Haig year was restricted to a victory over *Lindsell* by 101 runs.

Elmstead Market, who claim their 'square' on Vicarage Meadow to be one of the best in north-east Essex, got through the first two rounds without too many problems but went out in their next match to *Tillingham* who reached their target of 102 with four wickets outstanding. In the first round *Elmstead* dismissed *Tolleshunt D'Arcy* for 99 and won by eight wickets.

Rettendon C.C.s secret weapons, according to treasurer

R. F. Frost, are the club president's horses which graze in a field adjoining the ground and are alleged by visiting sides to have been trained to congregate behind the home side's bowlers' arms. Obviously not white horses, which would make a fine sight-screen, were responsible for *Rettendon's* progress in the Haig through to the semi-finals where they lost to *Tillingham*. You *can't* take a white horse to Lord's on September 9th.

Group 22 – Berkshire

Littlewick Green C.C. were founded in 1810, and their traditional ground must be rated among the more picturesque cricketing venues of Berkshire, but they failed in the first round of this competition, being all out for 101 to which their visitors, *Sonning,* replied with 107 for 7. *Sonning* awarded their Haig tie to Bob Sheridan for his 36 not out and three wickets for 21.

Braywood, near Maidenhead, says Tom Wild, their secretary, have in the past three years a superb record of achievement, both on and off the field of play. The members, plus some professional aid, have built the pavilion and laid out a car park. In the Haig they had a somewhat cliff-hanging third-round match against *Pinkneys Green,* whom they dismissed for 73, struggling to win with only two wickets to spare. They beat *Sulhamstead & Ufton* in their semi-final round, qualifying to meet *Welford* in the final.

Mike Nunn, fast bowler and forcing batsman, is the only player in the memory of secretary G. D. A. Turner to have hit a six into the 'Hare and Hounds' – headquarters of *Cookham Dean C.C.* 'But,' says Mr Turner, 'with wickets pitched on the edge of the "square" the boundary can be as little as 20 yards away – "six" is above hedge height.' *Cookham* raised funds last year by a sponsored 'pub-crawl' around the many hostelries of the 'Three Cookhams'.

W. G. Grace and Percy Chapman played in their respective eras at the pleasant – 'almost flat', says secretary P. S. Fowler – ground of the *Hurst* club. *Hurst* were founded in about 1850, but met their match in the third round of this year's Haig, making only 126 in reply to *Welford Park's*

146 for 8 from their allotted overs. As an avid Forsyte man I must confess to hoping that *Mapledurham* – where the ageing Soames endured and expired, learned his golf and had his cow milked – would complete the saga in their own group of the Haig. *Buscot Park* put a sharp end to their ambitions in the third round, only to fall to *Welford Park* by a considerable margin (41 runs) in their semi-final.

Before losing their semi-final to *Braywood*, *Sulhamstead & Ufton* had an uneven passage. They beat *Buckland and District* in the first round, with K. Dade (28 not out) winning their Haig tie, and in the third round made 71 against *Taplow* who fell four runs short of the target.

Letcombe, near Wantage, were early victims of *Buscot Park* and P. Craggs' score of 12, plus one wicket and a good catch, earned him *Letcombe's* Haig tie. *Moreton C.C.* in the Didcot area were founded in 1858 and have as secretary wicketkeeper Gerald Howat, a professional historian. Mr Howat co-operates closely with the Rev. J. H. Pickles, vicar of Blewbury, in promoting matches for schoolboys during the summer holidays. Their ground has an attractive setting beside the 13th century church.

Group 23 – Devon and Cornwall

Troon, a very strong cricketing club near Camborne, emerged quite predictably as group champions of Devon and Cornwall, for they have over the years contributed nine players to the Cornwall team in the Minor Counties Competition. In the first round they beat *Boconnoc* – recognised by general consent as the oldest cricket club in the county – by six wickets. In *Boconnoc's* 113 for 6, J. Key, their captain, scored a valuable 41, but *Troon* went on to beat *Werrington* in a match reduced by rain to 15 overs a side in the third round, put out *Gorran* in the semi-final and took the title by defeating *Thorverton,* before going on to greater Haig glories.

Gorran, too, have provided four members of Cornwall's Minor Counties team, including their club captain, Roger Mason, a self-confessed 'exiled Yorkshireman', who leads a side almost all of whom were bred and born in Gorran. *Lustleigh,* in the third round of the Haig, could manage only 50 runs against *Gorran's* 196 for 6.

All my sympathies went out to J. Webber who had mournfully to report that as secretary of *Stoke Gabriel* – a delightful village on the bank of the River Dart – 'Our greatest wish is for a ground of our own.' *Whitestone C.C.,* near Exeter have, on the other hand, no ground problems, except possibly of altitude, for they play some 650 feet above sea level on a field provided by a local farmer with the fine old Devonshire name of John Brewer. *Whitestone* scored 96 against *Stoke Gabriel's* 108 in their first Haig encounter.

Group 24 – Somerset

Ken Harvison of Haig made a 220-miles round trip on April 30th to watch the first round match between *Evercreech* and *Ruishton. Evercreech,* the eventual county group champions, won the toss and batted first, making 91 by the tea interval. *Ruishton,* in reply, could only manage 31 runs before being all out in the ninth over of their innings. *Ruishton,* incidentally, have a 'Jewel' of an umpire – Freddie by name – whom B. L. W. Jones describes as 'extremely conscientious.' *Ruishton* had to give up their ground in 1970 as the M.5 motorway was encroaching on the outfield, and now play at West Monkton school near Taunton, although most of the cricketers still combine in alley skittles in winter at the Bell Inn in their adjoining village of Creech St Michael.

Mr Harvison praises the *Evercreech* bowlers and fieldsman as 'magnificent' and presented the Haig tie to Graham Wood for his five wickets for 15 runs which wrecked *Ruishton's* innings. *Evercreech* put out *Timsbury* in the final. Trevor Benwell, their secretary, tells me that this season the club toured Scotland, playing matches in Elgin, Nairn, Inverness and Perth, and in the *Somerset C.C.C. Handbook* for 1968/69 I was delighted to see in the *Evercreech* photograph an old friend of mine, Sir Rowley Baker, who in the mid 1950's was president of the Ottawa

Valley cricket association when I was playing there and he was assisting the Royal Canadian Navy.

Temple Cloud, near Bristol, who were *Evercreech's* semi-final victims had their moments of Haig glory, particularly in the first round when Andrew Dyer, their star batsman, led them to a total of 303 for 5 with an unbeaten 122. N. Harding then completed *Dulverton's* discomfiture, taking four wickets for 16 runs of their all-out total of 49.

Rex Saviour, not inappropriately albeit unsuccessfully, made a great effort to redeem *Mells C.C.* in the first round after they had been dismissed by *Brent Knoll* for a mere 38. Rex not only had the exceptional bowling figures of four wickets for two runs from his nine overs but added a run-out to his tally, hitting the stumps from 40 yards. *Brent* survived to win by three wickets, but Rex Saviour received the Haig tie as some recompense.

Blagdon, who claim to have one of the prettiest grounds in the county, with its setting of the parish church complete with Norman tower and the famous trout fishing lake, had of necessity to play their first round match away to *Lydford*, near Somerton. The *Blagdon's* club ground belongs to a local farmer who, according to secretary Keith Board, takes a greater crop of hay from it than from any of his other fields – so *Blagdon* play away from home until after hay-making.

In the best Somerset tradition, Ted Burrough, a former captain and now president of *Butleigh C.C.*, provides two flagons of home-made cider per match on this attractive ground in a parkland setting with a direct view of Glastonbury Tor and backed by the ruins of Butleigh Court. 'Cricket here can become poetry,' says J. G. Lovell their skipper. 'Our opening bowler is at his best on three pints of rough cider, but tends to be below par over that limit.' Butleigh, whose wicketkeeper is a chatty auctioneer, went out however, in the third round to *Milverton*, falling somewhat short of the target of 148 for 8 in the allotted overs.

Dinder and Croscomb C.C. have a unique ground-rental arrangement. They play rent-free on part of the Bath and West Show site, but the members have to do a certain amount of work for the show – 'seems very fair,' says E. R. Thorne, their secretary.

Group 25 – Dorset

Shillingstone, near Blandford, duly became the champions of Dorset, beating *Wimborne St Giles* convincingly in the final. I'm sure, though, that *Shillingstone's* A. E. Power, landlord of the Old Ox Inn, would be the first to agree that an entry of only 17 village clubs from this most rurally sporting of counties was disappointing; better things, I hear, are planned for the 1973 Haig. This low entry meant, of course, that all the clubs had a first-round bye, except *Studland* who beat *Thornford.*

Once again, some of the attractive village names went down – *pace* that inquiry – including *Witchampton* who play at Crichel Park and lost away to *St Giles* in their semi-final by two wickets (73–74 for 8). *Witchampton* have the Hon. Mrs G. G. Marten as their president, and Lieut.-Commander Marten and Air Marshal Sir John Bradley as vice-president and honorary life member respectively. *Wimborne* countered with the Earl of Shaftesbury as their president.

Marnhull, with Dr P. E. Watts as their secretary, survived until the third round of the Haig, then departed by a narrow margin to *Beaminster.* Against *Stratton* in the second round, Reg Dye made an invaluable 38 runs in *Marnhull's* total of 101, gained the Haig tie and saw his club to victory by 33 runs. On *Stratton's* ground at Wrackleford, near Dorchester, you can score four runs by hitting through the line of trees on one boundary, or six by landing on top of, or clearing, them.

Compton House C.C. whose ground is at The Park, Over Compton, near Sherborne, did not expect to get far in the inaugural Haig competition, according to D. Farley their secretary. However, they were beaten, but far from disgraced – although 'W. G.' played for them on occasions – by *St Giles* in the third round. It is probably as well that the 'Amazing Grace' is not still around, for Mr Farley reports A. Troakes, the club scorer as having 'writing no one can read' and G. Brewer, who operates the club bar, as having 'run out three of our batsmen in one match.'

Martin Holdaway, the *Milton Abbas* leading all-rounder,

was in top form for their game against *Cattistock*. The match was rain-reduced to 25 overs a side and in *Milton's* 97 Holdaway scored 41 and his three wickets for 11 runs were the main contributing factor to *Cattistock's* all-out total of 45. *Milton Abbas* met champions *Shillingstone* in the third round and made 128 for 9 only to lose by one wicket.

Group 26 – Wiltshire

Only contestants in the Wiltshire group's first round – the other 15 village clubs received byes – were *North Bradley* and *Compton Chamberlayne*. *Bradley*, the home side, put out their opponents for 29 after batting first and making 76. *Bradley* went on to the semi-final round, away to *Shrivenham* who dismissed them for 81 and then knocked off the 82 runs needed with eight wickets in hand.

North Bradley, however, according to M. A. Lane, are no strangers to defeat; at the Peace Memorial Ground in 1926 they were all out for one run . . . 'that debatable, because of our umpire's "no" to an appeal for a run-out.' Also in the 1926 season they played two matches in one day, losing 35 to 37 in the afternoon and 'evening' the score later by 78 to 13 – quite a tea-break for the opposition!

Goatacre C.C's president is Mr E. V. Iles, known throughout North Wiltshire as 'Mr Village Cricket,' who watched, in his 85th year, as many of the club's matches as possible. Playing for Purton before moving to Goatacre Farm, Mr Iles bowled the great 'W. G.' first ball. *Goatacre*, though, and to Mr Iles's sorrow, lost to *North Bradley* by 16 runs in the third round.

Little Durnford play on a ground overlooked by the Manor House and Lord Chichester charges them only a nominal rental. Chris Biddle, their captain, led his club to the final of the group championship but they finished 18 runs short of the target set them by *Shrivenham*. In the semi-final *Durnford* disposed of *Seagry and Startley*.

Group 27 – Hampshire

Steep C.C. who play at Steep Farm, Petersfield, won the Hampshire final with a seven-wicket victory over *Crown Taverners,* but their most satisfying result of the Haig competition, says John Hayes, was over 'historic Hambledon' in the semi-final round. That mighty club, who in the days of Richard Nyren, around abut 1750, could take on and beat 'All England', could only muster a mere 20 runs in reply to *Steep's* 123. Noah Mann, a great Hambledonian, lived and worked as innkeeper and shoemaker in Northchapel in Sussex and thought nothing of riding 27 horseback miles to Broad Halfpenny Down to play, eat and drink his beloved cricket before riding home before dawn. What would he think of his proud club today... 'a lot of young cobblers?'

Steep, though, have long been a side to contend with in the county and never averse to record-making; their secretary Malcolm Clements claims the three Judd brothers of Cowplain as hat-trick victims. *Steep's* most enjoyable Haig match, says John Hayes, was against *East Tisted* in the Meon Valley, near Alton, which they won by six wickets, then going on to put out *Bramshaw* by 91 runs.

Compton and Shandford combined a few years ago to form an amalgamated villages cricket, soccer, and social club, whose general secretary and treasurer R. Wilmhurst has served the club for 24 years since joining as a boy of 16. *Compton,* after beating *Sarisbury* in the third round went out to *Crown Taverners* by three wickets in the semi-final.

Hambledon, it must be said, have now only 25 full playing members, although Desmond Eager, former Hampshire captain, is their president and John Arlott a vice-president, plus life members from all the cricketing countries in the world. Before their crushing defeat by *Steep, Hambledon* had already beaten *Preshaw and Holt* by 10 wickets and *Easton and Martyr Worthy* by three wickets in the Haig, and my personal tip for the 1973 competition is that the 'home of cricket' will hit back with a vengeance. One had high hopes of *Martyr Worthy* in the early Haig days but they did not fulfil these, despite their basin-shaped ground at Cockett's Mead which has always produced a fine crop of mushrooms.

Group 28 – Surrey

Shamley Green, across the end of whose ground runs the Guildford-Cranleigh road, was founded between 1820 and 1830, and for years was maintained by family tradition, the XI consisting at one time of the Stevens and the Jarrads, plus Seymour Glew. The Stevens family, says H. B. Cooke, are related to 'Lumpy' Stevens of Hambledon fame as a demon bowler. Mr Cooke, who played his cricket in the Isle of Wight and in the Midlands, only came to *Shamley Green* some 18 years ago – 'since when the village appears to have adopted me.'

The club scored 235 for 8 in their first Haig match against *South Nutfield* whom they then dismissed for 78, despite D. Wilderspin's gallant 34 which gained him the Haig tie. Not quite so convincingly, they beat *Bisley* in the third round and *Effingham* in the semi-final, before beating *Brook* by a mere five runs to emerge as Surrey's champion village.

F. T. Gauntlett, now the secretary of *Brook* and their captain from 1950–63, was full of praise for the Haig competition which he felt 'fits into the pattern of village cricket admirably, representing what the Gillette Cup does for the first-class game.' *Brook* had a convincing win over *Peper Harow* in the first round, scoring 89 for 2 and dismissing them for only 26. *Peper Harow,* though, trace their history back to 1727 and a match between themselves and Cowdray Park, although the present *Peper Harow* club was started in 1840.

Long before *Chipstead C.C.* was formed in 1860 says secretary R. J. Jarrett, cricket was played in the village. Then the parish church was used as the pavilion and match results were announced from the pulpit. Alas, going from ancient to modern times, *Chipstead* did not survive the second round in the Haig, despite the presence of Harold

Watt, policeman, medium-pace bowler and chairman and inspiration of the bar sub-committee.

Groups 29 and 31 – Sussex

For draw purposes Sussex, with its wealth of cricketing villages, was divided into two groups for the Haig. In the first, made up of 20 clubs, *Eastergate* became the group champions, although probably not as conclusively as this sporting Chichester club would have wished, their victory over *Findon* being decided on the toss of a coin.

Fernhurst, the group champions first-round victims, scored 141 for 6 but went down by three wickets, a rather disappointing end for a club whose opening pair R. Butler and D. Quinnell the season before had broken all *Fernhurst* records with a partnership of 155 against *Hindhead*. In another close first-round match *Balcombe* dismissed *Anstye* for 94, R. Moll scoring a brave 32, and then struggled home by two wickets. Ken Mitchell was *Balcombe's* hero taking four *Anstye* wickets for 13 and scoring 19 runs, a performance which earned him the Haig tie. *Balcombe,* founded before 1860, have a pleasant ground near Haywards Heath, but with a decided slope as the land falls away to woodland on the east side. 'Deep square leg can't see deep point,' says A. H. D. Constable.

Until his death A. T. L. Watkins, playwright and film censor, was president of the club whose new pavilion, erected in 1971, is named in his memory. Mr Constable also supplied details of *Balcombe's* match against Ifield, played on May 24th 1869 which must have its own special niche in cricket history. Both teams scored 44 in their first innings and completed a 'double tie' when they each totalled 24 for the second knock. I gather that when the centenary match was played in 1969 the result, for *Balcombe,* was not quite so historic. Mr J. R. Greenwood, High Sheriff of Sussex, has succeeded Mr Watkins as club president.

Although Mr John Baker of Horsham has recorded in his diary for August 9th, 1773, watching a single wicket match at *Findon,* the present club really traces its origins to 1867. That Whit Monday they played their first competitive match, losing to West Worthing by a single run, although the then *Findon* secretary vehemently claimed a tie because before 'lost ball' was called five runs had been made 'which as everyone knows according to the rules of the Marylebone Club, scores six runs, but through the stupidity of the scorers was scored only as five.'

Findon in their third round of the Haig beat *Lurgashall* by eight wickets with M. Hill taking 4 for 11 and B. Pannell 4 for 14 in their opponents' total of 66. With a fine 37 from I. Smith, *Findon* easily reached 70 for 2. I. Smith, this time with 29 not out, then saw *Findon* to victory by nine wickets over *West Chiltington* who were dismissed for 56.

Lurgashall had 'one of the most exciting matches ever seen on our village green,' according to B. E. Swannell, when they met *Barcombe* from the Lewes area in the Haig second round. *Lurgashall* batted first and reached 86 for the loss of only two wickets, with F. Thiselton scoring 55; then the remaining wickets tumbled to K. Walters (5 for 24) and J. Trower (2 for 9) and the home side were all out for 113 off 37.5 overs. *Barcombe* fared badly at first – three wickets were down for 11 runs – only to recover to 110 for 6, only four short of victory. G. Coury then stepped in and in nine balls dismissed the last four *Barcombe* batsmen without any addition to the score and *Lurgashall* were home by the odd run, Coury finishing with 5 for 30. At *Warnham,* near Horsham, cricket has been played since 1772, but alas for this village, birthplace of the George Coxes of Sussex County Cricket Club fame, they did not survive the first round of the Haig.

Nor did *Watersfield* of Pulborough who lost by 102 runs to *Barns Green.* The latter batted first and reached 136 for 9 with R. Parker undefeated on 37; R. Fisher, 4 for 7, and R. McCormick, 3 for 1, then cut loose and *Watersfield* could only manage 34 runs.

In the second of the Sussex groups, comprising 23 village clubs, *Glynde and Beddingham,* near Lewes, won the final by 48 runs over *Withyham,* and from the first round *Glynde* always seemed the probable winners, with D. Pullen their outstanding batsman. Pullen scored a fine 105 not out in *Glynde's* declared score of 226 for four against *Rotherfield* in the third round and won on the higher scoring rate – not surprisingly – against their opponents' 66 for 3 three wickets in the semi-final. The *Glynde* club is nothing when rain halted play. *Glynde* went on to beat *Bolney* by if not progressive and the members have raised more than £3,000 for improvements to their ground, bounded by the Ouse and overlooked by South Downs.

Withyham had a close call in their semi-final against *Chiddingly*, only winning by four runs (81–77). They owed their victory to a fine spell of bowling by secretary R. Standring who took five wickets for five runs. Things were easier for them, though, in the first round when they reached 176 for 9 and proceeded to dismiss *Burwash Common* for only 52.

Bolney, who play on Glebe Field, had a tense third-round match against *Crowhurst Park,* winning by one wicket. Crowhurst had made 143 for 9 off their allotted overs, and *Bolney,* thanks to 62 from H. Clarke, just got home. *East Hoathly,* near Lewes, claim to be the second oldest cricket club in Sussex, dating their foundation from 1757. Due to lack of support the club nearly went out of existence in 1969 but staged a revival with the advent of newcomers to the village. *Ditchling,* however, proved too strong in the first round, scoring 50 for 5 to beat *Hoathly* by five wickets.

Wally Jopson, the club captain, was the hero of *Rotherfield's* first-round victory over *Stonegate.* He came in when five wickets were down for only 18 runs and rattled up a sterling 64 to take the total to 140 for 9 off the agreed 30 overs. Jopson then shared the attack with Alan Moody, the youngest player, and they took 3 for 23 and 3 for 22 respectively; completing his all-round stint. Wally held two good catches, and his right to the Haig tie was indisputable.

Groups 30 and 31 – Kent

Kent, as was the case with the Sussex clubs, produced a strong entry for the Haig and again was divided into two.

In the first of these, there resided near Maidstone the illustrious side who play at *Linton Park*. They more than justified their well-wishers' hopes by not only winning their group final, but also by going on to greater glories in the Haig competition. *Linton* is a ground not only beautiful for its trees and rhododendrons and superb views of the Weald of Kent, that almost uncontested 'cradle of cricket' – but is also famous for its history. Here in the 18th century Sir Horatio Mann played matches for 2,000 guineas a side against the best the Duke of Dorset of Knole Park could field and 'knocked off the heads of the daisies with his cane on Linton ground in his anxiety.' And in our time George Fenner, who died in 1970, had been connected with the club for 60 years, its secretary for 30 of those, and head coach at Lord's from 1928–34.

Linton removed some other fine Kentish cricketing history in the first round of the Haig when they beat *Leeds and Broomfield* by two wickets (88 for 8 against 81 for 8). In days now long gone *Leeds* could field eminent cricketers, such as Alfred Mynn and Fuller Pilch, in whose era the club took on the might of M.C.C. and, says secretary J. A. Ault, 'beat them twice in the same year.' Linton beat *Stocke and District* in the second round, and then overwhelmed *High Halstow* to the tune of 70 runs, before defeating *Stansted Invicta* by eight wickets in their semi-final round. For *Linton,* P. Bowles scored 42 not out; G. Mountford took 3 for 21 in *Stansted's* total of 78.

One doubts, though, if *High Halstow* would have been so defeated had Bryan Valentine, who played for the club after his days with Kent were done, been at the crease. Valentine was close to leading M.C.C's first post-war side to Australia in 1946–47 and according to E. W. Swanton's enthralling memoirs, (*Sort of a Cricket Person,* Collins £2.75) published this September, the series would then have resumed on far happier note than was the case under Hammond's austere captaincy ... 'his side would have responded to his guts and cheerfulness with the utmost effort. . . .'

Betsham of Wombwell Park, Northfleet, celebrated their coming of age by putting *Cudham* out of the first round by some 75 runs, although subsequently *West Farleigh* were too strong for them. *Cudham* are far from short of personalities: the president is the Rev. Bryan Isaac, vicar of the 11th century church and father-in-law of David Sheppard, Bishop of Woolwich, captain of Sussex and England; the club's headquarters were once the Blacksmith's Arms – birthplace of Little Tich of music hall 'soft shoe' dancing music hall fame. Their pavilion, too, although modern, has its place in cricket lore – it was designed by Orpington U.D.C. to fulfil three needs, mortuary, gas cleansing station in the 1939–45 war and at the end of hostilities, a cricket pavilion.

By the end of the second round of the second Kent group the eventual local champion seemed almost anyone's bet with eight strong club sides, *Saltwood, Benenden, Horsemonden, Nonnington, Yalding, Sissington, Sheldwich* and *Biddenden* all ready for the third-round fray.

Benenden were the first to take my fancy if only for the beauty of their ground on the village green, their headquarters at the Bull – a minor cricketing museum – and the enthusiasm for the competition by Ray Harding and his team, all of whom, says the skipper 'have something odd about them... like Mike Chambers, demon fast bowler, demon barber.' Benenden made an attractive third-round 217 for 5 and duly dismissed *Saltwood* for 169, but did not fare too well, weatherwise, in the group semi-final. There they met *Horsemonden* who reached 99 all out in the allotted overs and *Benenden* were all set to coast to victory when at 38 for 3 the inevitable rain stopped all further play and Ray Harding found that they had lost through not scoring quickly enough in the first 15 overs which decided the match. Somehow I can't see *Benenden* lapsing like this in the 1973 Haig; typically though, they cancelled their fixture for September 9th and planned an excursion to Lord's for the final.

Horsemonden, established more than 100 years, play on the village sports ground bounded on three sides by orcharding. Building of their new pavilion started in 1972 and the club is lucky in their groundsman, C. W. Fletcher, who is allowed by the landowner to maintain the ground during working hours. Mr Fletcher, oldest member, also puts in many hours of his own time in the evenings and at weekends.

Sheldwich beat *Horsemonden* in the final by 33 runs, but had an easy passage through the semi-final where the toss of a coin gave them victory over *Sissinghurst* after this Cranbrook club had encountered problems in meeting revised fixture dates. *Sheldwich* in the third round passed *Biddenden's* 67 for 7 for the loss of only four wickets while *Sissinghurst* having piled on 246 for 3, thanks to an unbeaten 104 by G. White, held *Yalding* to 205 for 8 and won by 41 runs.

When Jeff Thomas, an Australian, arrived in the village of *Little Chart,* the cricket club there had gone out of being, largely for financial reasons. He set about its revival with such success that as club captain he was able to report that by the 1970 season *Little Chart,* although still short of money, were on the up grade and had won 16 out of the 36 matches played. They now play only 10 home matches at Little Chart Forstal but the team – a good mixture of farm workers, doctors, dentists, and schoolteachers – are always made welcome by nearby clubs with more available ground facilities. In the old days of the club H. E. Bates, the author, who lives locally, captained and organized the side between 1946 and 1954 and is now president of the revitalised *Little Chart C.C.* They beat *Fordcombe* in the first round of the Haig but did not survive against *Biddenden.*

Smarden, near Ashford, where cricket was played in the 1870's lost their first-round match against *Sheldwich* but in 1971 their opening batsmen Glenn Wicken and Robert Small had a record partnership of 168, remarkable in that the previous best, 148, had been made by their respective fathers some 21 years before.

CHAPTER THREE

The Enduring Village

'See you at Lord's'

One statistic was omitted from the survey in the earlier chapter, for the simple reason that it was hardly a statistic in the accepted sense as it consisted entirely of 'yesses' – not a 'don't know' or a 'no' in any of the mass of club questionnaires I examined. Club officials were unsolicitedly unanimous in their opinion that their club – plus one other to make a match of it – would be in the final of Lord's! One or two, certainly not many more, felt they might be somewhat fortunate to get there, but would do so all the same. Within days of the news of The Haig, in its final form, appearing in the press and on radio and television, the organisers had received many inquiries for tickets for the ninth of September – this in mid-January, some two months before advance bookings opened for the Lord's Test against the Australians!

If further evidence were needed of the clubs' enthusiasm for their own truly national, truly rural, competition, here it was. And equal proof too, of the ever-enduring character of the game at the village level – *'Plus ça Change, plus c'est la même Chose'* could well be anglicised as the motto of the village game. For surely no other game at any level has survived so many vicissitudes, or so absorbed changes in the fair name of 'progress', imposed by outside sources on village life.

In our own time, which includes two major world wars, the face of the countryside has changed almost out of recognition. Many hamlets and villages have disappeared into the maw of suburbia. The expansion of light industry has swollen villages into small towns and the road-building programme has cut great swathes through farming lands. Smaller landowners have been bought – or forced – out, taking with them the patronage of 150 years and though the survey indicates that much still remains, it shows, too, that village clubs in many areas have been obliged to become more self-dependent. In addition, plenty of people who live in the country no longer work there. They are refugees from the towns and they have brought their influence to bear.

Living standards in general have increased so that you are unlikely these days to see old George, the handyman, standing at long-on in his blue shirt, baggy grey flannels, red braces and tennis shoes. Modern transport, give or take a strike or two, has placed the recreational and entertainment facilities of the town within reach of all.

The local rivalries still burn deep, however, and the teas that the Ladies' Committee provide are still just as good, although the beer isn't (it never was). And the game is just as good, and that's the thing.

The Shepherd's Crook

Cricket is, above all others, a country game with its roots buried deep in country places. All cricketers are sure of it. The compilers of dictionaries, however, think otherwise. They insist the word 'cricket' derives from the French *criquet*, a stick pushed into the ground to act as marker for an early form of the game of bowls. This implies that bowls and cricket were once closely allied, but though for hundreds of years the cricket ball was delivered underarm that surely is the only similarity.

Cricket's historians, unwilling to concede or countenance that the most English of games has Frenchified origins, have looked elsewhere for the derivation of 'cricket' and feel sure they are on the right track in asserting that it comes from the Anglo-Saxon *creag*, a curved stick. This *creag* through the years became *cricce* and it is reasonable to suppose that a smaller version of this weapon would have been called a criccet or crickket or cricket. But let the French claim croquet by all means as their aristocratic amusement!

The correct explanation will always remain a mystery, but this curved stick, much akin to a shepherd's crook and in all probability used as such by Anglo-Saxon sheepminders and drovers, immediately places the game in the countryside, and the name of the bowler's target, the stumps, indicates that it emerged on the fringes of forest land being cleared, almost certainly the edge of the Weald, for that was Saxon country. In time the distance between bowler and batsman became settled at 22 yards, a tenth of a furlong, the distance a man and an ox could be expected to plough a furrow, before resting.

So the pastoral, forestry and arable communities joined to produce three of the basic elements of the game. Only one more was needed – the ball. Here there is no evidence at all. The ball as a means of recreation was known to many earlier civilisations and all we can be sure of is that in 1744 when the first rules we know of were written down, the weight of the ball was ordered to be between five and six ounces. Today's limits say not less than five and a half ounces, not more than five and three-quarters. Other early eighteenth century sources make it clear the ball was leather-covered and the Dukes family of Penshurst in Kent are thought to have made cricket balls as early as the middle of the sixteenth century. So in all probability the ball has changed less than any other implement over the years.

As the game moved out from the edges of the Weald on to the adjoining Downland, tree stumps became scarce. A new target was required, a wicket gate, for instance. This had the added advantage of being easily transported and the overlapping sides could be jabbed into the turf.

Enter the Batt

The *cricce* gained a new name, too: the *batt*, a heavy stick or club much favoured by peasants who had a score to settle... Wat Tyler's men, for example. These *battes* would have been any manageable shape or size, but for cricket purposes they would almost certainly have been cut to retain the pronounced curve of the crook at the bottom in order to block or score off underarm 'grounders'.

The first mention of the word cricket occurs in 1598 in the *Guildford Guild Merchant Book*. There, 'John Derrick, gent.', one of the 'queene's majestie's coroners of the county of Surrey' records that as a boy 'he and several of his fellowes did run and play... at crickett and other plaies'. John Derrick, gent., was fifty-nine in 1598, which would put his boyhood cricketing days about fifty years before, when Henry VIII was preparing for death. And the fact that Derrick's is the first mention of the game seems to indicate that for a very long time indeed cricket in its earliest forms was solely a pastime of the lower classes and began climbing up the social scale only in the sixteenth century.

Nor did it climb very fast, for it is not mentioned as one of the games permitted to be played on Sundays by James I's bishops in 1617. But the people continued to make merry at it all the same. In 'the profane town' of Maidstone, the biographer of Thomas Wilson, the Puritan rector of Otham, a village near the town, tells us there was 'morrice dancing, cudgel playing, stoolball, crickets, and many other sports openly and publickly [played] on the Lord's Day'. The county of Kent seems to have been synonymous with vice in those days, for in 1654 the Eltham churchwardens fined seven of their parishoners two shillings each – probably a week's wages for most of them – for playing cricket on Sunday.

The game shrugged aside these pinpricks and in 1676 Henry Teonge, the naval chaplain, records that a party from three royal ships landed at Aleppo in the Levant and diverted themselves at various sports, including 'krickett'. Presumably this party was composed entirely of officers, so that cricket's social improvement was clearly gathering pace. By the end of the century its grip had taken in London, where a commentator observed, 'cricket... will be very much in fashion and more Trades-men may be seen Playing in the Fields than Working in their Shops'.

Coffee House Betting

H. S. Altham in his *History of Cricket* suggests that the game's rapid rise in the second-half of the seventeenth century was probably due to the Royalist defeat in the Civil War. He argues that the King's supporters, diplomatically retiring to their estates, out of boredom took up the game played by their servants and workers, and returned to London after the Restoration with a new diversion. Clubs of all sorts were the rage then, based in the coffee houses of St James's, and there matches were made, without doubt for some sort of stake. Certainly by 1700 there appears in a March issue of *The Post Boy* the announcement that 'a match at cricket' is to be played, evidently a series of five games, the first 'on Clapham Common near Foxhall [Vauxhall] on Easter Monday next, for £10 a head each game and £20 the odd one'. Cricket and gambling had joined hands and would remain joined for 150 years until the M.C.C. were obliged to drive the bookies out of the temple at Lord's. Now they're back again!

The first description of the game and its implements appears in 1706. Until now all research has been mainly conjecture, but in a lengthy poem, all in Latin, by William Goldwin, an Etonian, comes confirmation. He describes 'curving bats' – the *creag*, in effect – a leather ball, the wicket and the jeers of the 'rustic crowd' at the batsman being run out. The wicket by this time had assumed another shape, very familiar indeed in the countryside. The players had adopted the small entry hurdle from the sheep pens and used that as their target. This was an infinite improvement, for the entry hurdle consisted of two upright sticks forked at the top with a crosspiece, known as the bail, resting in the forks. When the ball hit this wicket the bail would be dislodged, so that there could be no question whether a batsman was out. But the old terminology survived: stumps and wicket, not hurdle.

The Milk-white Bail

Goldwin's wicket is described delightfully as 'twin rods that forked heads uprear ... (nor wide the middle space between), and next a milk-white Bail is laid from fork to fork'. No dimensions are given but it is unlikely to have been two feet wide and only one foot high as one old player is supposed to have said. Assuming that in adopting the entry hurdle as the new target, cricketers used it without alteration, it is reasonable to suppose that it must have measured rather more the reverse; that is, approaching two feet high and one foot wide. The somewhat smaller sheep of those days could easily move through a space a foot wide and would be deterred from trying to slip back out by the bail at roughly eye level, whereas the silliest of them would find no obstacle at all in a wide barrier only a foot from the ground.

Cricket begins to appear in paintings early in the eighteenth century and although artists, professional and amateur, were pretty lax in the matter of perspective and proportion, at least one picture may be taken as nearing accuracy. It is the famous *Cricket on the Artillery Ground 1743*, believed to be by Francis Hayman, a Royal Academician and a close friend of Hogarth, whose attention to detail was beyond reproach. Hogarth himself could well be the player depicted as wicket-keeper in the painting, and, as the stumps are roughly the height of his knee, it would put the top of the stumps about 20 inches or so from the ground.

Hayman is more helpful with the bat. His batsman, preparing a drive off the front foot, wields a weapon with a pronounced curve, almost like a modern hockey stick but with much more wood in the pod.

The Laws of 1744

The year after Hayman's painting, 1744, saw the drawing up of the first written laws of the game to come down to us. They provide the basis for the far more sophisticated rules we know today. It was probably more than time that some effort had to be made to come to an arrangement about how the game should be conducted. Members of the London Cricket Club accordingly met in the *Star and Garter* in Pall Mall to settle on the code. These rules could well have been founded on a much older set of instructions, for various modern authorities point out that there is a sharp difference in the style of phrasing between what may be broadly described as seventeenth century language, unsophisticated and direct, and the more refined mode of expression heavily based on the revival of Greek and Latin learning. Maybe those older laws are still in existence somewhere, jumbled p in some ancient parish records.

The 1744 laws were not published immediately. They were intended as a guide for those members of the nobility and gentry, even of the royal family, who loved to play and yet clearly found themselves at variance with their fellows on what was and what was not permissible.

The *Star and Garter* meeting laid down among other things that the stumps should be twenty-two inches high and six inches apart and that the popping crease should be cut (that is, cut into the turf) 3 ft. 10 in. in front of the wicket. Many authorities have tried to make something of these figures, not entirely convincingly. Twenty-two inches sounds a reasonable size for the height of an entry hurdle, and although six inches is narrow enough to keep in even a skinny, shorn, early eighteenth century sheep it does not seem wide enough to admit them. Probably the width was adapted to the size of the ball.

Popping Crease theories

One cricket historian has suggested – and it seems most likely – that the Tudor ell, a measure of cloth forty-five inches long, was used as the standard distance from stumps to popping crease with an inch added to allow for the crease itself. Might it on the other hand have something to do with the manageable size of the bat? We know that bat-making by then had become something of a specialist, if part-time, occupation. The maker probably cut bats to a standard length and we know he used string round the handle end to lessen the sting. So those old-timers may have done what we did as boys, establish the batting crease by the length of the entire bat, plus the handle.

Two instructions come as something of a shock. One says: 'if he [the striker] runs out of his ground to hinder a catch, it's Out'. And later: 'When ye Ball is hit up, either of ye Strikers may hinder ye catch in his running ground, or if she's hit directly across ye wickets, ye other Player may place his body anywhere within ye swing of his Batt, so as to hinder ye Bowler from catching her, but he must neither strike at her nor touch her with his hands.'

From this we can deduce that those rough country boys played a no-holds barred game, which the gentlemen of the London Club brought under some restraint by forbidding the striker to dash out of his crease and hinder a fielder from catching the ball, although he and the non-striker were allowed to do so between wicket and wicket.

This gives some clue to the riotous way in which the game must have been played, particularly in its cradling ground. Cricket matches had become accepted as among the great events of the countryside's year. Any number could play and matches against odds were to remain a feature of the game well into the twentieth century, though not of course at first-class level. Matches were the occasion for hearty eating and drinking with plenty of gambling and general revelry thrown in, including doubtless some offhand wenching on the side. The spectators were fiercely partisan and – as we have learned from Goldwin, our Old Etonian – always ready to roar out support, abuse and advice. To take part in one of these inter-village games was a fearsome occasion for the faint-hearted.

The visiting team, or the side winning the toss, had the right to select the pitch and though the turf between wicket and wicket was almost certainly scythed it is unlikely to have been rolled or flattened in any way. Few country districts were likely to have had access to the 'rowling Stones' with which the gentry's bowling lawns were smoothed to a level which astonished visitors from the Continent. In any case, a rough patch with all its tufts and general inequalities made for more fun. And more danger. Every ball, as G. M. Trevelyan has suggested, became a crisis.

Brawling, happy days ...

Few of those ancient under-arm bowlers had any idea about propelling the ball other than to hurl it as fast and as straight as they could along the ground, leaving the bumps in the pitch to do the rest. Even to block the ball with that great clumsy club must have been an achievement. To score a run made the batsman a hero. Few, unless they were out first ball, could have played an innings without having their unprotected ankles, shins and knees cruelly hammered and rattled, bruised, grazed and cut.

The batsman could have had only two courses open to him: swing his bat hard at every ball and trust to luck, or delay his shot until the very last second to avoid popping a catch to the wicketkeeper, short slip or to the fielder who stood almost equally close at the 'point' of that massive curved bat.

All the time came the din from the crowd, so that these ancient encounters called for exceptional nerve, character and presence of mind on the part of the players, the fielders no less than the batsmen – imagine trying to take a towering catch at mid-on with the striker dashing at you brandishing his bat ... great sprawling, brawling happy days indeed!

But they were not to last much longer. The laws of 1744 were published in pamphlet form in 1755 and five years later came the first of the series of Acts of Parliament which were to change the face of the English countryside – the Enclosure Acts. Right through George III's reign and on deep into the 19th century, private Bills were hustled through Parliament allowing the wealthy to seize vast tracts of common land and the open fields.

Suddenly the small peasant found himself with no rights in the land. Until now he had regarded himself as independent. He could grow his patches of barley and rye on the open fields, pasture his cow, goat and geese on the commons and gather his fuel from copses and woodlands there. Now this legalised land-grab removed all his rights and the best he could hope for was to be taken on as a field hand at wages. His independence was gone. So, too, were his recreation grounds. The South was not so hard hit by the Enclosure Acts as the Midlands and Yorkshire, for there enclosure had been going on quietly for a much longer period.

The First Professionals

The new improved farming methods inspired landowners to buy out the smaller fry and the effect was the same. Many peasants drifted off to the towns seeking work in the new ways of industrial production. Of those who remained, a small number were particularly indebted to cricket.

Their skill at the game prompted cricket-loving landowners to keep them at hand, employing them in almost a formal capacity so that they could make up a strong local team. Patronage, which had been steadily growing in the game for the past century, now began its great flourish. These country cricketers became in effect the first professionals. Many squires kitted them out in special uniforms, even to special buckles on their shoes, and provided them with better-prepared new grounds. They played according to the laws framed by the London Club and later by those drawn up by the White Conduit Club, the fore-runner of M.C.C.

It was all so different from the old, carefree, ill-disciplined

Action at Greenmount's ground, in pleasant surroundings outside Bury, Lancashire

Birlingham, near Pershore in Worcestershire, consider their ground to be one of the prettiest in England

Gowerton, champions of the Hereford and South Wales group, play on this ground of which they are justly proud

days. And it was all so much more improved. Life for most of those who remained in the countryside grew better, too, and though cricket must have departed from many villages and hamlets who had lost, or been cut off from, their common lands, a fair proportion of communities found ways round the problem. Not all the land had been enclosed, many of the aggrandised landowners were sensible enough to let the people play in one of their meadows, and, where it was big enough, there was always the village green. Indeed, probably from this period begins the great tradition of village green cricket matches, which in the nineteenth century became the dominant feature of any mention of countryside recreation.

Hambledon Days

As country people struggled to reorganise their beloved team game, there emerged the greatest village side of all: Hambledon.

The village sits among the folds of the hills ten miles north of Portsmouth, four miles off the London Road. How a club which came to gain such renown, which produced players who revolutionised the game, and administrators and patrons who went on to establish the most famous of all clubs, M.C.C., could develop in such a tucked-away corner of England is possibly the biggest mystery in cricket history. What combination of circumstances attracted handfuls of dukes and earls, to say nothing of gentlemen of quality by the gross, to clamour to be members probably never will be explained. We are not even sure when the club was founded.

Possibly there was a village side of the old sort in the area some years before 1746 when Richard Nyren's family moved there from Slindon, just across the Sussex border near Arundel. Nyren was twelve at the time and remained in Hambledon all his cricketing days, so he must have learned the game with a local side. Later he developed into their best all-rounder, became captain of the side (his nephew John says 'General') and finally secretary and guiding spirit.

By the time the club's surviving minutes and account

books begin in 1772 Nyren *was* Hambledon, but Hambledon was no longer a village club in the old sense.

It was now one of the most fashionable clubs in England. It could afford to engage the best players and pay them not only good match fees but additional money when they turned up for practice. Talented cricketers came thirty miles and more to play for Hambledon – grocers, carpenters, innkeepers, shoemakers, calico printers, bailiffs, gamekeepers, small farmers, glovers, bakers, maltsters appeared; but, so far as we know, no field hands were asked to join the ranks of these semi-professionals.

Among the members were the Dukes of Dorset and Chandos, the Earls of Darnley and Tankerville, Lord John Russell, later sixth Duke of Bedford, Bysshe Shelley, uncle of the poet, and a cable of assorted naval officers, including Sir Hyde Parker, Nelson's bumbling C-in-C at Copenhagen, and Robert Calder, whose failure to press home an engagement with the French fleet in the summer of 1805 left the way open for Trafalgar. And there was the Earl of Winchelsea, who in 1787, his presidential year at Hambledon, was the prime mover in founding M.C.C.

Hambledon's power was so great that they frequently beat sides representing Surrey, Kent and even All-England, sometimes by an innings. On their well-prepared pitches at Broad Halfpenny Down, and later Windmill Down, their bowlers abandoned the old fast sneaker type of bowling for well-judged deliveries pitched on a length. Nyren, and in particular David Harris, perfected the new type of attack, so that the curved bat had to be abandoned in favour of one perfectly straight, the prototype of those we use today.

The Third Stump

The new bowling brought one other change, the third stump. Bowlers frequently saw the ball pass between the two stumps standing six inches apart. The climax came in a five-a-side match against Kent at the Artillery Ground in London. Hambledon's last man went in with fourteen runs needed to win. He stuck there two-and-three-quarter-hours and got them, but several times Lumpy Stevens, almost as great a bowler as Harris, bowled the ball through the wicket without removing the bail. The third stump became inevitable and in a few years was generally adopted.

Hambledon's glorious dominance over English cricket began to die rapidly when the war with France broke out in 1792. Many of their naval members went off to sea at once and Nyren found it increasingly difficult to collect subscriptions, some of which were several years in arrears, and the club's affairs were wound up in 1796. One curious footnote is that at the last meeting at which anyone turned up, on August 29, there were present three members and twelve non-subscribers, one of whom was 'Thos Paine, Author of *The Rights of Man*'. The minutes of the meeting sadly record 'No business'. Cricket was to revive in Hambledon, but never again was the club to attract crowds of 20,000 and more, for matches with £2,000 at stake.

Elsewhere village cricket was changing, too. Now it began fusing all sections of the community and as England moved through the almost uninterrupted peace of the nineteenth century there developed that unique amalgam of personalities that became so beloved of authors trying to set a rural summer scene for their readers.

'Crusoe' at Large

Postman and parson, farmworker and farrier, gamekeeper and grocer, ploughman and poacher ... they became familiar enough types in late nineteenth and early twentieth century fiction. The reality is more remarkable, as R. C. Robertson-Glasgow's charming, reflective vignettes on country life and country cricket show. He spent most of his adult life connected with the first-class game as player and journalist. Always he slipped back to play country cricket.

'Crusoe' once told the writer: 'I don't know what I'm doing hanging around here watching these blokes [it was the Saturday of a tedious Test match at Lord's]. I could be down in Berkshire now enjoying myself with the village side. At least they get some fun out of the game.'

He loved to tell of when he and a teammate chasing a six into the next field found the ball had dropped in a fresh cow pat. 'That's yours, Charlie,' said Crusoe. 'Not mine,' said Charlie, 'I ain't got diarrhoea. Mine's under the hedge back there.' And Crusoe would add: 'Test matches could do with a few fresh cow pats now and again. Liven things up a bit.'

Certainly, village cricket is unlikely ever to have been so dull. Charles Dickens' report of the great match at Dingley Dell, although a shade shaky on technicalities, is probably little exaggerated as a summary of games he had seen. Possibly Mrs Mitford is a more reliable observer, woman though she was. In outlining the game's growth it was not intended to be assumed that cricket was purely a man's affair. We know that by the late eighteenth and early nineteenth century women's matches were not uncommon, and it is more than possible that women often made up the numbers in local matches elsewhere.

It was, after all, a girl, so the legend goes, who introduced roundarm bowling, because in trying to deliver the ball underarm her hand frequently became entangled with the voluminous skirt of those days. And, of course, the greatest name in all village cricket history, W. G. Grace, was taught the game in large part by his mother. Grace, his elder brother E.M., and his younger brother G.F., and other relations all at various times turned out for Thornbury, a dozen miles north of Bristol.

As life in the towns became more complex, human affairs in the country remained more straightforward, clinging to the pattern established with the Enclosures. As England's great open fields and vast stretches of common land became broken up by hedges in the chequerboard appearance it wears today, country cricketers for long continued to play the game the way it had been defined by the Hambledon men.

Round-arm and later over-arm bowling, were not adopted immediately and there are many people alive today who can remember seeing under-arms on the village green, teasing, well-spun lobs that could dip and turn wickedly to trap the unwary. Batting frequently remained founded on even earlier principles and the country game gained a reputation for wild swiping that became summed up in the village blacksmith's haymaking hits – a caricature born of sheer snobbery and, perhaps, envy.

Cricket has so often proved that what works for you won't work for others and the big man who heaves across the line and plonks the ball high up against the church tower does so because he knows he can do it. Or, because he's always wanted to smack one against the clock face.

One of these primitive hitters emerged from Wiltshire in the 1930's and made a deathless reputation with Middlesex as the only batsman whose appearance immediately emptied the old Tavern bar. Big Jim Smith stood close on six and half feet, weighed more than seventeen stone and strode out like a champion of Alfred the Great. He had one stroke – a great, clubbing, firm-footed, heaving cowshot that began outside his right shoulder and finished outside his left. If he connected the ball flew far, wide and always high, enormously high. Towering catches were offered off almost every ball. Never in first-class cricket was a man dropped so often in so many innings. Never have mis-hits carried the ball so far. And never did spectators so enjoy themselves, roaring with delight as some smack off the splice soared into St John's Wood Road, and almost delirious with laughter as some bemused fielder circled uncertainly and unhappily under a hit that seemed to have been made ten minutes before. Big Jim carried everyone back to their forebears' simple pleasure and enthusiasm for the game. He gave us a glimpse of cricket's tap root.

CHAPTER FOUR

Village Cricket Tales –
For After-Dinner Speakers

'Who would think,' wrote Mary Russell Mitford, many, many years ago, 'that a little bit of leather and two pieces of wood had such a delightful and delighting power?' And still, you know, the erudite and the inarticulate are seeking the answer, for to each cricketer his game has its own special appeal. For my own part the lure of cricket is not only the magic of performance but that the game can go on and on as long as you wish. It has its own brand of humour and nostalgia and so often a match replayed in pavilion bar or pub acquires a new dimension. This, as every proper cricketer knows, is even more true at the club dinner in the murk of mid-winter when new glories emerge – and there is no match tomorrow to wreck the image.

Very few of us, indeed, fail to enjoy the occasion and very few, in the course of time, escape the inevitable task of speaking at our own or some other club's dinner. Equally few fail to see themselves as a budding Cardus or Arlott – until, that is, they get to their feet before the ribald rowdies who have heard each tale not once, but oft and oft. I have never quite managed to work out who suffers most – orator or audience.

Among many other refreshing aspects which the village clubs have brought to their national competition is their own brand of humour and leg-pull and the spirit in which extreme insult is proffered, accepted and reciprocated; and I don't mean by leg-pull the good old 'cow shot'. So for those who, like myself, so often find themselves shorter in originality than in length I submit several tales from the clubs which should not defy the speaker's imagination and invention to turn against his captive audience. Where necessary, anonymity is respected, and if a few personal reminiscences creep in I am fain not to apologise.

I have a very good friend both at bar and bat who was always in great demand as an after-dinner speaker. In fact, from long experience he had graded his host clubs by their degree of conviviality, from 'sloshed' to 'teetotal'. Once by mischance, he found himself on the toast list of a lesser grade and suffered through the meal and the first couple of speeches in complete aridity.

Called upon in his turn he stood remarkably erect and waving an empty glass at the top table said! 'Gentlemen, I give you the toast of Absent Friends – coupled with the name of that blasted wine waiter'. The applause rang around the room and Hon. Treasurer sat in silence.

You, like me, have probably suffered more from variations of the Cricketing Horse story than from any other chestnut, so the gallant beast will not appear here, except as a connotation. A famous political journalist, now with the feathered choir, told me that in his cub-reporting days in Fleet Street his editor gave him a plum assignment – to take to lunch Dorothy Parker, the famous American columnist and epigram specialist. 'For God's sake', said the editor, 'keep her amused, but don't give her a chance to do her funny bits'.

So, after a fine expense-account meal my man decided to chance his arm and announcing 'this is true British humour' embarked on the Cricketing Horse story, which in those far-off days was quite the thing. Triumphantly he ended the horses's historic match with its refusal to take the last over – 'whoever heard of a horse bowling'. Miss Parker had heard him out in complete silence and all seemed well. She considered for a moment and then said : 'I'm so sorry but I don't know the first thing about cricket.' Squelch, perfect and complete.

A northern Haig club played the neighbouring village, home and away, in time immemorial fixtures, but were always discountenanced by their hosts who had a magnificent horse to pull the roller and who, it was explained year after year, was responsible for the superior playing condition of their pitch. Comments about the state of their own hand-rolled pitch for the return encounter had to be endured with near-politeness.

Until a couple of years ago, that is, when the superior lot appeared with due condescension to play on the 'cart track', only to find the groundsman leading a donkey trailing the heavy roller up and down the pitch. Superiority severely shaken, the visitors changed in silence as they watched the ceremonial rolling from the dressing room window. At last one village stalwart could stand the insult no longer and, leaning out of the window, bellowed at the groundsman: 'What's so bloody special then about a so-and-so donkey?' The groundsman completed his progress, halted the donkey and bellowed back even more loudly: 'This bugger's got gold teeth'.

Village rivalry is always intense, if sometimes apochryphal, and often the Church gleans its share of chaff. A curate, no mean batsman, served two parishes and, loving his cricket, chose to play for one club and regularly scourged the other. They tell the tale that one occasion, however, the Rev. failed to get off the mark being given out caught at the wicket first ball off a palpable wide. The officiating umpire was the sexton of the 'neglected' church and slowly wending his way off the pitch the curate halted at the bowler's end. 'George', he said sadly, 'I fear you'll never go to Heaven'. Unabashed old George replied: 'I'm real glad to hear that Sir – I ain't never had no 'ead for 'eights'.

And from Arley C.C. in Cheshire they tell of past glories against the neighbouring village of Moulton when the first of three Doctors Love was their mainstay. In one match the Vicar of Moulton – not wearing his dog collar – strolled over the fields to Arley to see how his team were prospering and found only one or two people tidying up the ground. On asking what had happened to the match he was told: 'You're too bloody late, mate. Moulton were all out for three – t' Doctor hit first ball for fower and they've all gone back to the 'aymaking'.

At Arley, too, Jeremy Weston tells me that they do not have women players, although there was a move to stage a mixed match at the end of the 1971 season – 'but the chief protagonist got pregnant, so it didn't happen'. The match, that is.

On a semi-clerical note Clifton in Derbyshire played a Sheffield Collegiate side some years ago and one of their players remarked to a Clifton member that there seemed to be more men than usual in the match being played two fields away. It was pointed out to him then – and often since – that that 'game' was in fact the local cemetery and the 'men' were white tombstones.

Holme, a Cumberland club, played at nearby Appleby and one of the home batsmen hit a huge six into the adjoining graveyard. 'Dead ball' appealed the Holme square-leg.

In his *Whispering Gallery* Thomas Hood had this to say of cricket in 1842: 'Of all games or sports Cricket appears to be the most trying to the temper, for a player cannot lose his wicket without being put out'. I would imagine that an unknown player of Outwood, Kent, in the early 1920's would have agreed with Hood. Outwood were then captained by a Major J. R. E. Cunliffe who, although not the most popular of skippers, was undoubtedly a colourful personality who would arrive for a match on horseback and lead his side on to the field immaculately dressed and complete with white kid gloves and a monocle. When batting the gallant major was only interested in scoring fours and sixes and on one occasion an enterprising partner called him for a short run, and got himself run out in the process. The Major thus consoled the irate victim... 'Sorry old boy – I dropped my monocle'.

From Outwood, too, Captain F. A. Clutterbuck's notes for his report to the annual general meeting of 1928: 'Conclusion: 1. Tomorrow as ever is – come up in full strength. 2. All good friends. 3. Thanks to umpire and scorer.

For other ways of getting out I like Derrick Broome's story of Pott Shrigley's misfortunes, 'In a local game, played on a very wet day we bowled all afternoon with the ball like a sponge. The opposing captain, a useful bowler, and their spinner did not appear to be troubled. Then towards the end of the game our umpire went to the pile of sawdust to re-mark the crease.... and found that the pile contained a nice little supply of dry balls'.

Bill Schofield, a member of Delph club in Yorkshire, tells a tale about the visit of West Indian tearaway bowler Roy Gilchrist for a friendly match against the club. Mr Schofield stood as umpire and no-balled Gilchrist each time he offended. 'He asked me about it and I thought there was going to be trouble. "I thought it was a friendly match", he said. I told him: "There's nowt friendly about it to me"'.

I feel that for gamesmanship this 'authentic record of the cricket match between Ilkeston and Hathern', published in 1881, takes some beating.

> The first match of the season was with Hathern and came off on the Rutland Ground, on Monday and Tuesday, June 5th and 6th, 1856. Some excellent cricket was played on both sides and towards the close of the game, great excitement prevailed. It was arranged that the stumps were to be drawn at six o'clock. When the Rutlanders went to their wickets for the second time, 113 runs were wanted to win. Four wickets having fallen. T. Attenborough and C. Ross found themselves together and all attempts of their opponents failed to separate them. The ball was being knocked about right merrily and many an anxious eye was turned towards the church clock. The hour of six was approaching, and nearly 40 runs were yet wanting. At this juncture an idea occurred to one or two that it would be advantageous if the Church clock could be stopped. The permission to do so was obtained and two well-known Ilkestonians were deputed to carry out the scheme. While one of the two kept watch through the glass in the centre of the dial facing the cricket ground, the other was instructed to hold the pendulum a few seconds at a time. Still the batsman were making runs and the fielders longed for the hour which would put a stop to the game. Suddenly it appeared to some of the players that the clock was moving very slowly, watches were compared and the question was decided by the Hathern umpire drawing the stumps when only

18 runs were required to win, with six wickets to fall. The game thus resulted in a draw. The conduct of the Hathern players, when they saw Ilkeston gaining upon them, was not at all gentlemanly. The batsman never lost time in taking position; but the bowlers, one particularly, between every ball made a most minute inspection of his person, even to the soles of his feet and very often indulged in a roll on the ground and in grimace at the spectators, whose disgust with such conduct sought expression in frequent exclamations of contempt. The intention to prevent Ilkeston playing out the game by inexcusable delays at each over and in bowling, was too evident, and contrasted strongly with the conduct of the home team in the morning when their opponents were at the wicket.

And these extracts from the minutes of Groombridge C.C. in Kent tell their own stories.

6th April 1892 – 'That 1/- be paid to Mr L who will then give up a ball found in his field by one of his workmen to whom he gave a shilling for finding same.'

5th April 1894 – 'New rule – 'Anybody entering the field otherwise than by the gate be suspended for 7 days.'

8th March 1898 – 'That the H.Q. be removed from the Crown Inn to the Welcome Coffee bar (Rev. J. H. Masters, President, in the Chair)'

14th February 1910 – 'Hon. Sec. read an apology from the Hon. Sec. Cowden C.C. relating to some unfavourable remarks in the newspaper of the Groombridge umpire at the match at Cowden.

Resolved to leave Cowden out of fixtures for 1910.'

Praise for sapient captaincy was not the general tone of the Haig clubs' reports so that this tribute to A. Cherry, captain of Westcott, Bucks, is worthy of mention. 'Our captain', says secretary C. A. Searle, 'is a man who, seeing one dark cloud on a clear day when a spin bowler is on, will change to our fast bowler and actually get a wicket because of a slight change of light'.

Not all secretaries are quite so complimentary, however, and one Bedfordshire official comments on his captain: 'Excellent rugby player with large nose and foul mouth'.

And of a star player: 'Temperamental and ugly opening batsman, bowler, fielder and umpire – but last to buy a round'. And of another batsman: 'largest varicose veins in Bedforshire, caused by his ineffective forward defensive play'.

From the Diary of Mr John Baker of Horsham, August 9th, 1773:

> Walked to see a single wicket cricket match between Mills, Sharp and May of Horsham and Swift and two others of Findon. In the morning Mills fetched 12, neither Sharp nor May one, then Findon went two out of 5 and the last fetched 11, 16 in all. Then May went in and fetched none again. When we came at about half-past four Mills was in and had fetched 13 or 14, and he made it 29. Then Sharp fetched 12. So they were 37 ahead. Then the first two Findon men fetched none and the last only one. So they lost by 36.

About 1928 it was decided that Findon Cricket Club were worthy of having colours of their own. There was at that time, a horse in training at The Vale which had won several races and as the colours of its owner were black and amber, it was agreed that these should be the colours of the club. The caps were similar to those of today, having amber rings running round the cap. Their first appearances drew some ribald remarks from opponents, 'scrambled eggs' being the only printable one.

It was a happy band of men who formed the Findon club in the twenties and thirties and if the cricket was taken seriously on the field, so also was the 'supping up' after the games. On one evening returning from Northchapel, the club's cricket bag fell unnoticed from the transport and remained so until the police constable from Southwater returned it, having found it lying in the road at dead of night looking uncommonly like a body.

Another incident, which could have had a much more serious ending occurred during a return journey from Roffey. A car driven by Cecil Young and carrying at least five other members of the club, hit the wall at Shorts Farm, just north of the Gun Inn, overturned and slid on its roof and its side, eventually facing back in the direction whence it had come. The car was very badly smashed, but luckily the injuries sustained by the occupants were relatively light.

Jack Kennett had his nose pushed sideways and subsequently straightened by an unknown bystander, while poor 'Chummy' Constable had the misfortune to have his rear end hanging through the open side window when the car slid along on its side. Being so close to the Gun, brandy was instantly available for the injured, who availed themselves of the opportunity. Cecil Young called Wade's garage in Worthing to have the car seen to and when asked if the breakdown lorry should be despatched, said, 'No, bring a bloody shovel'. The very next day, the less injured were playing once again, such was the spirit in the club.

In the early days of the Haig we asked the clubs to supply some details of playing strength, membership costs and equipment. This part included 'Umpires' coats' to which Peter Lawrence, match secretary of Sampfords C.C., replied: 'one and half – donkey ate rear end of one last year'.

One of the most exasperating aspects of the 1972 season was the abominable weather in the early and middle sections. So bad, indeed, that even the keenest Haig clubs had on occasion to be content with deciding a match on the toss of a coin. A dull way to win or lose and it seemed a pity that they didn't try the old Derbyshire recipe of Alfred Cochrane (1865–1948):

We'd never a penny to toss for choice,
So we'd chuck up t' bat would we.
'Ump!' says Jim. 'Oller!' says I
And 'ump it is', says 'e.

Old members of clubs, cricket and otherwise, have an unfortunate tendency to fasten themselves upon the newest member as being the only person who hasn't heard their stories of past glories many times before. A young friend of mine joining a club, suffered just this fate from a retired Service officer who concluded his free drinking session by borrowing an amount of money. The new member progressed successfully through the club but without being repaid, and toward the end of the season felt emboldened to ask the oldest member if the fiver he had loaned him in the spring could be returned. 'Haven't finished with it yet' was the only reply he got.

In hospital, sick stories are pretty obvious and on one day of my recent sojourn, a sporting doctor decided that a cricket-loving patient could leave his bed to walk to the day room to watch a one-day International match. On getting out of bed, he was immediately returned to it by an officious ward sister who completely countermanded the doctor's orders. Another cricketing patient said that this was rather like Arthur Fagg giving Stackpole out lbw only to have it countermanded by a bibulous spectator from the square leg bar.

I have also had told to me the tale of the short-sighted umpire who insisted on speaking at every club dinner. Apparently his stories got cornea and cornea.

I once had a Royal Naval uncle whose opinion of cricket was in completely adverse proportions to his sense of humour. I remember at a school house match he arrived on leave and I was batting at the time. My house master mentioned to him that it was peculiar that his nephew should bowl left-handed and bat right-handed, to which the Navy replied that nephew had learned his cricket in the streets of Liverpool where to have batted left-handed against a lamp-post would have meant standing in the gutter!

CHAPTER FIVE
The Battle for the Group titles

By early July the 795 Haig village clubs had been reduced to 32 – that is, to the champion club of each of the county groups. With the assistance of the sponsors who provided new balls for each match and organised the umpires, these clubs were now ready to flex their muscles for the Regional rounds *en route* to Lord's. *Meigle* became the Scottish group winners by six wickets when a fine 38 not by B. Reid took them to 104 for 4, against *Glendelvine's* 102 all out, A. Gleig taking three wickets for nine runs. Club officials, with few exceptions, provided full score details of the county final rounds and these can provide interesting winter reading for club strategists preparing for the 1973 Haig competition, (* indicates captain, † wicket keeper).

Group 2 – Warenford v. Burneside

Burneside won the toss and before the biggest crowd then seen at Warenford's ground, chose to bat first, but got off to a bad start, T. Thompson taking four wickets in his first four overs. Only a fighting seventh-wicket stand of 21 by Slinger and Walker prevented a complete Burneside débâcle. *Warenford,* of whom much more anon, lost wickets steadily, but A. Patterson stayed firm, only being run out four runs short of the target. Skipper J. Riddell fittingly struck the boundary needed for Warenford's four-wicket victory.

BURNESIDE

B. Scott, b T. Thompson	0
R. Wilson, b T. Thompson	14
M. Scott, b T. Thompson	0
G. Scott, b T. Thompson	5
S. Moffatt, c I. Patterson, b A. Patterson	2
*I. Wilson, run out	1
M. Slinger, c Curry, b T. Thompson	8
B. Walker, c I. Patterson, b A. Patterson	18
D. Scott, run out	6
†J. King, c Curry, b A. Patterson	0
A. Major, not out	3
Extras (Lb 1, w 1)	2

21 overs. Total   59

Fall of wkts: 1–0, 2–0, 3–19, 4–20, 5–23, 6–24, 7–45, 8–50, 9–50.

Bowling: T. Thompson 9–2–20–5; I. Patterson 6–0–20–0; A. Patterson 6–2–17–3.

WARENFORD

A. Patterson, run out	33
W. Robson, c D. Scott, b B. Scott	7
A. Hedley, lbw B. Scott	3
I. Patterson, c King, b D. Scott	3
B. Thompson, b B. Scott	0
B. Squibbs, c & b G. Scott	9
*J. Riddell, not out	4
L. Alexander, not out	0
Extras (B 1)	1

28 overs. Total (6 wkts)   60

Did not bat: †J. Turnbull, G. Curry, T. Thompson

Fall of wkts: 1–11, 2–20, 3–38, 4–38, 5–56, 6–56.

Bowling: B. Scott, 9–2–23–3; A. Major 9–2–12–0; D. Scott 5–1–17–1; G. Scott 5–2–6–1.

Warenford won by 4 wkts.

Group 3 – Tong v. Great Preston

In the first Yorkshire section, *Tong* batted first against *Great Preston* and made 174 including 56 by B. Webster and despite M. Clark's 6 for 33. *Great Preston* were then dismissed for 123 to leave Tong with victory by 51 runs.

Group 4 (Yorkshire II) – Folkton & Flixton v. Altofts

Again there was a large crowd to watch the home side win the toss. Stubborn batting by Blackburrow and a quick 19 from T. Baker, each hitting one six, took *Flixton* to 119 all out off 38 overs. When *Altofts* batted, the *Flixton* close-to-the-wicket fielders were in top form and only Leek looked like getting the runs, hitting three sixes in his valuable but vain 33.

FLIXTON

G. Nichol, b Greaves	22
M. Stewart, lbw Greatorex	1
M. Brown, b Greatorex	0
M. Blackburrow, b Wilson	43
T. Baker, b Greaves	19
*†J. Philipson, b Wilson	1
D. Elvidge, b Wilson	6
M. Hotham, not out	7
T. Carr, b Wilson	1
T. Wood, b Greaves	2
D. Sellars, b Greaves	1
Extras (B 9, lb 3, nb 3, w1)	16
38 overs. Total	119

Fall of wkts: 1–2, 2–2, 3–60, 4–90, 5–93, 6–101, 7–106, 8–112, 9–115.
Bowling: Greatorex 9–1–15–2; Greaves 9–0–20–4; Wilson 9–0–43–4; Baston 9–2–10–0.

THE BATTLE FOR THE GROUP TITLES

ALTOFTS

J. Gunn, lbw Baker	0
C. Jackson, b Wood	4
B. Newby, c Sellars, b Wood	4
T. Greaves, b Baker	11
†J. Wilson, lbw Baker	6
W. Greatorex, c Blackburrow, b Sellers	17
D. Leek, lbw Wood	33
D. Baston, c Elvidge, b Sellars	6
B. Greatorex, b Sellars	2
*T. Mason, not out	1
M. Mason, c Brown, b Elvidge	0
Extras (B 1, lb 2, nb 1)	1
27 overs. Total	88

Fall of wkts: 1-0, 2-5, 3-22, 4-28, 5-38, 6-57, 7-73, 8-87, 9-88.
Bowling: Baker 9-3-33-3; Wood 9-2-33-3; Elvidge 5-0-15-1; Sellars 4-2-3-3.
Umpires: G. Mountfield & K. Boddy.

Flixton won by 31 runs.

Group 5 – Lindal Moor v. Read

Considering that at that time *Read* were running away with the Ribblesdale League championship and had not been beaten so far in the season, *Lindal* won the Lancashire group final with comparative ease before a home crowd of about 600. *Read* took first innings on an easy-paced pitch, but apart from Harwood's 41 and a last-wicket stand of 25 by Waddington and Pollard, they were always struggling for runs. Set to make 124 to win, *Lindal* got off to a good start from Gardiner and Coward who added 33 together and consistent batting by the middle-order batsmen took them to their target with five wickets in hand.

READ

B. Fairclough, c Clarke, b Gifford	28
M. Georgeson, c Cornthwaite, b Herman	1
J. Harwood, st Cornthwaite, b Gifford	41
P. Tatton, c Herman, b Gifford	12
R. Goodway, b Gifford	0
M. Grainger, b Shuttlewoth	2
P. Howarth, c Marshall, b Shuttleworth	2
†P. Grainger, run out	4
*E. Sumner, c Knight, b Shuttleworth	2
J. Waddington, not out	14
D. Pollard, not out	12
Extras (B 2, lb 3)	5

40 overs. Total (9 wkts)   123

Fall of wkts: 1–1, 2–50, 3–73, 4–74, 5–85, 6–85, 7–90, 8–93, 9–98.

Bowling: Herman 8–3–23–1; Shuttleworth 9–4–13–3; Liddicott 9–0–44–0; Gifford 9–1–22–4; Knight 5–0–16–0.

LINDAL MOOR

J. E. Gardiner, b Pollard	25
B. Coward, b Sumner	16
*E. Shuttleworth, c Goodway, b Sumner	14
W. Knight, not out	27
T .Clarke, lbw Sumner	8
T. E. Gifford, b Tatton	26
M. T. Marshall, not out	5
Extras (B 1, nb 3)	4

35 overs. Total (5 wkts)   125

Did not bat: G. V. Dawson, S. Liddicott, R. Herman, †J. Cornthwaite.

Fall of wkts: 1–33, 2–53, 3–60, 4–75, 5–113.

Bowling: Tatton 9–1–24–1; Waddington 6–0–40–0; Sumner 9–1–30–3; Pollard 55–3–14–1; Goodway 4–0–13–0.

Umpires: W. Melville and K. Glover.

Lindal Moor won by 5 wkts.

Group 6 – Northop Hall v. Compstall

Compstall, Cheshire's last hope, won the toss at Northop Hall but apart from a fighting 47 not out by Chris Lees after the first five wickets had gone for 25 runs, they were always struggling. John Richards and Lees added 33 for the ninth wicket to take Compstall to 105 off their 40 overs. *Northop Hall* also struggled at the start of their innings and had only made 66 for 6 when Eddie Millington and Jones came together. This pair put on 40 for the seventh wicket and were still there when victory was achieved.

COMPSTALL

F. Wilson, c Lloyd, b Jones	26
H. Lewis, b Williams	0
J. McGowan, b Williams	6
B. Shaw, b Martin	1
B. Arrowsmith, c Millington, b Jones	1
W. Anderson, lbw Jones	2
C. Lees, not out	47
A. Mitchell, b Hughes	1
P. Brown, c Hughes, b Millington	2
J. Richards, not out	12
Extras (B 1, lb 4, nb 1, w 1)	7
40 overs. Total (8 wkts)	105

Did not bat: M. Hawkin
Fall of wkts: 1–6, 2–13, 3–16, 4–16, 4–21, 5–25, 6–60, 7–69, 8–72.
Bowling: Williams 9–2–23–2; Martin 9–4–8–1; Jones 9–1–24–3; Millington 9–1–20–1; Hughes 4–0–23–1.

NORTHOP HALL

W. J. Hughes, b Richards	14
S. W. Oultram, b Anderson	13
J. Peers, c Lewis, b Richards	6
C. E. Lynch, c Brown, b Hawkin	7

H. Lloyd, c Anderson, b Hawkin 15
D. Riley, b Hawkin 11
J. E. Millington, not out 23
W. I. Jones, not out 11
   Extras (Lb 4, nb 1, w 1) 6

37 overs. Total (6 wkts) 106

Did not bat: P. L. Millington, G. Martin, J. D. Williams.
Fall of wkts: 1–21, 2–33, 3–34, 4–42, 5–66, 6–66.
Bowling: Anderson 9–0–29–1; Richards 9–3–12–2; Brown 8–1–26–0; Hawkin 9–1–23–3; Wilson 23–0–10–0.
Umpires: M. Lewis and T. E. Owens.

Northop Hall won by 4 wkts.

Group 7 – *Holmesfield* v. *Shipley Hall*

Holmesfield won the toss at the County Ground, Ilkeston, but lost an early wicket when Roberts was caught at slip. Pearson and Smith, and then later Crossley all batted well until Crossley was out with the score 90–3. Skipper H. Price then switched the batting order and his hitters Seaton, Soutter and Hobson put on quick runs to give *Holmesfield* a respectable total of 139 for 8 off their 40 overs. *Shipley Hall* started well but, despite a fine innings of 59 by Stott, they fell behind the required scoring rate and lost wickets in attempting to catch up, although a few quick runs at any stage could have swung the game. *Holmesfield* won by 26 runs in an exciting match.

HOLMESFIELD

T. G. Pearson, b Cockaiyne 17
W. Roberts, c Pratt, b Smith 6
G. Smith, b Cockaiyne 42

J. Crossley, c & b Sumner 25
R. Guest, c Young, b Pratt 1
*H. Price, not out 1
D. H. Barber, b Pratt 3
G. J. Seaton, c Smith, b Pratt 15
J. Soutter, not out 15
J. Hobson, c Fairholme, b Smith 12
Extras (Lb 6, w 1) 7

40 overs. Total (8 wkts) 139

Did not bat: †S. Huckerby.
Fall of wkts: 1–8, 2–40, 3–90, 4–91, 5–112, 6–113, 7–128, 8–137.
Bowling: Smith 9–2–18–2; Sumner 9–2–30–1; Cockaiyne 8–0–32–2; Fairholme 9–1–19–0; Pratt 5–0–26–3.

SHIPLEY HALL

D. Stott, c Huckerby, b Seaton 59
R. Pratt, b Crossley 11
P. Young, b Crossley 5
M. MacDonah, c Price, b Crossley 0
D. Cockaiyne, c Hobson, b Roberts 9
E. Greensmith, b Hobson 4
J. Sumner, b Guest 1
*Parkinson, b Guest 7
B. Fairholme, c Huckerby, b Guest 4
P. Straw, run out 3
W. Smith, not out 0
Extras (Lb 8, nb 2) 10

37.4 overs. Total 113

Bowling: Crossley 9–1–18–3; Seaton 8–1–23–1; Roberts 9–1–22–1; Hobson 7–0–20–1; 4–4–0–20–3.
Umpires: B. Meakins and L. Simpson.
Holmesfield won by 26 runs.

Group 8 – Collingham v. Cuckney

In Group 8, *Collingham,* at home to *Cuckney* in the Notts and Lincs final, won the toss and G. Croft put the visitors in. With N. Thompson taking four wickets for 24 and Williams and Peel taking two apiece, *Cuckney* were all out for 97 in the 40th over – then it was *Collingham's* turn to struggle for runs. Against the accurate opening attack of Palmer and Wright they lost the first four wickets for only 27. C. A. Watson arrived on the scene and his 33, including two sixes, swung the game the other way, and with the tailenders all contributing, *Collingham* reached 98 for 9 to win with two overs and one wicket to spare.

Group 9 – Fenns Bank & Iscoyd v. Swynnerton Park

Fenns Bank took first innings on their home ground but could make little of the bowling of C. Ellis, ably supported by Wagg and Walters. They were all out for 87 in 35 overs and *Swynnerton* romped home by three wickets, with A. D. Giles their wicketkeeper-opening batsman only two runs short of an unbeaten half-century. Giles batted for 70 minutes, hitting one six and six fours.

FENNS BANK

J. Faulkner, lbw Wagg	0
D. Gallagher, stpd Giles, b Wagg	18
†T. Winter, c Giles, b Walters	4
D. Price, b Ellis	25
R. Windsor, b Walters	1
P. Crump, lbw Ellis	7
W. Griffith, b Davies	10
A. Faulkner, not out	8
A. Molyneux, b Ellis	3
*E. Faulkner, b Ellis	4
T. Fisher, b Ellis	1
Extras (B 4, lb 2)	6
35 overs. Total	87

Fall of wkts: 1–0, 2–15, 3–37, 4–38, 5–51, 6–68, 7–70, 8–77, 9–85.
Bowling: Wagg 9–2–22–2; Walters 9–0–21–2; Ellis 9–1–23–5; Davies 8–1–16–1.

SWYNNERTON PARK

†A. D. Giles, not out	48
*D. S. Metcalfe, c Faulkner, b Gallacher	4
K. Aspinall, c Winter, b Price	28
M. Ellis, b Price	4
G. Baldwin, not out	4
Extras (Lb 3)	3
21.1 overs. Total (3 wkts)	91

Did not bat: C. Ellis, N. Young, K. Wagg, B. Walters, M. Capper, G. Davies.
Fall of wkts: 1–13, 2–78, 3–82.
Bowling: Gallacher 7–2–21–2; Molyneux 8–2–24–0; Windsor 4–0–23–0; Crump 1–0–10–0; Price 11–0–10–2.
Umpires: B. Stevenson and G. Dove.

Swynnerton Park won by 7 wkts.

Group 10 – Empingham v. Newtown Linford

J. Hibbitt won the toss for Empingham and put the visitors in. His bowlers Pell and Woodbridge were quickly among the wickets and *Newtown* having reached 28 for 4 then lost three more batsmen at the same score. Only opener T. Austin (18) and tailender A. Veasey (19) offered any resistance and the side were all out for a lowly 62 in the space of 27 overs, Pell taking 4 for 20. *Empingham* lost their opening pair of Fuller-Smith and Hibbitt for 20 runs but an unfinished third wicket partnership of 44 by Pattison and Want saw them to victory.

NEWTOWN LINFORD

M. Taylor, c Thraves, b Pell	5
T. Austin, c Connelly, b Pell	18
B. Redston, b Woodbridge	0
M. Collington, run out	0
J. Morgan, b Woodbridge	5
B. Parkin, b Pell	0
L. Juba, c & b Want	3
*K. Sammons, c Pattison, b Pell	0
†M. Penny, c Woodbridge, b Want	9
A. Veasey, b Thraves	19
J. Palmer, not out	3
Extras	0
27 overs. Total	62

Fall of wkts: 1–13, 2–14, 3–18, 4–28, 5–28, 6–28, 7–28, 8–34, 9–57.
Bowling: Pell 9–1–20–4; Woodbridge 9–3–18–2; Thraves 5–1–5–1; Want 4–0–19–2.

EMPINGHAM

C. Fuller-Smith, c Collington, b Sammons	3
*J. Hibbitt, c Parkin, b Sammons	9
†M. Pattison, not out	13
D. Want, not out	31
Extras (B 5, lb 3)	8
19.4 overs. Total (2 wkts)	64

Did not bat: J. Thraves, R. Woodbridge, M. Pell, D. Bingham, P. Baker, J. Connelly, J. Smith.
Fall of wkts: 1–7, 2–20
Bowling: Sammons 9–1–36–2.
Umpires: W. Peck and I. Balfour.

Empingham won by 8 wkts.

THE BATTLE FOR THE GROUP TITLES

Group 11 – Avoncroft v. Willersey

Avoncroft of Bromsgrove won the Worcestershire title by five wickets on their home ground against *Willersey*, a Broadway club. Sent in to bat, the visitors owed much of their total of 144 to J. Byrd, who scored 50 in 35 minutes, including three sixes and four fours, and M. Garaway who, coming in at No. 6, took out his bat for an unbeaten half century. Coultas was the most effective bowler with 6 for 31, his last five wickets coming from 19 balls for only 10 runs.

Good bowling by J. Clements had *Avoncroft* struggling at 53 for 5 but K. Rose, 68 not out, and P. Shaw put on an undefeated 92 to give *Avoncroft* victory in the 36th over. P. Shaw again kept wicket brilliantly for *Avoncroft*, taking two fine catches and not allowing any byes. That brought his performance in three Haig matches to one bye in 341 runs, five catches and one stumping and a tally of 81 runs for once out.

WILLERSEY

G. Bate, b Coultas	6
G. Care, c Shaw, b Banner	1
E. Richmond, b Banner	7
J. Byrd, c Banner, b Burne	50
J. Beale, b Burne	2
M. Garaway, not out	50
*†V. Garaway, b Coultas	13
J. Clements, c Shaw, b Coultas	0
B. Drinkwater, c & b Coultas	4
B. Beale, b Coultas	1
Extras (Lb 3, nb 2)	5
34.1 overs. Total	144

Fall of wkts: 1–3, 2–16, 3–44, 4–57, 5–76, 6–124, 7–124, 8–136, 9–142.

Bowling: Coultas 8.1–1–31–6; Banner 8–0–34–2; Burne 5–0–29–2; Braithwaite 9–0–23–0; Gilbert 4–0–22–0.

AVONCROFT

M. Neal, b Clements	13
*R. Braithwaite, run out	1
R. Giles, c M. Garaway, b Clements	14
J. Sketchley, b Beale	6
K. Rose, not out	68
E. Coultas, b Clements	0
†P. Shaw, not out	29
Extras (B 5, lb 7, nb 2)	14
36 overs. Total (5 wkts)	145

Did not bat: G. Banner, M. Wyres, N. Gilbert, R. Burne.
Fall of wkts: 1–7, 2–26, 3–35, 4–53, 5–53.
Bowling: Beale 9–1–32–1; Clements 9–2–15–3; M. Garaway 8–0–40–0; Richmond 2–0–12–0; Byrd 7–0–24–0; Care 1–0–8–0.
Umpires: Phillips and Bayliss.

Avoncroft won by 5 wkts.

Group 12 – Hockley Heath v. Astwood Bank

Astwood Bank, who went on to great deeds in subsequent rounds of the Haig, beat *Hockley Heath* by 73 runs in the Warwickshire final played at Redditch C.C's ground. *Astwood* won the toss and skipper J. Yoxall's superb innings of 138 not out, including 15 fours and three sixes, dominated the match. *Astwood* in reaching 209 for seven wickets batted in perfect conditions on a good pitch, but heavy rain during the tea interval, although forcing *Astwood* to bowl with a wet ball, made high scoring difficult for *Hockley* and the rain continued almost throughout their innings. For all that they reached 136 for 5 off their 40 overs, thanks largely to an unbeaten 62 by opener G. White.

ASTWOOD BANK

*J. Yoxall, not out	138
J. Robinson, b Yates	0

B. Spittle, c Thornton, b Curtiss 9
C. Robinson, c Yates, b Dawes 5
M. Wedgebury, c Curtiss, b Dawes 10
J. Poole, lbw Eathorne 17
R. Davies, run out 4
J. Crumpton, c Wright, b Yates 2
F. Morrall, not out 5
Extras (B 9, lb 10, w 3) 19

40 overs. Total (7 wkts) 209

Did not bat: T. Bird, †R. Nash.
Fall of wkts: 1–5, 2–57, 3–66, 4–106, 5–160, 6–170, 7–180.
Bowling: Yates 8–0–45–2; Eathorne 9–2–31–1; Dawes 9–1–31–2; Curtiss 5–0–18–1; White 9–0–65–0.

HOCKLEY HEATH

G. White, not out 62
T. Wright, lbw Robinson (C) 6
P. Dawes, c Wedgebury, b Robinson (C) 1
G. Eathorne, run out 4
N. Perry, b Robinson (C) 6
B. Curtiss, b Robinson (C) 20
M. Jones, not out 24
Extras (B 9, lb 2, nb 1, w 1) 13

40 overs. Total (5 wkts) 136

Did not bat: C. Yates, D. Bullivant, J. Maund, R. Thornton.
Fall of wkts: 1–17, 2–19, 3–33, 4–41, 5–66.
Bowling: Morrall 9–0–26–0; Crumpton 9–0–22–0; C. Robinson 9–3–9–4; Yoxall 3–0–25–0; Spittle 5–2–16–0; Bird 3–0–12–0; J. Robinson 2–0–13–0.
Umpires: H. N. Cook and M. Tyson.
Astwood Bank won by 73 runs.

Group 13 – Overstone v. Horton House

Horton made full use of winning the toss in this Northamptonshire final at Overstone; John Nutter's 88 was the backbone of their innings and Mike Adams, missed shortly after he came to the crease, contributed a valuable 28. *Overstone* bowled and fielded with rare spirit, Dick Chalcroft taking 3 for 32 in Horton's 182 off 36 overs. *Overstone,* though, batting in drizzle and grey light had to contend with the hostile attack of Mike Jubb, John Hall and Nutter. Dave Bradbury and Barry Freeman batted sensibly for an hour only to be both out in trying to speed up the scoring rate. Wittering (32 not out) and Pickering (18 not out) added an entertaining 60 runs for the seventh wicket but *Horton,* justifying their high local reputation, won an excellent match by 50 runs.

HORTON

M. Learoyd, c Civil, b Chalcroft	9
B. Russell, b Chalcroft	5
J. Nutter, c May, b Vann	88
J. Musson, c Bradbury, b Chalcroft	13
M. Adams, b Vann	28
J. Hall, run out	1
T. Joyce, run out	27
J. Owen, c Wittering, b Bradbury	6
R. Evans, c Bradbury, b Woods	1
P. Terry, c Civil, b Woods	2
M. Jubb, not out	2
Extras (B 1 lb 1)	2
36.4 overs. Total	182

Fall of wkts: 1–10, 2–23, 3–51, 4–102, 5–103, 6–169, 7–174, 8–179, 9–182.
Bowling: Chalcroft 9–0–32–3; Freeman 9–1–42–0; Bradbury 3–0–8–1; Woods 6.4–0–42–2; Vann 9–0–50–2.

THE BATTLE FOR THE GROUP TITLES

OVERSTONE

D. Collins, c Russell, b Hall	5
B. Freeman, c Russell, b Nutter	22
D. Bradbury, c & b Nutter	16
H. Moore, b Hall	0
O. Vann, c Learoyd, b Jubb	16
L May, b Terry	12
P. Pickering, not out	18
S. Wittering, not out	32
Extras (B 9, lb 2)	11
40 overs. Total (6 wkts)	132

Did not bat: M. Woods, *R. Chalcroft, †T. Civil.
Fall of wkts: 1–5, 2–37, 3–38, 4–52, 5–67, 6–76.
Bowling: Jubb 9–2–17–1; Hall 9–2–23–2; Nutter 9–1–28–2; Terry 8–2–25–1; Owen 3–0–14–0; Musson 2–0–14–0.
Umpires: P. W. Watson & P. Williams.

Horton House won by 50 runs.

Group 14 – Kimbolton v. Terrington St Clements

G. Beeby, *Kimbolton's* opening batsman dominated the home side's innings with an unbeaten 113 by the end of the 40 overs. Beeby hit 13 fours and one six and shared a first-wicket stand of 98 with R. Hart, when the latter was run out for 43. Facing a formidable total of 213 for 5, *Terrington* set off in a brave chase for the runs after losing Arnold for five. Five of their batsmen scored more than 20, but by the end of the allotted overs *Terrington* were 162 for 9, still 52 short of the target.

KIMBOLTON

G. Beeby, not out	113
R. Hart, run out	43
T. Newman, b Williams	13
R. Folds, c Biggar, b Williams	11

J. Hart, c Chamberlain, b Arnold 11
B. Facer, c Meek, b Newby 10
D. Peacock, not out 3
   Extras (B 5, lb 4) 9

40 overs. Total (5 wkts) 213

Did not bat: R. Stevenson, †D. Quirke, T. William, P. Bance.
Fall of wkts: 1–98, 2–123, 3–161, 4–189, 5–209.
Bowling: Arnold 8–0–38–1; Newby 6–1–29–1; Pearson 6–0–24–0; Meek 4–0–22–0; Williams 9–1–43–2; Brodie 7–0–48–0.

TERRINGTON ST CLEMENTS

R. Arnold, b Bance 5
S. Meek, b Facer 26
B. Pearson, c Folds, b Stevenson 31
D. Legget, c Folds, b Stevenson 20
B. Chamberlain, c Quirke, b J. Hart 21
D. Williams, c Hart (R), b Facer 1
S. Biggar, b J. Hart 0
D. Brown, b Williams 10
†G. Smith, not out 23
*I. Newby, b Folds 0
V. Brodie, not out 21
   Extras (Lb 4) 4

40 overs. Total (9 wkts) 162

Fall of wkts: 1–10, 2–44, 3–76, 4–88, 5–106, 6–106, 7–106, 8–134, 9–134.
Bowling: Bance 9–2–19–1; Williams 9–2–42–1; Facer 7–1–42–2; Stevenson 9–1–19–2; Hart 2–1–4–2; Folds 3–0–18–1; Newman 1–0–14–0.

Kimbolton won by 51 runs.

The magnificent pavilion at Shrivenham's ground in Wiltshire – surely one of the finest club pavilions in the country

P. Forty is presented with a Haig tie by Shrivenham's treasurer, Mr O. Collett, after the Wiltshire group final with Little Durnford, which Shrivenham won

The Summer Game: a match in progress at Littlewick Green, Berkshire

Contrasts in light and shade at Stanway C.C.'s ground, near Winchcombe, Gloucestershire

THE BATTLE FOR THE GROUP TITLES

Group 15 – Burrough Green v. Bradfield

Bradfield travelled to Burrough Green for the final of the Norfolk and Suffolk group and returned to the Norwich area with that title under their belts and giving special thanks to their bowlers, particularly Wilgress, whose four wickets for seven runs off four overs was the main factor in destroying *Burrough Green* for a lowly 33 in only 18 overs. Shreeve (2 for 5) and Howarth (2 for 12) were his main allies and only B. Claydon (15) reached double figures for the Green. *Bradfield* lost opener D. Sadler before a run had been scored but R. Colman (12 not out) and C. Bidewell (18) saw them to 37 in the 14th over and a victory by seven wickets. I. Lowe took two *Bradfield* wickets for 13 runs.

Group 16 – Gowerton v. Kington

Gowerton took the first innings on their own ground near Swansea, but got off to a bad start losing their first two wickets, both to E. Cronin, for only 16. A stand of 34 between skipper Robert Evans and John Morris improved the position, but it was not until John Richards joined Evans that *Gowerton* moved into top gear. This pair put on 103 for the fifth wicket, Richards reaching his 50 in 12 overs. Evans stayed on to score 80 and *Gowerton* were all out in the 38th over for a hard-hit 221.

Kington made a steady start in their reply scoring 51 without loss off the first 15 overs. Then Bill Thomas struck with two wickets in his first over and a further two in the fourth over. An aggressive 63 by M. Cronin helped *Kington* to respectability, but they were all out for 149 and *Gowerton* were home by 71 runs.

GOWERTON

E. Bevan, b Main	14
A. Dew, c Richardson, b E. Cronin	0
A. Daniel, lbw E. Cronin	10
R. Evans, c Jones, b Richardson	80

J. Morris, lbw E. Cronin — 22
J. Richards, stpd Bowdler, b M. Cronin — 65
B. Sterio, lbw M. Cronin — 10
G. Morgan, std Bowdler, b Richardson — 5
D. Jenkins, c E. Cronin, b M. Cronin — 1
T. Davies, c E. Cronin, b Richardson — 3
W. Thomas, not out — 2
Extras (B 2, lb 1, nb 4, w 2) — 9

37.4 overs. Total — 221

Fall of wkts: 1–4, 2–16, 3–32, 4–66, 5–169, 6–189, 7–213, 8–216, 9–216.
Bowling: Richardson 1.4–0–6–3; E. Cronin 9–3–18–3.

KINGTON

B. Richardson, c Morris, b Davies — 25
C. Campbell, c Evans, b Thomas — 32
E. Cronin, stpd Dew, b Thomas — 0
M. Cronin, c Richards, b Bevan — 63
J. Burgoyne, c Sterio, b Thomas — 12
E. Jones, c Davies, b Thomas — 0
*T. Main, c Dew, b Davies — 2
W. Nicholls, run out — 5
J. Davies, stpd Dew, b Bevan — 2
†R. Bowdler, c Jenkins, b Bevan — 1
T. Richardson, not out — 0
Extras (Lb 4, nb 2, w 1) — 7

35.2 overs. Total — 149

Fall of wkts: 1–51, 2–62, 3–62, 4–94, 5–94, 6–97, 7–134, 8–144, 9–149.
Bowling: Thomas 9–1–42–4; Bevan 3.2–0–25–3.

Umpires: W. Stretch and L. J. Davies.

Gowerton won by 72 runs.

THE BATTLE FOR THE GROUP TITLES

Group 17 – Dowdeswell & Foxcote v. Frocester

A large and vociferous crowd at *Dowdeswell* saw a most exciting match with the result wide open until the last over, *Frocester* failing by only five runs to beat *Dowdeswell's* 139 for 9 which was admirably sustained by D. Parrott's stubborn 62. For *Frocester* F. Clifford had a field day with the ball taking six wickets for 26 in his nine overs. Clutterbuck and Hudd gave *Frocester* a good start with a partnership of 43, E. Hawkins made a useful 25 but the scoring rate then dropped and the economical *Dowdeswell* fielding and bowling just landed the county title for the home team.

DOWDESWELL & FOXCOTE

D. Parrott, b Clifford	62
R. Waring, run out	9
R. Todd, lbw Clifford	27
R. Williams, lbw Clifford	5
I. Waterston, b Clifford	0
D. Waterston, c Baker, b White	5
T. Greaves, b Clifford	0
A. Cox, b Clifford	6
A. Todd, c Clutterbuck, b White	2
J. Lane, not out	8
I. Williams, not out	4
Extras (B 6, lb 6)	11
40 overs. Total (9 wkts)	139

Fall of wkts: 1–22, 2–98, 3–101, 4–101, 5–106, 6–108, 7–118, 8–126, 9–126.
Bowling: White 8–2–14–2; Herbert 9–2–24–0; Clifford 9–3–26–6; Young 8–1–30–0; Baker 6–1–34–0.

FROCESTER

R. Clutterbuck, b Waring	29
G. Hudd, b Waring	25

E. Hawkins, c R. Williams, b Waring	25
T. Baker, b Lane	5
J. Hawkins, c R. Williams, b Cox	13
R. Young, not out	16
M. Walker, run out	5
F. Clifford, run out	0
P. Herbert, b Lane	0
P. White, not out	8
Extras (B 5, lb 3)	8
40 overs. Total (8 wkts)	134

Did not bat: R. Spyvee.
Fall of wkts: 1–43, 2–83, 3–87, 4–104, 5–108, 6–115, 7–115, 8–117.
Bowling: Waterston 9–1–22–0; Lane 9–2–10–2; Waring 9–2–26–3; Cox 3–0–18–1; R. Williams 4–0–18–0; I. Williams 6–0–32–0.
Umpires: G. Cook and L. J. Smith.

Dowdeswell won by 5 runs.

Group 18 – Aston Rowant v. Bledlow

Bledlow duly won the Oxfordshire group title beating *Aston Rowant* by five wickets in a low-scoring final. P. Lambourne scored 69 and R. McQueen 28 of *Aston Rowant's* total of 126, but their remaining batsmen had little or no answer to the accuracy of S. Goldthorpe (3 for 31) and B. Baker (3 for 33). A. Spencer with an unbeaten 65 led *Bledlow* to 127 for 5 and victory.

Group 19 – Eversholt v. Winchmore Hill

The Buckinghamshire group final proved to be a tense match in which the home club, *Eversholt*, gained an early initiative by dismissing the *Winchmore Hill* openers for six runs and retaining it throughout to win eventually by four wickets. Despite an aggressive innings of 40 by J. Payne, assisted by 20 from D. Calder, *Eversholt's* bowlers attacked consistently and were backed by excellent catching and fielding. *Winchmore Hill* finally totalled 104 from 37.2 overs. Brian Lawson was the most successful bowler with 3 for 16, plus two good slip catches. Persistent drizzle started during the tea interval and continued throughout the *Eversholt* innings. Roy Cook followed his three catches behind the stumps by giving *Eversholt* a positive start, scoring 16 out of 23 for the first wicket before he was bowled by Calder. Calder went on to dismiss Garratt and Larbey but Inchbald was now well-established. David Spruzen scored 17 before falling to Saunders. Excitement mounted as J. Morris took two more quick wickets but Clarke batted coolly and enabled Inchbald to score the remaining runs for victory. Calder finished with 3 for 24 for *Winchmore Hill*. The triumphant home team were presented with their winners' medals by Ian Redpath, the Australian Test cricketer.

WINCHMORE HILL

*D. Payne, c Cook, b Lawson	2
A. Payne, c Cook, b Lawson	4
C. Haines, b Anstee	7
J. Payne, c Lawson, b Woodwards	40
K. Francis, lbw Anstee	3
B. Collins, c Lawson, b Larbey	2
J. Saunders, b Woodwards	0
D. Calder, c Woodwards, b Lawson	20
J. Adams, run out	7
†D. Thomas, c Cook, b Garratt	10
J. Morris, not out	2
Extras (B 2, lb 3, nb 3)	7
37.2 overs. Total	104

Fall of wkts: 1–3, 2–6, 3–22, 4–39, 5–61, 6–61, 7–61, 8–81, 9–100.

Bowling: Lawson 9–3–16–3; Anstee 9–2–24–2; Woodwards 9–1–30–2; Garratt 6.2–2–0–10–1; Larbey 4–1–17–1.

EVERSHOLT

J. Inchbald, not out	44
†R. Cook, b Calder	16
*C. Garratt, c Thomas, b Calder	3
R. Larbey, b Calder	7
D. Spruzen, b Saunders	17
A. Pickersgill, b Morris	2
G. Butt, c Thomas, b Morris	1
A. Clarke, not out	4
Extras (B 8, lb 2, nb 1)	11
31.3 overs. Total (6 wkts)	105

Did not bat: B. Lawson, R. Woodwards, M. Anstee.
Fall of wkts: 1–23, 2–33, 3–47, 4–72, 5–77, 6–89.
Bowling: Adams 7–1–23–0; Calder 9–2–24–3; Saunders 9–2–23–1; Morris 6.3–0–0–24–2.
Umpires: F. Wells and E. Sherry.

Eversholt won by 4 wkts.

Group 20 – Blunham v. Aspenden

Blunham, one of the strongest sides in the Haig as subsequent rounds were to prove, were at home to *Aspenden* from Buntingford in the Beds and Herts final. The visitors won the toss only to receive an immediate setback when Saunders was out with the score at 2. Dowler, the other opening batsman, held the side together with a stubborn 55, receiving valuable support from his captain R. Willett (28), stumper Hampton (16) and Glasscock (15). Page was *Blunham's* most successful bowler, taking 4 for 33 and *Aspenden's* innings closed in the 37th over for 152. Ranson (37) Fordham (33) and D. Lawson with a not out 46 demonstrated *Blunham's* all-round strength and they passed *Aspenden's* total in two less overs and with four wickets in hand.

ASPENDEN

R. Saunders, c Ashwell, b Watson	1
C. Dowler, c Ranson, b Page	55
†P. Hampton, c Thompson, b Ranson	16
T. Glasscock, stpd Ranson, b Rawlins	15
W. Wallace, stpd Ranson, b Fordham	12
A. Warner, c Thompson, b Page	1
*R. Willett, b Ranson	28
M. Oregan, c Watson, b Ranson	10
J. Mason, c Lawson, b Page	8
D. Hampton, c Ranson, b Page	3
D. Mole, not out	0
Extras (B 3)	3
36.2 overs. Total	152

Fall of wkts: 1–2, 2–25, 3–42, 4–54, 5–114, 6–130, 7–131, 8–149, 9–152.
Bowling: Page 7.2–0–33–4; M. Ranson 9–0–34–3.

BLUNHAM

†P. Ranson, c Hampton, b Mason	37
B. Thompson, b Glasscock	11
P. Fordham, run out	33
D. Lawson, not out	46
R. Ashwell, c Saunders, b Mason	4
R. Rawlins, b Wallace	6
J. Tester, b Wallace	1
M. Watson, not out	15
Extras (B 3)	3
36 overs. Total (6 wkts)	156

Did not bat: W. Watson, R. Lawrence, T. Page.
Fall of wkts: 1–26, 2–83, 3–83, 4–93, 5–106, 6–112.
Bowling: Wallace 9–0–34–2.

Blunham won by 4 wkts.

Group 22 – Welford Park v. Braywood

Braywood, the visitors, batted first and set a fairly stiff target of 160 for 7 wickets off their 40 overs, with C. Knight, their captain, setting the pace with a fine 89. *Welford* started their reply with an opening partnership of 53 by Sampson (15) and Alton (66). Then things started to go wrong and it looked *Braywood* all the way until M. Thomas joined skipper D. Uzzell with eight wickets gone for 124. This pair then staged a cliff-hanging finish until Thomas settled the issue, making the winning hit in the 39th over. Uzzell's captain's knock brought him an undefeated 31 and his side a two-wickets victory, Langley and Webb sharing the eight *Welford* wickets.

BRAYWOOD

*C. Knight, c Thomas, b Church	89
B. Barditch, c Sampson, b Alton	19
D. Belworthy, run out	4
S. Langley, b Alton	0
R. Webb, b Whale	19
†T. Holden, b Whale	12
P. Haywood, b Uzzell	4
R. Arnold, not out	2
M. Hurst, not out	6
Extras (B 2, lb 3)	5
40 overs. Total (7 wkts)	160

Fall of wkts: 1–57, 2–81, 3–81, 4–107, 5–133, 6–149, 7–153
Bowling: Whale 9–3–21–2; How 6–0–34–0; Alton 9–1–32–2; Church 8–0–42–1; Uzzell 6–0–24–1; Hamblin 2–0–11–0.

WELFORD PARK

G. Sampson, c Webb, b Langley	15
K. Alton, b Webb	66
D. Edwards, c Hurst, b Webb	11

THE BATTLE FOR THE GROUP TITLES

†R. How, c Holden, b Langley	6
*D. Uzzell, not out	31
M. Whale, b Langley	0
B. How, b Langley	1
C. Hamblin, c Hayward, b Webb	5
M. Rumble, b Webb	5
M. Thomas, not out	12
Extras (B 4, lb 5)	9
39 overs. Total (8 wkts)	161

Did not bat: C. Church.
Fall of wkts: 1–53, 2–94, 3–104, 4–104, 5–104, 6–105, 7–112, 8–124.
Bowling: Langley 9–1–34–4; Webb 9–0–30–4; Knight 4–0–28–0; Hayward 9–0–30–0; Belworthy 8–1–30–0.
Umpires: G. Marshall and P. Dunthorne.
Welford Park won by 2 wkts.

Group 23 – Troon v. Thorverton

Troon, correctly fancied for highest Haig honours, had to fight hard before winning the Devon and Cornwall group by a mere 12 runs from *Thorverton*. Batting first on their home ground, *Troon* used all their 40 overs in reaching 169 for 9, including a strong 54 from T. Edwards who with skipper T. Carter (18) put on 47 for the first wicket. All *Troon's* nine wickets fell to catches, four of which were off the bowling of J. Courtney (9–1–39–4). *Thorverton* also batted well down the order but were behind the scoring rate required and with K. Baker (11) and Courtney (12) together at the close were 13 runs short of glory and with three wickets in hand. Earlier Molineux (32) and Andrews (46) had added 60 for the third wicket.

TROON

*T. Carter, c Wardle, b Dyson	18
T. Edwards, c & b Molineux	54

B. Carter, c Wardle, b Courtney	14
J. Vincent, c Langdon, b Courtney	27
J. Spry, c Courtney, b Andrews	18
M. Sweeney, c Andrews, b Courtney	1
B. Moyle, c Molineux, b Northcott	18
K. Lean, c Carter, b Andrews	0
†D. Rashleigh, c Molineux, b Courtney	6
G. Dunston, not out	5
P. Thomas, not out	8
Extras (B 3, lb 1, nb 2, w 2)	8
40 overs. Total (9 wkts)	169

Fall of wkts: 1–47, 2–85, 3–91, 4–133, 5–138, 6–142, 7–142, 8–159, 9–165.

THORVERTON

†J. Carter, run out	16
D. Langdon, b Dunstan	16
*S. Molineux, b Lean	32
C. Andrews, c B. Carter, b Lean	46
L. Wardle, run out	15
D. Dyson, b Lean	0
P. Williams, lbw B. Carter	1
K. Baker, not out	11
J. Courtney, not out	12
Extras (B 1, lb 3, nb 1, w 3)	8
40 overs. Total (7 wkts)	157

Did not bat: J. Frankpitt, M. Northcott.
Fall of wkts: 1–33, 2–35, 3–95, 4–128, 5–129, 6–130, 7–133.
Bowling: Lean 9–0–37–3.
Umpires: T. Shoreland and E. Thomas.

Troon won by 12 runs.

In Group 24, *Evercreech* for whom great Haig things had been planned, duly took the Somerset title. They put *Milverton* in first and out for 148, then C. Perera (72 n.o.) led them to a six wickets victory.

Group 25 – Shillingstone v. Wimborne St Giles

Shillingstone, probably still rankling at some unfavourable local Press comments on their good fortune in beating mighty *Beaminster* by one run in the group semi-final, demonstrated in the Dorset final that this was no mere flash in the pan. Their visitors *Wimborne St Giles* won the toss and gave *Shillingstone* first knock. The home side started with an opening stand of 31 by Hardy and Crane and when the captain departed for 17, Hardy and Mace put on 78 for the second wicket before Hardy was stumped for a hard-hit 52, Mace being 62 not out when the innings closed at 152 for 2. St Giles put up a stiff resistance with good innings by P. Robinson (43) and N. Andrews (36). G. Ridout's five wickets for 22 turned the game however and *St Giles* were all out in the 38th over still 15 runs short of victory. F. J. Hamilton the *Shillingstone* secretary, said that the match was played before the largest crowd he had ever seen at the ground.

SHILLINGSTONE

†N. Hardy, st Park, b Cheater	52
*D. S. Crane, b Shepard	17
D. Mace, not out	62
C. Ridout, not out	7
Extras, (B 6, lb 4, w 4)	14
40 overs. Total (2 wkts)	152

Did not bat: A. Hunt, E. Sheen, P. Hawkins, G. Wells, T. Hawkins, C. Hawkins, P. Crane.
Fall of wkts: 1–31, 2–109.
Bowling: Shepard 9–1–21–1; Clarke 6–1–17–0; Andrews 7–0–40–0; Robinson 7–0–22–0; Cheater 9–1–30–1; Davis 2–0–8–0.

WIMBORNE ST GILES

D. Cheater, c Hardy, b Sheen	14
P. Robinson, b Sheen	43
N. Shepard, run out	28
J. Park, c Hunt, b Ridout	2
N. Andrews, c Hawkins, b Ridout	36
R. Scott, c Ridout, b Wells	0
M. Lowe, b Ridout	4
M. Davis, not out	1
R. Clarke, c Hunt, b Ridout	0
R. Shepard, run out	0
F. Snow, c Mace, b Ridout	0
Extras (B 5, lb 5)	10
40 overs. Total	138

Fall of wkts: 1–31, 2–72, 3–75, 4–81, 5–113, 6–133, 7–137, 8–137, 9–138.
Bowling: Sheen 9–1–29–2; Wells 6–0–31–1; Mace 9–3–10–0; Crane 7–0–36–0; Ridout 6.5–2–22–5.
Umpires: Paulley and Newell.
Shillingstone won by 14 runs.

Group 26 – Shrivenham v. Little Durnford

Shrivenham, given a good start by Hambridge and Pratt, were always thereafter looking for runs and T. and B. Hayward shared a bright stand of 45 for the fourth wicket. The others kept up the pace until the last wicket fell at 164. *Little Durnford* got within striking distance of the Wiltshire title with sound innings from Yates (28), Seddon (31) and Combes (38), but could not accelerate the pace and were 14 runs short at the close with a wicket in hand.

SHRIVENHAM

F. Hambridge, c Reeves, b Hubbard	8
G. Pratt, b Wilkins	14

T. Hayward, c Thomas, b Wilkins   57
R. Harvey, c & b Wilkins   7
B. Hayward, run out   34
D. Bradfield, b Wilkins   4
†P. Forty, c Yates, b Biddle   14
B. Wilson, b Reeves   14
*R. Burrough, c & b Biddle   2
K. Wallace, c Parry, b Biddle   0
R. Cox, not out   0
Extras (B 2, lb 5, nb 2, w 1)   10

38.4 overs. Total   164

Fall of wkts: 1–22, 2–34, 3–62, 4–107, 5–122, 6–138, 7–160, 8–164, 9–164.
Bowling: Reeves 8–2–17–1; Biddle 8.4–0–26–3; Wilkins 9–1–28–4; Hubbard 9–0–49–1; Thomas 4–0–34–0.

LITTLE DURNFORD

T. Yates, c & b Hayward   28
D. Wilkins, c Forty, b Bradfield   0
D. Thomas, c Wallace, b Wilson   19
Q. Seddon, c Burrough, b Harvey   31
M. Combes, c B. Hayward, b Hambridge 38
R. Barnard, b Hayward   2
R. Reeves, c Harvey, b Hayward   6
J. Veck, st Forty, b Harvey   14
†T. Parry, not out   3
*C. Biddle, c Forty, b Hambridge   3
D. Hubbard, not out   2
Extras (Lb 4)   4

40 overs. Total (9 wkts)   150

Fall of wkts: 1–4, 2–31, 3–77, 4–78, 5–84, 6–122, 7–133, 8–142, 9–148.
Bowling: Wilson 9–2–19–1; Bradfield 9–2–20–1;

Burrough 2-0-12-0; Hayward (B) 9-0-34-3; Harvey 9-1-48-2; Hambridge 2-0-13-2.
Umpires: D. Froud and D. Wakefield.
Shrivenham won by 14 runs.

Group 27 – Steep v. Crown Taverners

Crown Taverners, electing to bat first at Steep, never really recovered from a slow start and had scored only 38 off the first 20 overs. Malcolm Clements then caused all sorts of problems with his leg-spinners and despite an enterprising 23 not out by Swinstead, the visitors could only muster 105 for 9 from the 40 overs. Clements finished with four wickets for 10 runs. *Steep* then coasted along to take to take the Hampshire title in the 21st over with seven wickets to spare and with Roy Passingham undefeated two runs short of his half century.

CROWN TAVERNERS

*Farrington, b King	26
Powell, c Passingham, b Clements	11
Pilgrim, st Lewis, b Clements	0
Stroud, c Lewis, b Batstone	6
Wright, lbw King	1
Patrick, c King, b Clements	7
Galer, c King, b Clements	12
Swinstead, not out	23
†Keeble, b Antrobus	13
Carbury, b Antrobus	1
Dowle, not out	0
Extras (B 1, lb 3, w 1)	5
40 overs. Total (9 wkts)	105

Fall of wkts: 1-37, 2-37, 3-39, 4-47, 5-62, 6-62, 7-72, 8-73, 9-105.
Bowling: Clements 9-4-10-4; King 9-2-12-12; Antrobus 9-2-20-2; Batstone 9-1-35-1.

STEEP

C. Gordon, c Galer, b Dowle	20
R. Starnes, c Stroud, b Dowle	8
J. Hetherington, b Wright	20
R. Passingham, not out	48
R. Antrobus, not out	9
Extras (Lb 1)	1
20.3 overs. Total (3 wkts)	106

Did not bat: M. Clements, †T. Lewis, *J. Hayes, B. Rea, C. King, J. Batstone.
Fall of wickets: 1–18, 2–37, 3–78.
Steep won by 7 wkts.

Group 28 – Brook v. Shamley Green

Shamley Green scraped home by five runs to win the Surrey title at Brook. Winning the toss they reached 185 for 9 at the end of their 40 overs, thanks largely to a good 71 by S. Stevens, M. Wrixson (24) and M. Stevens (34). *Brook* lost opener A. Wood at 4, and then Hardy and Hodges advanced the score to 48 and the total mounted steadily but the closure came at 180 in the 40th over with L. Smithers not out 11.

Group 29 (Sussex I) – Eastergate v. Findon

Eastergate 193 for 7 (A. Cockburn 68, E. Richards 53) beat Findon 39 for 1 on the toss of a coin, a disappointing end to a match which had offered in its pre-rain period every prospect of a thrilling finish.

Group 30 (Kent I) – Linton Park v. Shipbourne

This was an excellent match from all angles with some fine bowling and fielding matched by good batting on both sides. *Linton Park's* fielders took every chance that was offered – including an acrobatic effort at mid-off by Benny Bell to get rid of *Shipbourne's* heavy scoring opener Axten, and a sharp slip chance held by Mike Iliffe to dismiss Sly for 0. In fact, of the eight wickets that fell six were catches and two run outs.

Shipbourne's hero was skipper Alan Morris, a stylish left-hand bat who rallied his side from the depths of 38–4 and hit five fours in his 63. But *Linton's* pace quartet of Alan Cooper, Graham Mountford, Tony Gauna and Ron Hickman always kept control and the innings closed at 145.

Linton Park's run chase was given an ideal start in a well-paced partnership from Andrew Moss and Paul Bowles. Starting steadily and then accelerating they reached 66 before Bowles was well caught at short mid-wicket. Moss went on to hit five boundaries in his 50 and when he was third out, caught at long-on, the result seemed a formality. But Peter Buss grabbed three wickets in an over to set *Linton* hearts palpitating before they eventually got home in the 38th over.

SHIPBOURNE

†F. Axten, c Bell, b Mountford	11
*A. Morris, c Cooper, b Gauna	63
R. Davey, c Chance, b Cooper	0
J. Sly, c Iliffe, b Cooper	0
E. May, run out	2
P. Phillips, run out	19
D. Allaway, c Anscombe, b Hickman	18
P. Buss, not out	18
G. Kilby, c Cooper, b Gauna	2
N. Axten, not out	8
Extras (B 1, lb 2, w 1)	4
40 overs. Total (8 wkts)	145

Did not bat: J. Wakeman.
Fall of wkts: 1–22, 2–24, 3–30, 4–38, 5–73, 6–109, 7–121, 8–125.

Bowling: Mountford 9-0-21-1; Cooper 9-0-25-2; Bowles 7-0-49-0; Gauna 9-0-32-2; Hickman 6-1-14-1.

LINTON PARK

A. Moss, c Allaway, b Axten	58
P. Bowles, c Davey, b Kilby	35
†C. Anscombe, c Kilby, b Axten	21
*J. Thirkell, b Buss	19
M. Iliffe, b Buss	0
R. Chance, lbw Buss	0
B. Bell, not out	4
A. Cooper, not out	5
Extras (B 1, lb 3, nb 2)	6
38.4 overs. Total (6 wkts)	148

Did not bat: G. Mountford, R. Hickman, T. Gauna.
Fall of wkts: 1-66, 2-114, 4-139, 5-139, 6-140.
Bowling: Wakeman 9-2-18-0; Kilby 9-0-39-1; Morris 5-0-27-0; Phillips 8-1-29-0; Buss 3.4-0-14-3; Axten 4-2-15-2.
Umpires: M. Hill and D. Pantony.

Linton Park won by 4 wkts.

Group 31 (Sussex II) – Withyham v. Glynde & Beddingham

Glynde and Beddingham took first innings on winning the toss and after losing G. Baker for 4, D. Pullen, missed at slip early on and M. Sutton added 51 for the second wicket. Steady accurate bowling by the home side, however, restricted *Glynde* to 91 for 5 off 30 overs. Then W. Jones and K. Parris came together and launched a furious attack in an unbeaten partnership that in the final 10 overs took *Glynde* to a total of 158. When *Withyham* batted, they soon lost Shackleton to a magnificent running catch by Martin and Head was bowled by Jones for 1. B. Standring and

Tankard than added 27 before both were run out in the space of two overs. McDonald and Crowe added 43 for the fifth wicket, but McBrown struck with three wickets in an over and *Withyham's* challenge was over. McBrown returned the excellent bowling figures of 8–0–26–6.

GLYNDE

D. Pullen, c & b Standring (R)	38
G. Baker, b Froude	4
M. Sutton, b Standring (R)	19
R. Clayton, c Head, b Stewart	15
R. Martin, b Standring (G)	2
W. Jones, not out	39
K. Parris, not out	28
Extras (B 8, lb 2, w 3)	13
40 overs. Total (5 wkts)	158

Did not bat: D. Turrell, A. McBrown, P. Moorey, T. Hill.
Fall of wkts: 1–16, 2–67, 3–79, 4–87, 5–91.
Bowling: Froude 9–2–33–1; McDonald 9–1–26–0; Head 5–0–23–0; R. Standring 8–1–18–2; G. Standring 3–0–15–1; Stewart 6–1–30–1.

WITHYHAM

P. Head, b Jones	1
K. Shackleton, c Martin, b McBrown	2
R. Standring, run out	23
C. Tankard, run out	4
D. MacDonald, b McBrown	22
P. Froude, b McBrown	23
G. Standring, b McBrown	7
S. Depr, c Baker, b McBrown	0
J. Stewart, b McBrown	0
K. Martin, not out	6

T. Sullivan, not out 16
Extras (B 3, lb 1, w 1) 5

40 overs. Total (9 wkts) 109

Fall of wkts: 1–5, 2–6, 3–33, 4–36, 5–79, 6–82, 7–82, 8–82, 9–87.
Bowling: Jones 9–4–11–1; McBrown 8–0–26–6; Clayton 9–1–35–0; Moorey 9–2–26–0; Turrell 3–1–3–0; Baker 2–1–3–0.

Glynde & Beddingham won by 49 runs.

Group 32 (Kent II) – Horsmonden v. Sheldwich

Sheldwich won the toss and batted first. Runs came steadily, with opener Mitchell 31 and Hobbs 21 contributing largely to their reaching 91 for 4. In trying to force the pace the later wickets fell quickly and *Sheldwich* were finally dismissed for 128. Good bowling by Knight (2 for 17) and Larkin (1 for 21) was mainly responsible for the moderate score.

Horsmonden, a good batting side, started disastrously, losing J. Couchman in the first over, but the situation was retrieved by D. Couchman and Bagwell who took the score to 37 after 15 overs. Then good bowling by R. Heward and Creed brought five wickets in five overs and *Horsmonden* were 50 for 6. Some first-class batting by Bateup (35), assisted by the later batsmen, resulted in *Horsmonden* reaching a total of 95 in 33 overs before being all out. Ian Redpath presented the medals to the group winners.

SHELDWICH

A. Mitchell, b Tester 31
†J. Holt, c Couchman, b Larkin 6
D. Hobbs, b Tester 21
J. Stanford, c Couchman, b Knight 18
F. Scott, b Knight 13

B. Newman, c Knight, b Tompsett   2
T. Heward, run out   6
R. Heward, run out   4
A. Creed, not out   9
*T. George, b Tester   2
D. Elliot, b Tompsett   9
    Extras (B 1, lb 5)   5

38.4 overs. Total   128

Fall of wkts: 1–27, 2–57, 3–66, 4–91, 5–94, 6–98, 7–103, 8–114, 9–119.
Bowling: Tompsett 4.4–0–23–2; Knight 9–2–17–2; Larkin 9–0–21–1; Bateup 9–0–41–0; Tester 7–1–21–3.

HORSMONDEN

J. Couchman, b Elliot   0
*D. Couchman, c Hobbs, b Creed   14
J. Bagwell, b Creed   25
S. Knight, c Holt, b R. Heward   1
P. Bateup, lbw T. Heward   34
W. Tompsett, lbw R. Heward   0
K. Knight, b Creed   1
†N. Fisher, run out   8
J. Wybourn, not out   7
E. Larkin, b Elliot   0
T. Tester, b Creed   0
    Extras (B 1, lb 3, nb 1)   5

33 overs. Total   95

Fall of wkts: 1–0, 2–37, 3–38, 4–46, 5–47, 6–50, 7–63, 8–63, 9–94.
Bowling: Elliot 6–2–6–2; George 6–0–31–0; R. Heward 9–0–17–2 T. Heward 3–0–14–1; Creed 9–2–22–2.

Sheldwich won by 33 runs.

Ladbrokes set the odds

And so these 32 village champions had started their run to the final stages of the Haig, and in the sixth round, with travelling assistance, they had to meet their neighbouring title-holders. As an added incentive Ladbrokes opened a book on the eventual winner at Lord's, a somewhat brave step at this stage as most of the clubs were relatively unknown, apart from local 'form'. However, for the sixth round *Folkton and Flixton* were made favourites at 8–1, with Midland clubs *Kimbolton* and *Horton House*, plus *Linton Park* at 10–1; *Tong* 12–1 and such teams as *Warenford*, *Empingham*, *Troon* and *Blunham* outsiders at 25–1. After this round the odds changed somewhat as national form began to take shape.

Now they are sixteen

Meigle v. Warenford

Warenford crossed the Border for their sixth-round match against *Meigle* on St Boswell's ground, and losing the toss were invited to bat first. *Warenford* could not have had a worse start when A. Patterson was caught behind the wicket in the first over. But the wicket was good, and so was the weather, and the visitors than settled down to run-getting. I. Patterson and Robson proceeded to add 96 runs for the second wicket and after they were out Thompson (24) and Squibb (27 not out) carried on so that *Warenford* reached 203 for 5 from their 40 overs. *Meigle*, in contrast, started well with an opening stand of 33 by Halder and Whitelaw but their middle order batsmen could not sustain the high scoring rate and, apart from 31 by R. Dow and a gallant 34 by P. Drummond (senior) could achieve little against Warenford's accurate bowling and sure catching. They were all out for 164 and both teams adjourned to the Buccleugh Arms.

WARENFORD

A. Patterson, c B. Reid, b Walton	0
I. Patterson, c A. Reid, b Drummond	69
W. Robson, b Gleig	59
B. Thompson, c Whitelaw, b Drummond	24
B. Squibb, not out	27
*J. Riddell, b Halder	3
C. Curry, not out	9
Extras (B 8, lb 4)	12
40 overs. Total (5 wkts)	203

Fall of wkts: 1–0, 2–96, 3–141, 4–175, 5–196.
Bowling: Drummond 9–1–47–2; Halder 7–0–37–1; Gleig 9–0–41–1; Walton 6–1–37–1.

MEIGLE

G. Halder, c Alexander, b I. Patterson	34
*N. Whitelaw, b A. Patterson	11
M. Walton, c & b Thompson	12
†B. Reid, c Hedley, b I. Patterson	4
R. Dow, lbw Squibb	31
A. Reid, b Thompson, b Robson	2
G. Gerrie, b I. Patterson	12
P. Drummond, c I. Patterson, b Robson	34
W. Scott, c Riddell, b Squibb	3
W. Brown, c I. Patterson, b Curry	2
A. Gleig, not out	18
Extras (W 1)	1
36.2 overs. Total	164

Fall of wkts: 1–33, 2–48, 3–62, 4–65, 5–65, 6–90, 7–121, 8–129, 9–136.
Bowling: Thompson 7–1–31–1; A. Patterson 4–0–25–1; I. Patterson 9–0–27–3; Robson 2.2–0–12–2; Squibb 9–0–46–2; Curry 5–0–22–2.
Umpires: Major A. A. Wright and Major C. Allen.
Warenford won by 39 runs.

THE BATTLE FOR THE GROUP TITLES

Tong v. Folkton & Flixton

A Yorkshire side had to win this White Roses clash, and *Tong* it was who put out *Flixton* the original favourites. Winning the toss on their home ground, *Tong* started slowly losing two wickets to some excellent bowling by T. Baker and T. Wood, only 40 runs coming from the first 18 overs. Then some lusty hitting from H. Cummings, 91 not out (10 sixes and 4 fours) and B. Bradley 30 and a fine, controlled innings by the opener P. Marriott, 70 (3 sixes 7 fours). *Tong,* ever more eager for runs, slumped from 189 for 5 to 199 for 8 with M. Stewart dismissing Greenwood and Pickersgill, both caught and bowled off successive balls. Cummings, joined by Noll Glennon, saw the *Tong* total to 239 for 9 off their 40 overs.

Flixton, needing six per over to win, started soundly against the father and son bowling combination of Fred and Tony Pickersgill, but were halted at 37 by Tony's 2 wickets in two balls. After being 92–7 the *Flixton* tail wagged to such purpose, thanks to T. Carr, 60 not out (6 sixes 3 fours), assisted by D. Elvidge 21 and T. Wood 28, that 6 sixes from the last over would have won the match. That proved impossible even on this small ground, Tong winning by 31 runs.

TONG

F. Pickersgill, c Stewart, b Wood	4
P. Marriott, c Blackburrow, b Elvidge	70
D. Wilkinson, c Elvidge, b Wood	1
B. Bradley, b Elvidge	30
H. Cummings, not out	91
H. Webster, c Brown, b Stewart	13
C. Greenwood, c & b Stewart	0
A. Pickersgill, c & b Stewart	0
T. Fawthrop, c Wood, b Sellars	0
*J. Robinson, c Baker, b Stewart	1
L. Glennon, not out	16
Extras (B 10, lb 3)	13
40 overs. Total (9 wkts)	239

Fall of wkts: 1–7, 2–13, 3–67, 4–141, 5–189, 6–190, 7–190, 8–199, 9–207.
Bowling: Baker 9–1–26–0; Wood 9–3–12–2; Sellars 9–1–52–1; Brown 3–0–32–0; Elvidge 5–0–56–2; Hotham 1–0–12–0; Stewart 4–0–36–4.

FOLKTON & FLIXTON

M. Blackburrow, b A. Pickersgill	18
M. Stewart, b Fawthrop	39
*M. Hotham, b A. Pickersgill	0
†J. Phillipson, c & b Glennon	23
M. Brown, c Greenwood, b Glennon	0
G. Nichol, c Cummings, b Glennon	1
T. Baker, c F. Pickersgill, b Fawthrop	1
T. Carr, not out	60
D. Elvidge, c A. Pickersgill, b Fawthrop	21
T. Wood, c Webster, b Glennon	28
D. Sellars, not out	2
Extras (B 5, lb 6, nb 4)	15
40 overs. Total (9 wkts)	208

Fall of wkts: 1–37, 2–37, 3–73, 4–73, 5–77, 6–86, 7–92, 8–142, 9–206.
Bowling: F. Pickersgill 9–2–29–0; A. Pickersgill 9–0–27–2; Fawthrop 9–0–54–3; Glennon 9–0–52–4; Robinson 2–0–18–0; Greenwood 2–0–13–0.
Umpires: Major F. Upfold and F. Lawson.

Tong won by 31 runs.

Lindal Moor v. Northop Hall

On the day this was an easy win for *Lindal* after an opening stand of 109 by Gardiner and Coward and a quick 27 by Gifford bringing the total up to 180 for 4. This total seemed to be too great for *Northop* who never went for the runs, or were not able to against accurate bowling. The game's highlights were *Lindal's* opening stand and their excellent fielding and catching. Even in defeat the *Northop* players and supporters were all sportsmen and welcome guests at *Lindal Moor's* celebrations.

At Lindal Moor: *Lindal:* 180–4 (40 overs) E. Gardiner 43, B. Coward 54, T. E. Gifford 27 not out. *Northop Hall:* 98–8 (40 overs). D. Riney 20, G. Martin 17 not out; Gifford 3–21, Shuttleworth 2–17, Liddicott 2–26. *Umpires:* T. Dainty and L. Green. *Lindal* won by 82 runs.

Collingham 174 for 4 beat Holmesfield 103.

Swynnerton Park v. Astwood Bank

Swynnerton, although taking first innings on their own ground, could do little against the accurate bowling of Crumpton, aided by Robinson and Morrall. All out for 101 they set *Astwood* little challenge, the winning hit coming in the 29th over with only four wickets gone.

At Swynnerton Park: *Swynnerton* 101 (40 overs). G. B. Baldwin 43; J. Crumpton 4–18, F. Morrall 1–28, C. Robinson 2–36. *Astwood Bank:* 102–4 (28.3 overs). J. Yoxall 38; C. Ellis 2–35; *Umpires:* R. Wormington and C. Baskeyfield. *Astwood* won by 6 wkts.

Empingham v. Horton House

Empingham made a brave reply to *Horton House's* total of 210 for 5 but could not match their visitors' opening stand of 109 by Learoyd and Russell. *Horton* with an added 57 not out by M. Adams ended their 40 overs on 210 for five wickets. *Empingham* were all out in the 40th over of their innings for 183 despite a fine eighth-wicket stand of 54 by Woodbridge and Boalch.

At Empingham: *Horton House:* 210–5 (40 overs). M. Learoyd 52, B. Russell 52, M. Adams 57 not out, J. Owen

21 not out; R. Woodbridge 2–39, J. Thraves 2–30. *Empingham:* 201 (40 overs). Woodbridge 38, R. Boalch 26; J. Hall 3–46, Owen 3–33.

Avoncroft v. Gowerton

This was a splendid match, played in wonderful spirit on a fine day in front of the biggest crowd ever seen at Avoncroft, including a coachload from South Wales. *Avoncroft* were shattered at first on a slightly damp wicket, Jenkins 1 for 9 and Richards 4 for 31, claiming the first five wickets for 28. Coultas with a whirlwind 27 in 26 minutes off 24 balls, and Neal with a gritty 40 not out in 109 minutes at least took the score past 100; to 113, in fact, with left-arm spinner Thomas taking 3 for 22. *Gowerton* fielded excellently. Bevan (17) and Dew (16) seemed to be coasting in for *Gowerton* with an opening stand of 36. However young Robert Burne hit back with three wickets in 17 balls and a spell of 4 for 14 in five overs leaving *Gowerton* at 52 for 4. Daniel (20) led a recovery before being magnificently caught by Banner; Cox (40 not out) kept his head and, in spite of several close shaves steered his team to a four-wicket win in the 39th over.

AVONCROFT

L. Keen, c Bevan, b Jenkins	6
K. Rose, c J. Davies, b Richards	0
R. Giles, c Bevan, b Richards	14
M. Neal, not out	40
*R. Braithwaite, b Richards	0
G. Banner, c Evans, b Richards	0
F. Coultas, b Davies	27
†D. Shaw, st Dew, b Thomas	2
M. Wyres, st Dew, b Thomas	7
N. Gilbert, b Thomas	9
R. Burne, c T. Davies, b Bevan	4
Extras (B 3, lb 1)	4
38.5 overs. Total	113

THE BATTLE FOR THE GROUP TITLES

Fall of wkts: 1–4, 2–8, 3–26, 4–28, 5–28, 6–57, 7–62, 8–74, 9–90.
Bowling: Jenkins 9–4–9–1; Richards 9–2–31–4; T. Davies 9–1–29–1; Thomas 9–2–22–3; Bevan 1.5–0–6–1; J. Morris 1–0–12–0.

GOWERTON

†A. Dew, b Burne	16
E. Bevan, c Rose, b Burne	17
A. Daniel, c Banner, b Giles	20
*R. Evans, lbw Burne	0
J. Richards, b Burne	1
J. Cox, not out	40
J. Morris, c Banner, b Coultas	7
J. Davies, not out	6
Extras (Lb 6, nb 4)	10
38.2 overs. Total (6 wkts)	117

Did not bat: D. Jenkins, T. Davies, W. Thomas.
Fall of wkts: 1–36, 2–45, 3–45, 4–52, 5–73, 6–99.
Bowling: Coultas 8.2–1–25–1; G. Banner 9–5–12–0; Burne 8–2–23–4; Braithwaite 8–0–30–0; Giles 5–1–17–10.
Umpires: G. Dark and O. G. Rhodes.

Gowerton won by 4 wkts.

Kimbolton v. Bradfield

Bradfield, journeying from Norfolk to Huntingdonshire – a county still enduring the bureaucrats' boundary changes – to meet *Kimbolton,* won the toss and put their hosts in to bat. *Kimbolton's* strength was the consistent application of the main batsmen with Nos 1–7 amassing 162 runs without any scoring above 31 and – it is worthy of record – the sun shone. *Brad*G*eld* bowlers Spinks, Wilgress and Shreeve shared the wickets and the home side were all out in the final over for an agreeable 181.

The Norfolk side, however, were not so solid at the top, but their middle-order batsmen, led by skipper Roper staged a late charge, albeit in vain, and *Bradfield* with one wicket to fall had to admit defeat by a mere 11 runs. How pleasant it was to hear from both sides how much they admired the fine impartiality of their umpires H. Mellows and R. Cohen.

KIMBOLTON

G. Beeby, run out	24
R. Hart, b Howarth	21
T. Newman, c Spinks, b Wilgress	22
†R. Folds, b Wilgress	10
*J. Hart, c Spinks, b Wilgress	23
T. Flint, c Coleman, b Spinks	31
B. Facer, c Craske, b Spinks	31
R. Stevenson, b Shreeve	9
P. Presland, b Spinks	2
J. Walker, b Shreeve	0
P. Bance, not out	0
Extras (B 2, lb 4, nb 2)	8
39.2 overs. Total	181

Fall of wkts: 1–46, 2–55, 3–76, 4–103, 5–114, 6–158, 7–179, 8–179, 9–181.
Bowling: Spinks 9–1–32–3; Shreeve 8.2–0–26–2; Wilgress 9–1–27–3; Howarth 8–0–44–1; Reynolds 2–0–23–0; Roper 3–0–21–0.

BRADFIELD

†R. Coleman, b Bance	12
D. Sadler, c Newman, b Bance	2
C. Bidwell, c Hart (J), b Stevenson	30
C. Shreeve, c Presland, b Walker	15
E. Craske, c Folds, b Stevenson	4
D. Beckett, c Facer, b Presland	14
*J. Roper, c Newman, b Facer	35

B. Spinks, c Stevenson, b Facer 25
I. Howarth, not out 21
J. Wilgress, b Bance 0
J. Reynolds, not out 2
 Extras (B 2, lb 5, nb 2, w 1) 10

40 overs. Total 170

Fall of wkts: 1–6, 2–35, 3–62, 4–66, 5–67, 6–117, 7–132, 8–160, 9–163.
Bowling: Presland 9–1–33–1; Bance 9–0–38–3; Stevenson 9–1–38–2; Walker 9–2–24–1; Facer 4–0–27–2.
Umpires: R. Cohen and H. Mellows.

Kimbolton won by 11 runs.

Dowdeswell & Foxcote v. Bledlow

Bledlow, the visitors, having won the toss and batting first accumulated runs steadily throughout their 40 overs. Ian Dillamore, the opening batsman, played a valuable anchoring role with W. Davey top-scoring with 72; *Bledlow's* innings closed at 192 for 7. In their reply, *Dowdeswell* lost an early wicket, but stumper-opening batsman D. Waterson, with 41, saw them to 77 for 4 and then came a good stand for the fifth wicket between Williams and Todd that was worth 50 runs. After that, though, the home side offered little further resistance, to be all out for 135 in the 37th over, B. Baker claiming four wickets for 43.

BLEDLOW

†I. Dillamore, c R. Williams, b Cox 48
 A. Spencer, c & b Waring 8
 M. Gill, b Lane 0
 W. Davey, b Lane 72
*B. Baker, c Lane, b R. Williams 2

G. Eggleton, b Waring 16
J. Samways, not out 0
J. Bristow, lbw Waring 3
R. Floyd, not out 30
Extras (B 7, lb 6) 13

40 overs. Total (7 wkts) 192

Did not bat: S. Goldthorpe, R. Whitney.
Fall of wkts: 1–18, 2–18, 3–120, 4–128, 5–142, 6–146, 7–188.
Bowling: Waring 9–0–43–3; Lane 9–2–30–2; I. Williams 9–0–45–0; Cox 4–0–16–1; R. Williams 9–1–45–1.

DOWDESWELL

†I. D. Waterston, c Gill, b Floyd 41
D. Parrott, c & b Bristow 6
T. Greaves, c Gill, b Baker 11
R. Williams, b Goldthorpe 47
*R. Waring, c Eggleton, b Floyd 3
R. Todd, lbw Baker 15
N. Dimmer, not out 2
J. Venn, c Floyd, b Baker 1
A. Cox, b Baker 0
I. Williams, b Goldthorpe 5
J. Lane, b Goldthorpe 0
Extras (B 3, lb 1) 4

36.4 overs. Total 135

Fall of wkts: 1–16, 2–56, 3–68, 4–77, 5–127, 6–129, 7–130, 8–130, 9–135.
Bowling: Samways 9–3–15–0; Bristow 9–0–27–1; Floyd 5–0–36–2; Baker 9–0–43–4; Goldthorpe 4.4–0–10–3.
Umpires: O. G. Rhodes and G. Dark.

Bledlow won by 58 runs.

Shrivenham v. Shillingstone

Shillingstone started off briskly for five overs, but were then contained by B. Wilson and D. Bradfield, the latter accounting for D. Crane in the 10th over, with the score 24. Hardy and Mace steadily increased the score, the 50 coming in the 22nd. Both batsmen found R. Harvey difficult to score from, but the partnership was worth 49 when Burrough bowled Mace for 18. Hardy completed his 50 by hitting Burrough for six, but was then well caught by Pratt. Wilson returned to the attack to take two wickets, including Sheen who had previously hit a straight six. The remaining batsmen ran well between the wickets to push the score to 139 after 40 overs.

Shrivenham lost Pratt run out in the fourth over, due to indecision, and when Hambridge was caught at cover in the eighth over, the total was only 7. Harvey then set about the bowling hitting three fours before falling to Mace with the score at 41. With T. Hayward scoring 13 including a six over mid-on from the next over by Mace the score had reached 65 after 20 overs. B. Hayward then tried to swing Ridout to leg and was bowled; Bradfield and T. Hayward took the score to 78 before Mace had both caught brilliantly by Sheen and Hunt in the 24th over. Ridout dismissed Wothers and Wilson in the 27th over and Forty fell to Mace in the 30th, Mace taking 4 for 40. Burrough and Cox saw the 100 on the board at the 34th over but Burrough holed out next over giving Sheen a hat-trick of catches.

SHILLINGSTONE

*D. Crane, c B. Hayward, b Bradfield	9
†N. Hardy, c Pratt, b Burrough	55
D. Mace, b Burrough	18
A. Hunt, c Bradfield, b Wilson	16
G. Ridout, b Wilson	7
E. Sheen, c Harvey, b Wilson	11
P. Hawkins, not out	3

G. Hawkins, run out 11
T. Hawkins, not out 3
  Extras (B 1, lb 2, w 3) 3

40 overs. Total (7 wkts) 139

Did not bat: G. Wells, P. Crane.
Fall of wkts: 1–24, 2–73, 3–92, 4–106, 5–114, 6–130, 7–136.
Bowling: Wilson 9–1–29–3; Bradfield 9–2–19–1; Harvey 9–0–26–0; B. Hayward 9–1–38–0; Burrough 4–0–21–2.

SHRIVENHAM

F. Hambidge, c P. Hawkins, b Wells 6
G. Pratt, run out 1
T. Hayward, c Sheen, b Mace 28
R. Harvey, c Wells, b Mace 28
B. Hayward, b Ridout 6
D. Bradfield, c Hunt, b Mace 8
†P. Forty, c G. Hawkins, b Mace 9
A. Wothers, b Ridout 1
B. Wilson, c Sheen, b Ridout 0
*R. Burrough, c Sheen, b D. Crane 9
R. Cox, not out 2
  Extras (B 1, lb 1) 2

34.4 overs. Total 100

Fall of wkts: 1–2, 2–7, 3–41, 4–65, 5–78, 6–78, 7–86, 8–86, 9–89.
Bowling: Sheen 9–3–15–0; Wells 7–2–14–1; Ridout 9–1–28–3; Mace 9–1–40–4; Crane 0.4–0–0–1.
Umpires: F. Dunn and P. J. Puntis.

Shillingstone won by 39 runs.

This is what village cricket is all about – the bat swings mightily during the game between Kimbolton (Hunts.) and Bradfield (Norfolk) in Round Six of the Haig

Mr Irvine (centre), the Haig representative for the North East, presents one-gallon bottles of whisky to Jack Riddell (right) the Warenford captain, and Gordon Croft, skipper of Collingham, when the teams meet in the Regional semi-finals

Warenford were the 1972 Haig's 'giant-killers'. Here are the team's opening batsmen, brothers Ian and Alan Patterson, whose father, Bob, is the licensee of the White Swan, the village's only public house

THE BATTLE FOR THE GROUP TITLES

Sheldwich v. Linton Park (played at Imperial Paper Mills ground, Gravesend)

Sheldwich won the toss and put Linton Park in to bat on a good wicket. A sound opening partnership of 54 between Bowles and Moss ended when the latter was out for 23. With the total at 72, Ancombe, who had come in at No. 3 was brilliantly caught at backward square-leg for 8 and almost immediately J. Thirkell was bowled for nought with the total at 74 for three after 20 overs. Bowles continued to bat well and, in company with Iliffe, took the score to 101 before Iliffe was out for 16.

At this point Sheldwich brought on off-sinner Brett and skipper Tim George returned to the attack; these two bowled well and kept the scoring down. George struck two blows in quick succession having Greenfield lbw and one run later bowling Bowles for a fine 57. Alan Cooper took two fours off George, but in trying to hand out the same treatment to Brett was bowled, the score then being 123 for eight off 35 overs. Mountford struck some lusty blows before Brett bowled him for 10. The innings ended in the 39th over when Hickman was bowled by Creed with the Linton Park total at 141. Pick of the Sheldwich bowlers were George 3 for 34 and Brett 3 for 24.

Sheldwich opened slowly against tight bowling by Mountford and Cooper, only 20 runs coming in the first 12 overs for the loss of Holt's wicket. A slow but sound partnership between Mitchell and Hobbs then took the score to 44 after 15 overs before Mitchell was bowled by Thirkell for 15 and four runs later Hobbs was caught and bowled by Hickman for 25. Scott was out for two and at this point Sheldwich were in trouble, wanting 84 runs with five wickets standing and 16 overs remaining. With the score at 67 the unfortunate run out of T. Heward made the position more critical. Brett joined Newman and the score crept up, mainly in singles, until Brett was run out with the total at 80 in the 30th over. Creed came in and with Newman took the score to 116 when Creed was bowled by Cooper, who struck another blow by bowling R. Heward 1st ball. George joined Newman, with Cooper on a hat-trick; he survived the last ball of the over but Newman after making 42 valiant runs was bowled by Mountford leaving *Sheldwich* all out for 118 in the 37th over.

The match was played under the auspices of the Association of Kent Cricket Clubs who presented a magnificent trophy to *Linton Park* as the Champions of Kent. Ian Redpath rewarded Linton Park with their medals as Group winners.

LINTON PARK

P. Bowles, b George	57
A. Moss, c Holt, b Theward	23
C. Ancombe, c Creed, b R. Heward	8
J. Thirkell, b R. Heward	0
M. Iliffe, c Holt, b Brett	16
F. Greenfield, lbw George	3
B. Bell, lbw George	3
G. Mountford, b Brett	10
A. Cooper, b Brett	9
N. Thirkell, not out	11
R. Hickman, b Creed	0
Extras (B 1)	1
39 overs. Total	141

Fall of wkts: 1–54, 2–72, 3–74, 4–101, 5–108, 6–109, 7–112, 8–123, 9–133.
Bowling: George 9–0–34–3; Creed 8–2–24–1; R. Heward 9–0–24–2; T. Heward 7–0–34–1; Brett 6–0–24–3.

SHELDWICH

J. Holt, b Cooper	2
A. Mitchell, b Thirkell	15
D. Hobbs, c & b Hickman	25
J. Stanford, b Hickman	5
F. Scott, c Anscombe, b J. Thirkell	2

B. Newman, b Mountford — 42
T. Heward, run out — 1
J. Brett, run out — 5
A. Creed, b Cooper — 13
R. Heward, b Cooper — 0
*T. George, not out — 0
Extras (B 4, lb 4, nb 2) — 10

36.2 overs. Total — 118

Fall of wkts: 1-2, 2-44, 3-48, 4-51, 5-57, 6-64, 7-80, 8-116, 9-116.
Bowling: Mountford 7.2-4-14-1; Cooper 8-2-23-3; Hickman 9-1-18-2; Bowles 2-0-12-0; J. Thirkell 8-0-31-2; N. Thirkell 2-0-10-0.

Linton Park won by 23 runs.

Glynde & Beddingham v. Eastergate

Eastergate, batting first after winning the toss, quickly lost D. Lynn with the score at three but T. Foot soon established himself and, after losing Wells at 36, he and A. Cockburn, the captain, took the score to 111 before the third wicket fell. *Eastergate* scored 78 runs off the first 20 overs and 98 off the final 20. Baker and Pullen were quickly into their stride and put on 51 for *Glynde's* first wicket. Then Pullen and Martin added a further 53 for the second wicket before Pullen was out for 54. Martin and skipper R. Clayton took the total to 156 for three and *Glynde,* scoring 115 from their final 16 overs won by five wickets in the 36th over.

EASTERGATE

†D. Wells, c Turrell, b Clayton — 18
D. Lynn, b McBrown — 0
T. Foot, c Clayton, b Moorey — 53
*A. Cockburn, b McBrown — 44

J. Etherington, c Parris, b Clayton   11
E. Richards, st Sutton, b Moorey   5
M. Bryant, c Moorey, b Clayton   3
J. Foot, c Martin, b Turrell   5
M. Blunden, c Jones, b Nibblett   13
G. Hobday, not out   2
P. Scragg, lbw Nibblett   5
Extras (B 5, lb 3, nb 1)   9

40 overs. Total   168

Fall of wkts: 1–3, 2–36, 3–111, 4–126, 5–133, 6–138, 7–148, 8–159, 9–162.
Bowling: McBrown 9–1–30–2; Jones 9–3–30–0; Clayton 9–0–45–3; Moorey 8–0–36–2; Nibblett 3–0–7–2; Turrell 2–0–11–1.

GLYNDE

G. Baker, c Foot (T), b Scragg   22
D. Pullen, c Wells, b Hobay   54
R. Martin, b Foot (T)   31
*R. Clayton, c Foot (J), b Hobday   38
W. Jones, c Wells, b Foot (T)   0
K. Parris, not out   11
J. Nibblett, not out   2
Extras (B 4, lb 5, w 3)   12

36 overs. Total (5 wkts)   170

Did not bat: M. Sutton, D. Turrell, A. McBrown, P. Moorey.
Fall of wkts: 1–51, 2–104, 3–156, 4–156, 5–157.
Bowling: Scragg 9–1–33–1; J. Foot 9–3–18–0; Cockburn 4–0–30–0; T. Foot 7–2–25–2; Hobday 7–1–52–2.
Umpires: V. Bruce and H. G. Ayers.

Glynde won by 5 wkts.

THE BATTLE FOR THE GROUP TITLES

Blunham v. Abberton

Abberton, the Essex group champions, made heavy weather of it after winning the toss at *Blunham* and apart from defiant knocks by skipper E. Rumney (22) and J. Ward (25) had little answer to the accurate bowling of M. Ranson (4 for 11) and Fordham (4 for 8). They were all out for a disappointing 66 and although *Blunham* lost six wickets in the process, they hit off the 67 runs required for victory in the 20th over.

ABBERTON

†K. Brush, c Lawson, b M. Ranson	5
A. Patmore, c P. Ranson, b M. Ranson	3
*E. Rumney, c Ashwell, b M. Ranson	22
M. Loughton, c P. Ranson, b Fordham	0
C. Taylor, c M. Ranson, b Fordham	0
I. MacDonald, c Thompson, b Fordham	1
J. Ward, b Watson	25
A. Hogarth, c M. Ranson, b Fordham	1
P. Stephens, not out	4
F. Taylor, c Tester, b M. Ranson	0
K. Goody, c P. Ranson, b Watson	0
Extras (B 3, lb 1, w 1)	5
35 overs. Total	66

Fall of wkts: 1–6, 2–12, 3–12, 4–12, 5–20, 6–22, 7–62, 8–66, 9–66.
Bowling: Watson 7–4–10–2; M. Ranson 8–2–11–4; Fordham 9–6–8–4.

BLUNHAM

†P. Ranson, c Goody, b F. Taylor	1
B. Thompson, c Goody, b Ward	0
P. Fordham, lbw F. Taylor	16
D. Lawson, c Brush, b C. Taylor	8

*R. Ashwell, c MacDonald, b Ward   10
R. Rawlins, not out   16
J. Tester, c F. Taylor, b C. Taylor   0
M. Watson, not out   16

19.3 overs. Total (6 wkts)   67

Did not bat: M. Ranson, R. Lawrence, T. Page.
Fall of wkts: 1–1, 2–1, 3–12, 4–25, 5–39, 6–39.
Bowling: Ward 5–0–21–2; F. Taylor 3–1–12–2; C. Taylor 5–0–20–2.
Umpires: M. Minter and K. Bright.

Blunham won by 4 wkts.

In other matches, details of which were not to hand, *Steep* beat *Welford Park, Troon* 145 for 6, beat *Evercreech* 142, and *Shanley Green* 140 for 9 beat *Eversholt* 130.

With now only 16 teams remaining in the competition, Ladbrokes adjusted the odds for the Regional semi-finals; *Tong* became favourites at 5–1, with *Kimbolton* and *Shanley Green* at 7–1, *Lindal Moor* and *Linton Park* 8–1 and *Warenford* still the outsiders and still quoted at 25–1.

CHAPTER SIX

The Road to Lord's

Round Seven—The Battle to go into the Last Eight

Shamley Green v. Blunham

Shamley Green, losing the toss, were quickly in desperate trouble when *Blunham* put them in, and the loss of four wickets with only seven runs on the board made the remainder of the match almost a formality. Mick Watson, *Blunham's* Jamaican-born fast bowler, took three of those wickets while only two runs were being added – demoralising blows. S. Stevens and M. Glew staged a partial rally, but the end came in the 40th over with the total at 116. The wicket seemed to improve when Blunham batted and their opening pair, Peter Ranson and Bob Thompson, knocked off the 117 needed to win with some comfort in less than 33 overs.

SHAMLEY GREEN

M. Wrixen, c Ashwell, b M. Ranson	4
G. Tuffs, c P. Ranson, b Watson	1
S. Stevens, b Rawlins	29
R. Linaker, c P. Ranson, b Watson	0
M. Watkinson, b Watson	0
M. Glew, c Lawson, b Fordham	38
M. Stevens, b Watson	14
†R. Tuffs, c Ashwell, b Rawlins	0

*L. Tuffs, b Fordham 10
J. Hill, run out 11
P. Jones, not out 3
   Extras (Bl 4, lb 4, nb 1) 6

   39.4 overs. Total 116
Fall of wickets: 1–5, 2–7, 3–7, 4–7, 5–48, 6–78, 7–79, 8–95, 9–109.
Bowling: Watson 9–2–16–4; Ranson 9–5–13–1; Fordham 9–1–32–2; Rawlins 9–0–25–2; Page 3.4–1–24–0.

BLUNHAM

†P. Ranson, not out 66
B. Thompson, not out 41
   Extras (B 1, lb 4, nb 1) 6

   32.4 overs. Total (0 wkt) 117
Did not bat: P. Fordham, D. Lawson, R. Ashwell, R. Rawlins, J. Tester, M. Watson, M. Ranson, R. Lawrence, T. Page.
Bowling: Stevens 7.4–1–25–0; Linaker 9–2–29–0; L. Tuffs 7–2–18–0; Glew 6–0–32–0; Jones 3–1–3–0.

Blunham won by 10 *wickets..*

Gowerton v. Kimbolton

A third-wicket stand of 56 by A. Daniel and R. Evan was a brave but vain effort to pull *Gowerton* round from an unhappy start that cost them their opening batsmen for 14 runs. And once the big stand had been broken the remaining resistance was sporadic, although *Kimbolton* could remove only eight men in the 40 overs. *Gowerton's* total of 126 scarcely seemed enough, and so it proved, though for a while they thought they could snatch the result when they had the first four wickets down for 56. Jeff Hart, the *Kimbolton* captain, then took command and with useful support, saw his side home with seven balls of the game to go.

GOWERTON

†A. Dew, c Newman, b Presland	0
E. Bevan, c Folds, b Bance	5
A. Daniel, c Presland, b Facer	36
*R. Evan, b Walker	36
J. Cox, c Stevenson, b Presland	10
J. Morris, run out	1
J. Richards, c Presland b Stevenson	7
J. Davies, not out	15
T. Davies, run out	5
D. Jenkins, not out	5
Extras	6
40 overs. Total (8 wkts)	126

Did not bat: W. Thomas.
Fall of wickets: 1–0, 2–14, 3–70, 4–89, 5–89, 6–94, 7–104, 8–113.
Bowling: Presland 9–4–10–2; Bance 9–1–27–1; Stevenson 9–2–27–1; Walker 9–0–39–1; Facer 4–0–17–1.

KIMBOLTON

G. Beeby, c Bevan, b Jenkins	3
R. Hart, c Dew, b Richards	3
J. Newman, lbw b T. Davies	17
†R. Folds, c Cox, b T. Davies	21
*J. Hart, not out	46
B. Facer, c Jenkins, b Morris	13
D. Peacock, not out	3
Extras	9
38.5 overs. Total (6 wkts)	127

Did not bat: P. Presland, J. Walker, P. Bance.
Fall of wickets: 1–6, 2–6, 3–37, 4–56, 5–85, 6–108.
Bowling: Jenkins 8.5–2–28–1; Richards 8–1–27–2; Thomas 9–3–17–0; T. Davies 9–3–25–2; Morris 2–0–12–1; Cox 2–0–9–0.

Kimbolton won by four wickets.

Lindal Moor v. Collingham

Collingham won with considerable ease in the end, but only because of an electric and courageous innings by Tony Watson. *Lindal Moor,* after losing their openers for two runs, batted steadily to reach 127 for eight wickets and, capturing *Collingham's* first three batsmen for 38, put the game back on an even keel. Coming in at No. 5, Watson soon played a ball into his face, but refused to go off (it was later discovered that he had fractured a cheekbone in two places). While Dennis Poucher played safely, Watson let fly, cracking five sixes as he scored 58 in an unbroken, match-winning third-wicket stand of 90 in 12 overs, ending the match with 13 overs to spare.

LINDAL MOOR

E. Gardiner, c and b A. Slater	1
B. Coward, b A. Slater	0
*E. Shuttleworth, lbw b Thompson	27
W. Knight, b Croft	20
T. Clarke, c Thompson, b Croft	5
T. Gifford, c Watson, b Thompson	11
M. Marshall, b Williams	20
B. Chappells, c Courtney, b A. Slater	12
S. Lindicott, not out	9
R. Herman, not out	13
Extras (B 7, lb 2)	9
40 overs. Total (8 wkts)	127

Did not bat: †J. Cornthwaite.
Fall of wickets: 1–1, 2–2, 3–42, 4–50, 5–62, 6–75, 7–102, 8–108.
Bowling: Williams 9–1–26–1; A. Slater 9–1–24–3; Thompson 9–2–29–2; Croft 9–3–21–2; Woodcock 4–0–18–0.

COLLINGHAM

G. T. Woodcock, lbw b Herman	11
R. Slater, b Herman	0
N. Thompson, c Cornthwaite, b Gifford	23
D. Poucher, not out	28
A. Watson, not out	58
Extras (B 4, lb 3, w 1)	8
27 overs. Total (3 wkts)	128

Did not bat: †R. Courtney, H. Peel, J. Kirkham, *G. Croft, A. Slater, G. Williams.
Fall of wickets: 1–1, 2–21, 3–38.
Bowling: Herman 9–1–21–2; Shuttleworth 5–0–16–0; Liddicott 6–0–29–0; Gifford 5–0–35–1; Knight 2–0–19–0.

Collingham won by seven wickets.

Warenford v. Tong

By the time the competition had reached this stage, the bookmakers, relying on tradition, had picked *Tong*, the surviving Yorkshire side, as 5–1 favourites – a tribute to the county's great achievements – and *Warenford* at 25–1. However, the Haig was new ground for making odds, so perhaps *Tong*, from just outside Bradford – a redoubtable cricket centre if ever there was one – had rather more pressure put on them than the situation justified. In cup games anything can happen. It certainly did in this case, for *Tong*, splendidly directed by P. Marriott, reached 84 for two wickets and seemed about to cut loose when Squibb stepped in with two quick wickets before the total had reached three figures. Suddenly the Yorkshiremen found problems with the *Warenford* attack and five more wickets fell for 26 runs. Then the Greenwoods came together in a fighting last-wicket stand of 31 to take *Tong* to 156 in 34.2 overs – good, fast scoring considering that there was such steady traffic between pavilion and wicket.

Warenford began their reply hesitantly, scoring only 16 in the first eight overs and losing one of their opening Patterson brothers, Alan, in the process. But the other, Ian, who had picked up three wickets in *Tong's* innings, was joined by Robson in a second-wicket stand of 131 which took six bowlers to bring to an end. Robson left with only 10 runs needed and Squibb, who had begun it all with his bowling, was at the crease to round off little *Warenford's* triumph by seven wickets. The crowd of about 2,000 had seen the biggest upset, probably, of the whole competition.

TONG

F. Pickersgill, b T. Thompson	16
P. Marriott, c Riddell, b Squibb	58
B. Bradley, c I. Patterson, b A. Patterson	1
H. Cummings, b I. Patterson	19
†H. Webster, c I. Patterson, b Squibb	2
C. Greenwood, not out	28
T. Fawthrop, b I. Patterson	1
A. Pickersgill, b Squibb	1
L. Glennon, c and b Squibb	1
*J. Robinson, lbw b I. Patterson	0
B. Greenwood, lbw b T. Thompson	14
Extras (B 8, lb 7)	14
34.2 overs. Total	156

Fall of wickets: 1–50, 2–51, 3–84, 4–99, 5–118, 6–121, 7–122, 8–124, 9–125.

Bowling: T. Thompson 8.2–1–37–2; A. Patterson 8–0–31–0; Squibb 9–0–26–4; I. Patterson 9–0–47–3.

WARENFORD

A. Patterson, b Pickersgill	7
I. Patterson, not out	58
W. Robson, b Robinson	69
B. Thompson, lbw b Glennon	0
B. Squibb, not out	4
Extras (B 6, lb 7, nb 7)	20
35.5 overs. Total (3 wkts)	158

Did not bat: *J. Riddell, A. Hedley, L. Alexander †J. Turnbull, G. Curry, T. Thompson.

Fall of wickets: 1–16, 2–147, 3–149.

Bowling: R. Pickersgill 7–0–27–0; A. Pickersgill 9–1–27–1; Glennon 9–1–33–1; B. Greenwood 6–0–31–0; Fawthrop 2–0–13–0; Robinson 2.5–0–7–1.

Warenford won by seven wickets.

Shillingstone v. Troon

Troon's powerful attack gave *Shillingstone* scarcely any scope from the opening over. Four of *Shillingstone's* first five batsmen collected only six runs between them and the last four scrambled only three. N. Hardy fought well for his 27 and P. Hawkins did equally well, with useful help coming from G. Ridout. But a total of 83, including 10 extras, was not nearly enough to cause Troon any worries and the runs were knocked off without undue hurry in 27 overs.

SHILLINGSTONE

N. Hardy, b Johns	27
D. S. Crane, c Rashleigh, b Dunstan	3
A. Hunt, b Dunstan	0
D. Mace, b Johns	0
E. Sheen, c B. Carter, b Dunstan	1
P. Hawkins, not out	25
G. Ridout, b B. Carter	12
T. Hawkins, b B. Carter	0
G. Wells, b Thomas	0
G. Hawkins, st Rashleigh, b B. Carter	2
P. Crane, run out	1
Extras (B 1, lb 5, nb 3, w 1)	10
29.1 overs. Total	83

Bowling: Johns 9–4–15–2; Dunstan 9–2–25–3; Lean 3–0–10–0; Thomas 5.1–2–7–1; B. Carter 3–0–16–3.

TROON

T. Edwards, c P. Hawkins, b D. S. Crane	27
J. Spry, not out	42
B. Carter, not out	12
Extras (Lb 4)	4
27.2 overs. Total (1 wkt)	85

Did not bat: *T. Carter, J. Vincent, †D. Rashleigh, P. Johns, B. Moyle, K. Lean, G. Dunstan, P. Thomas

Bowling: Sheen 5–2–14–0; Wells 4–1–5–0; Mace 9–1–30–0; D. S. Crane 9–2–28–1; Ridout 0.2–0–4–0.

Troon won by nine wickets.

Astwood Bank v. Horton House

Good, tight bowling and fielding got *Astwood Bank*

home against *Horton House* for what they regarded as a critical victory. *Horton House,* sent in to bat, had a hard time of it, only three players reaching double figures. Twice they lost two batsmen in an over, on the first occasion to Colin Robinson, and later to Brian Spittle, who cleaned up the tail in less than five overs. Conditions were awkward and with two men out for 31 *Astwood Bank* were by no means sure of reaching the 90 they needed to win. However, Brian Spittle then stood firm while John Robinson went for the runs. Their third-wicket stand of 55 left little else to be done and *Astwood Bank* emerged winners by six wickets, despite Jubb's staunch bowling for Horton House.

HORTON HOUSE

M. Learoyd, c J. Robinson, b Crumpton	3
P. Joyce, b C. Robinson	9
J. Nutter, b Crumpton	11
M. Adams, c Nash, b C. Robinson	0
J. Hall, b Spittle	27
A. Wright, b Crumpton	4
J. Owen, c Yoxall, b C. Robinson	0
P. Terry, not out	15
R. Spokes, b Spittle	15
R. Evans, c Poole, b Spittle	5
M. Jubb, lbw b Spittle	6
Extras (Lb 2)	2
31.5 overs. Total	89

Fall of wickets: 1–11, 2–21, 3–21, 4–25, 5–36, 6–47, 7–61, 8–75, 9–83.

Bowling: Morrall 9–2–25–0; J. Crumpton 9–4–21–3; C. Robinson 9–4–18–3; Spittle 4.5–1–23–4.

ASTWOOD BANK

*J. Yoxall, c Terry, b Jubb	13
J. Robinson, c Nutter, b Hall	46

R. Davies, c Spokes, b Wright	6
B. Spittle, c Learoyd, b Jubb	16
M. Wedgbury, not out	1
J. Poole, not out	0
Extras (B 10)	10
22.5 overs. Total (4 wkts)	92

Fall of wickets: 1–20, 2–31, 3–86, 4–86.
Did not bat: C. Robinson, J. Crumpton, T. Bird, R. Morrall, †R. Nash.
Bowling: Jubb 7.5–2–18–2; Wright 9–1–33–1; Terry 4–0–18–0; Hall 2–1–13–1.

Astwood Bank won by six wickets.

Glynde and Beddingham v. Linton Park

This clash between the Sussex and Kent champions began disastrously for *Linton Park*, who lost their first two wickets for two runs. Sound batting by Paul Bowles rallied them but they were still in real trouble before an eighth-wicket stand of 35 by Alan Cooper and Nigel Thirkell, the 16-year-old son of the Linton Park captain, carried them eventually to a total of 133 for nine in their 40 overs. *Glynde* could be well satisfied with their outcricket, particularly their opening attack and Seabright, one of the best wicket-keepers seen throughout the competition. Unfortunately *Glynde* could not maintain the standard when it came to batting. Fine bowling by Ron Hickman, who finished with 5–23, toppled them from 28 for one to 35 for four. The Sussex club had no real hope after that and Seabright, their last man, was appropriately stumped, leaving *Linton Park* victors by 59 runs.

LINTON PARK

P. Bowles, st Seabright, b Moorey	45
A. Moss, c Clayton, b Jones	0
J. Ames, b McBrown	1

†C. Anscombe, b Jones 15
*J. Thirkell, c McBrown, b Niblett 22
M. Iliffe, c Seabright, b Niblett 1
G. Mountford, b Clayton 2
A. Cooper, not out 29
N. Thirkell, run out 10
R. Hickman, b McBrown 1
T. Gauna, not out 1
Extras (B 3, lb 2, nb 1) 6

40 overs. Total (9 wkts) 133

Fall of wickets: 1–1, 2–2, 3–30, 4–67, 5–72, 6–90, 7–90, 8–125, 9–127.
Bowling: Jones 9–2–28–2; McBrown 9–1–21–2; Clayton 4–0–21–1; Niblett 9–2–23–2; Moorey 9–0–34–1.

GLYNDE

G. Baker, b Hickman 23
D. Pullen, c Anscombe, b Mountford 1
R. Martin, b Hickman 7
W. Jones, c N. Thirkell, b Hickman 17
*R. Clayton, c Anscombe, b Gauna 1
J. Niblett, c and b Gauna 1
K. Parris, b Hickman 10
D. Turrell, not out 5
A. McBrown, c N. Thirkell, b Hickman 0
P. Moorey, run out 1
†M. Seabright, st Anscombe, b Cooper 0
Extras (B 7, lb 1) 8

31.3 overs. Total 74

Fall of wickets: 1–9, 2–28, 3–33, 4–35, 5–47, 6–63, 7–63, 8–71, 9–72.
Bowling: Mountford 6–2–11–1; Cooper 6.3–1–14–1; Gauna 9–4–17–2; Hickman 9–3–23–5; N. Thirkell 1–0–1–0.

Linton Park won by 59 runs.

Bledlow v. Steep

Bledlow moved into the quarter-finals, defeating *Steep* by three wickets in an exciting match which saw the advantage constantly changing hands. In very pleasant weather *Steep* totalled 157 in 39 overs and one ball, a good brisk rate of scoring that owed much to the batting of Gordon, Antrobus (who played almost a lone hand) and Passingham. *Steep* reached 115 for three wickets before disaster struck, three wickets, including that of Antrobus, going for the addition of 11 runs. The remaining batsmen were chipped away steadily, leaving Witney and Baker with impressive bowling figures and *Bledlow* with a formidable tak. They and their supporters were none too happy as *Steep's* steady bowling and lively fielding whittled away the leading batsmen. Six were back in the pavilion for 99, three of them victims of Clements, when Eggleton, the *Bledlow* captain, was joined by Samways, the secretary, and these worthies boldy added 54 for the seventh wicket, a match-winning stand. *Bledlow's* runs came a shade more quickly even than Steep's – fine cricket all round that left the good crowd well pleased.

STEEP

C. Gordon, c Witney, b Baker	42
R. Starnes, b Floyd	3
R. Passingham, c Mitchell, B Witney	23
M. Pumfrey, c Gill, b Witney	8
R. Antrobus, c and b Bristow	45
C. Greastham, c Gill, b Witney	8
M. Clements, b Witney	0
B. Jarmen, b Baker	7
R. Wickstead, b Baker	4
J. Hayes, b Baker	14
C. King, not out	0
Extras	3
39.1 overs. Total	157

Fall of wickets: 1–6, 2–71, 3–72, 4–115, 5–125, 6–126, 7–135, 8–143, 9–152.
Bowling: Samways 9–2–22–0; Floyd 5–0–21–1; Bristow 7–1–42–1; Witney 9–2–27–4; Baker 7.1–2–29–4; Eggleton 2–0–13–0.

BLEDLOW

I. Dillamore, b King	11
†A. Spencer, run out	24
R. Floyd, c Antrobus, b Clements	28
B. Davey, b Clements	3
M. Gill, b Passingham	12
B. Baker, b Clements	2
*G. Eggleton, not out	38
J. Samways, c Passingham, b Clements	31
J. Bristow, not out	0
Extras	9
37.2 overs. Total (7 wkts)	158

Did not bat: R. Witney, R. Mitchell.
Fall of wickets: 1–27, 2–65, 3–68, 4–70, 5–72, 6–99, 7–153.
Bowling: King 7.2–2–2–20–1; Antrobus 9–0–25–0; Jarmen 9–1–38–0; Clements 8–1–43–4; Passingham 4–0–23–1.

Bledlow won by three wickets.

The Quarter-Finals

Giant-killers say Farewell – Warenford v. Collingham

Alas, poor *Warenford's* luck ran out in the quarter-finals. The exploits of the Northumberland hamlet (pop. 31) had captured the interest of the entire North-East and as the summer wore on made them the principal talking point of sport in the Borders. Just when they seemed about to enter the semi-finals, rain put an end to their meeting with *Collingham* and the game had to be replayed the following week. This time *Collingham* scored steadily and solidly all down the order, ending at 186 for seven wickets. *Warenford's* reply included three ducks in the first half of the order and that was that.

But theirs had been a magnificent effort. No wonder that the B.B.C.'s local radio station made this game the Match of the Day in the North-East. The public thought so, too, for the crowd for the first match was estimated at more than 2,500, a figure that many first-class counties would envy and more than a few professional soccer clubs would be glad to get. No wonder, too, that the one local pub does so well – the landlord's two sons are the opening batsmen!

Warenford straddles the A1 about 30 miles south of Berwick. The club was founded in 1936 and although few of their players now live there – the population is indeed only 31, including seven pensioners – all of them learned their cricket at the Winnie Park ground. The Haig was the first competition they had entered and Lord's fever grew as success followed success.

After several early looseners, they toppled the strong *Burneside* team from Kendal, crossed the Border to knock out *Meigle,* the Scottish village champions, and then drew the 5–1 Yorkshire favourites, *Tong,* from just outside Bradford. Something like 2,000 turned up for this battle to reach the last eight, parking their cars alongside the A1 and in fields which local farmers threw open. The seven-wicket victory, followed by the even bigger attendance for the *Collingham* encounters warmed match secretary Jim Davidson's heart. Collections at the games, amounting to more than £150, took *Warenford's* finances right out of the red. More than that, says farmer Jack Riddell, the club captain, 'we've put Northumberland cricket on the map.'

COLLINGHAM

G. T. Woodcock, lbw b Robson   48

R. Slater, b T. Thompson 20
N. Thompson, b Robson 17
A. Watson, b I. Patterson 31
D. Poucher, c T. Thompson, b Squibb 1
H. Peel, c B. Thompson, b A. Patterson 26
†B. Courtney, not out 32
*G. Croft, c and b Squibb 0
G. Williams, not out 2
Extras 9

40 overs. Total (7 wkts) 186

Did not bat: A. Slater, G. Woodcock.
Bowling: T. Thompson 8–0–36–1; A. Patterson 7–1–33–1; I. Patterson 9–1–29–1; Robson 9–0–50–2; Squibb 7–1–29–2.

WARENFORD

A. Patterson, st Courtney, b A. Slater 0
I. Patterson, c Courtney, b A. Slater 27
W. Robson, c R. Slater, b Croft 34
A. Hedley, run out 0
B. Squibb, c R. Slater, b N. Thompson 8
B. Thompson, b N. Thompson 0
C. Curry, b Woodcock 31
*J. Riddell, c Poucher b Woodcock 5
L. Alexander, st Courtney, b Croft 4
†J. Turnbull, b Croft 0
T. Thompson, not out 4
Extras 3

34 overs. Total 116

Bowling: A. Slater 7–0–34–2; Williams 6–0–18–0; Croft 8–1–26–3; N. Thompson 9–1–19–2; G. Woodcock 4–1–16–2.

Collingham won by 70 runs.

Linton Park v. Blunham

A gruelling battle saw *Linton Park* get home by 22 runs, and very thankful to do so. *Blunham's* attack allowed few liberties and Mick Watson, their fast bowler from Jamaica, got them away to a good start with a wicket in his first over. *Linton Park's* batsmen fought back sturdily but none could play with real freedom and they were glad to settle for 143 for five wickets in their 40 overs. *Blunham's* reply was governed by their very slow start – only five runs coming from the first seven overs. Then Peter Fordham rallied them so well that they reached 107 with five wickets and eight overs left. Alan Cooper, a flooring expert with a famous tile company, was brought back into the attack at this point, and showed he could floor an innings, too, by removing Fordham, the danger man. Two more wickets fell for one run and the end came in the 36th over. Ruefully *Blunham* wished they might have played the game over again on their fast pitch and sloping outfield cared for them by their secretary, Fred Tester, groundsman at Bedford Modern School. Yet they had done remarkably well.

They had chalked up two victories by ten wickets and one by nine wickets, though they had a close call against neighbouring Roxton, winning by only four runs. The club goes back before the First World War and for a long time now has played in various forms of competitive cricket. They run two Saturday sides, a Sunday XI and stage evening matches, too. Not bad for a village of 700. The Sunday side, incidentally, are real wanderers, fulfilling fixtures as far away from Bedford as Gloucestershire, Kent, Sussex and even Yorkshire. A lot of local enthusiasm is needed to make that sort of programme work.

LINTON PARK

P. Bowles, b Fordham	28
A. Moss, c P. Ranson b Watson	0
D. Ames, c Lawson, b Fordham	39
†G. Anscombe, run out	30

*J. Thirkell, c Page, b Watson 29
M. Iliffe, not out 1
A. Cooper, not out 0
    Extras (B 1, lb 7) 8

40 overs. Total (5 wkts) 143

Did not bat: G. Mountford, N. Thirkell, A. Cooper, T. Gauna.

Bowling: Watson 9–1–30–2; M. Ranson 9–1–38–0; Rawlins 9–1–22–0; Fordham 9–0–32–2; Page 4–0–13–0.

BLUNHAM

†P. Ranson, c and b Gauna 21
B. Thompson, c Bowles, b Mountford 9
*R. Ashwell, b Cooper 0
P. Fordham, b Cooper 41
D. Lawson, b Gauna 0
J. Tester, c Ames, b Gauna 12
R. Rawlins, b Cooper 18
M. Watson, b Hickman 0
R. Lawrence, not out 7
M. Ranson, run out 1
T. Page, st Anscombe, b Cooper 4
    Extras (B 1, lb 7) 8

35.4 overs. Total 121

Bowling: Mountford 7–2–20–1; Cooper 8.4–3–18–4; Hickman 9–1–35–1; Gauna 9–1–24–3 (remaining bowling figures unavailable).

Linton Park won by 22 runs.

Bledlow v. Troon

For nearly three-quarters of this match it seemed that *Bledlow* would cruise home against the Cornishmen.

Bledlow's batsmen, particularly Ian Gillamore and 18-year-old left-hander Bob Floyd, from Royal Grammar School, High Wycombe, set a fierce pace. This pair added 83 adventurous runs and the men who followed maintained the pressure so that their 40 overs produced a total of 205 for four wickets. Against almost any other side in the competition this score must surely have been decisive and for a long time it seemed that even *Troon* had met their match. John Samways, the *Bledlow* opening bowler, and incidentally geography master at R.G.S. High Wycombe, removed three batsmen cheaply and *Troon* were 57 for four wickets when Jim Vincent joined his captain, Terry Carter. Then the fun began. While Vincent kept his end going Carter charged the bowling and slaughtered it with a magnificent innings of 119 not out. He and Vincent put on 148 to win the match by six wickets with nearly eight overs to spare. Carter's tremendous hitting brought him eight sixes and ten fours – glorious stuff, a captain's innings if ever there was one. *Bledlow* and their 900 supporters could only shake their heads at it all and marvel. Yet, as John Samways, who is also the club secretary, said : 'We really didn't expect to get even this far. We had never played any competitive cricket before, but we knew that if we did reasonably well it would draw attention in the area to the club. It has certainly done that, so as a result the club is more part of the community.'

Bledlow's ground, at the foot of the Chiltern Hills, midway between Aylesbury and High Wycombe, is very attractive with a fine new pavilion replacing the old one which was destroyed by fire several years ago. Lord Carrington, who lives in Bledlow, is the club president and recently donated the ground to the club.

BLEDLOW

I. Dillamore, c Moyle, b Thomas	59
R. Spencer, c T. Carter b Johns	7
R. Floyd, st Rashleigh, b Dunstan	56
W. Davey, st Rashleigh, b Dunstan	29
B. Baker, c Moyle, b Dunstan	24

*G. Eggleton, not out 4
J. Bristow, not out 3
   Extras (B 6, lb 16) 22

40 overs. Total (5 wkts) 204

Did not bat: J. Samways, R. Witney, S. Goldthorpe, †M. Gill.
Fall of wickets: 1–22, 2–105, 3–153, 4–187, 5–201.
Bowling: Johns 9–0–29–1; Edwards 9–1–40–0; B. Carter 4–0–22–0; Thomas 9–2–34–1; Dunstan 9–1–57–3.

TROON

T. Edwards, c Eggleton, b Samways 29
J. Spry, b Samways 1
B. Carter, b Samways 8
*T. Carter, not out 119
M. Sweeney, c Davey, b Bristow 7
J. Vincent, not out 36
   Extras (Lb 5) 5

32.2 overs. Total (4 wkts) 205

Did not bat: D. Johns, G. Dunstan, †D. Rashleigh, P. Thomas, B. Moyle.
Fall of wickets: 1–7, 2–31, 3–42, 4–57.
Bowling: Samways 9–1–28–3; Bristow 9–0–46–1; Witney 2–0–21–0; Baker 2–0–20–0; Goldthorpe 5–0–31–0; Floyd 3–0–34–0; Eggleton 2.2–0–20–0.

Troon won by six wickets.

Astwood Bank v. Kimbolton

Kimbolton, put into bat, never got going on a pitch which enabled Joe Crumpton and Frank Morrall to make the ball lift nastily at times on a rapidly drying pitch. Graham Beeby and Bob Folds batted bravely, but only two others managed to reach double figures. *Astwood Bank's* later bowlers benefited from the hostility of the opening attack so much that Colin Robinson, for instance, returned the remarkable figures of 9-3-8-3. Left to score 86 for victory with conditions improving, *Astwood Bank's* batsmen always looked more convincing than *Kimbolton's* and an unfinished fourth-wicket stand of 42 by Brian Spittle and Mike Wedgbury, who batted an hour for his four runs, carried the club into the semi-finals.

Astwood Bank's fast pitch came as a surprise to the *Kimbolton* men, whose turf on their home ground defiantly refuses to be speeded up. *Kimbolton's* ground, set in The Park next door to the Kimbolton School playing fields not far from the castle which houses the school, is one of the most attractive of the many picturesque grounds where matches have been played during the Haig competition. The club, formed well back in the nineteenth century, pay one shilling a year – five new pence these days – as rent to the Duke of Manchester.

That must be about the best bobsworth in Britain. You have to visit the ground to appreciate the handsome poplars guarding the pavilion and the fine Wellingtonian firs on the other side of the ground. The whole area is so well wooded that you can hear the thinnest of edges from the boundary. Claude Banks, the chairman, says: 'It's so quiet and peaceful here that everyone remarks on it – it's a wonderful atmosphere to play the game in.'

Kimbolton entered the Haig 'just because it was something different. We thought we could do reasonably well given a little bit of luck.' They have every reason to consider that reaching the quarter-finals is doing more than reasonably well.

Kimbolton have another reason to be particularly proud. The Park ground, with its £700 pavilion extension built last winter, and its bigger bar put in during the spring, was chosen by Huntingdonshire as the venue for their match with Leicestershire 2nd XI.

The village's 900 inhabitants support their heroes loyally.

The club respond by setting aside a corner of the ground as a play area for the children who come along to matches with their parents.

One man in the side who knows more than most about all aspects of the game is all-rounder Bernie Facer. Not only has he appeared for the county, he works at a cricket bat factory at St Neot's!

KIMBOLTON

G. Beeby, c Bird, b Morrall	21
R. Hart, b Morrall	1
T. Newman, c Wedgbury, b Morrall	11
R. Folds, c Spittle, b Yoxall	19
B. Facer, c Davies, b Yoxall	5
R. Stevenson, c Wedgbury, b C. Robinson	2
*J. Hart, c Spittle, b C. Robinson	5
†D. Quirke, b Spittle	1
D. Presland, b C. Robinson	11
J. Walker, not out	4
P. Bance, c Wedgbury, b Spittle	1
Extras (B 1, w 2, nb 1)	4
31.4 overs. Total	85

Fall of wickets: 1–1, 2–34, 3–35, 4–58, 5–61, 6–63, 7–76, 8–70, 9–82.

30–0; C. Robinson 9–3–8–3; Yoxall 2–1–3–2; Spittle 2.4–1–11–2.

ASTWOOD BANK

*.J Yoxall, c Presland, b Facer	10
J. Robinson, b Facer	9
R. Davies, c Folds, b Stevenson	19
B. Spittle, not out	42
M. Wedgbury, not out	4
Extras (B 1, nb 1)	2
28.1 overs. Total (3 wkts)	86

Did not bat: J. Poole, C. Robinson, J. Crumpton, J. Bird, †R. Nash, F. Morrall.
Fall of wickets: 1–18, 2–30, 3–44.
Bowling: Presland 6–1–29–0; Bance 3–0–10–0; Facer 9–3–18–2; Stevenson 9–2–25–1; Hart 1–0–5–0; Newman 0.1–0–2–0.
Astwood Bank won by seven wickets.

The Semi-Finals

Collingham v. Astwood Bank

When *Astwood Bank,* chasing 135 to win this semi-final, lost four wickets for no runs – three of them to Andrew Slater – after an opening stand of 40, *Collingham* thought they had a trip to Lord's in the bag. An unbroken stand of 97 by Mike Wedgbury and Colin Robinson changed all that to put *Astwood Bank* in the final and all Nottinghamshire in mourning.

Collingham's members and helpers had worked so hard to get their charming ground looking its best that it seemed they had even polished every blade of grass. Spectators began arriving before midday, two hours before the match was due to start and by two o'clock the ground was alive with the sound of hunting horns and bells from the rival fans. Hundreds of cars were parked round the pitch and latecomers almost seemed faced with the prospect of standing on somebody else's shoulders to get a view of the game.

John Yoxall, the *Astwood Bank* captain, called correctly when *Collingham's* Gordon Croft tossed and, not for the first time in the competition, asked his opponents to bat first. It was shrewd thinking. Both sides were over-tense, so Yoxall reckoned that by fielding first they might well snatch a wicket or two cheaply before the *Collingham* batsmen settled down. He could not have expected, though, that Trevor Woodcock and Roger Slater would get themselves in such a tangle as Woodcock played the first ball of the game into the covers, that Slater would be run out!

The running between wickets improved for a while as Woodcock and Neville Thompson set about rebuilding *Collingham's* confidence. Woodcock defended firmly while Thompson began opening out and the score had reached 37 before Colin Robinson came on to remove Woodcock, plus the next two batsmen while 15 were being added. Thompson, however, continued unflustered and in Dennis Poucher found a partner ready to join in some exciting run-stealing. Thompson reached a splendid half-century in the 21st over but lost Poucher at 81 and departed himself six runs later, leaving Peel and Courtney to join in a bright eighth-wicket stand that carried the total towards respectability. Yoxall then stepped in and in sixteen deliveries ended the *Collingham* innings, taking three wickets for two runs.

The Notts men had more shocks coming to them, for Yoxall and John Robinson, the *Astwood Bank* openers, took 20 runs off the first five overs; then, after a breather, Robinson cut loose with three fours in an over off Williams. There followed Slater's three cheap wickets plus the running out of Yoxall and incredibly *Collingham* were not only back in the game, they clearly had the advantage.

Colin Robinson and Wedgbury, however, were not to be panicked and carried the score to 95 with sensible batting before, in the 29th over, Wedgbury was dropped. That was *Collingham's* last chance, for the pair hit off the remaining runs in six more overs. Robinson's winning hit was the signal for a mass invasion of the pitch.

That demonstration must have disturbed Harry Woodcock, who has cared for the ground since 1945 when he succeeded his father. Harry's son, Trevor, the *Collingham* No. 1, lends a hand, particularly with the maintenance of the mechanical equipment – and Trevor's nine-year-old son has been spotted driving the motor roller.

'Says Harry: 'With 80 games a season I'm kept pretty busy but this ground's a pleasure to work on. We get a reasonably low rainfall and what there is soon dries because the soil's very sandy.' Harry has twenty-four strips to look after in all, sixteen on the square and eight outside: not bad for a retired furnaceman of 65.

The Woodcocks' loving work over the years has brought

Collingham an annual two-day Notts 2nd XI fixture besides a regular meeting between the Notts and Lincolnshire Colts sides.

The pavilion was built in 1902 for £120. The new £2,500 clubhouse was opened in 1971 by Gary Sobers. The cost would have been considerably greater had not the club members and supporters done much of the work themselves. The clubhouse features a kitchen, a bar – which with so many games a season does brisk business – and a large clubroom.

Collingham, formed about 1880, field two Saturday teams, three Sunday sides and run a mid-week Colts XI. The senior sides take part in the newly-formed South Lincs and Border League and in the Notts Alliance besides entering local charity cup competitions and the Newark six-a-sides, in which they have been twice winners and twice runners-up.

An unusual contribution to the first eleven's success in the Haig has been that seven left-handed batsmen have appeared for them during the summer, including the first four in the order. The club has 70-odd playing members but it is not true that left-handed applicants for membership have preference!

COLLINGHAM

G. T. Woodcock, c Davies, b C. Robinson	9
R. Slater, run out	0
N. Thompson, lbw b Morrall	53
C. A. Watson, b C. Robinson	1
J. Kirkham, c C. Robinson, b Crumpton	1
D. Poucher, b C. Robinson	18
H. Peel, lbw b Spittle	18
†B. Courtney, b Yoxall	17
*G. E. Croft, not out	8
A. Slater, b Yoxall	1
G. Williams, b Yoxall	0
Extras (B 3, lb 3, nb 2)	8
34.4 overs. Total	134

Fall of wickets: 1–0, 2–37, 3–43, 4–52, 5–81, 6–87, 7–123, 8–132, 9–134.
Bowling: Morrall 9–1–33–1; Crumpton 9–0–42–1; C. Robinson 9–1–31–3; Spittle 5–0–18–1; Yoxall 2.4–1–2–3.

ASTWOOD BANK

*J. Yoxall, run out	17
J. Robinson, c Watson, b A. Slater	21
B. Smith, b A. Slater	0
B. Spittle, c Poucher, b Slater	0
M. Wedgbury, not out	40
C. Robinson, not out	43
Extras (B 6, lb 9, nb 1)	16
34.4 overs. Total (4 wkts)	137

Fall of wickets: 1–40, 2–40, 3–40, 4–40.
Did not bat: R. Davies, J. Poole, J. Crumpton, R. Morrall, †R. Nash.
Bowling: A. Slater 9–1–27–3; Williams 9–1–40–0; Thompson 8–1–14–0; Croft 8.4–0–40–0.
Astwood Bank won by six wickets.

Troon v. Linton Park

Troon gained a surprisingly easy victory by nine wickets in this high-scoring semi-final. Yet *Linton Park* got away to a splendid start after being sent in to bat. Paul Bowles and Andrew Moss put on 55, one of the highest opening stands recorded in the later stages of the competition, and everything looked set fair for the Kent side. John Ames, son of Leslie Ames, helped Bowles add 33 before the second wicket fell and 37 more came with eight wickets still standing. The packed Cornish crowd began to have their doubts but *Linton Park* suddenly lost three wickets for three runs. One of the casualties was John Thirkell, *Linton Park's* captain. The collapse had the ground in an uproar, but Cliff

Anscombe found good support from Alan Cooper and they carried the total to 162. With the overs running out *Linton Park* sacrificed wickets attempting quick runs, ending at 167 for nine.

Once *Linton Park's* third wicket had fallen *Troon* excelled themselves in the field and David Rashleigh kept wicket to his usual high standard. Full of confidence now, *Troon* went all out for victory. They lost Tommy Edwards at 25, but *Linton Park* had no other success. John Spry, the *Troon* No. 1, and Brian Carter collected the remaining runs without being parted, although they had the occasional near squeak. *Linton Park's* attack kept hard at it until the end, yet they seemed helpless to break the stand of 146 – one of the highest partnerships recorded in the Haig.

John Thirkell, the *Linton Park* captain – he has led them for 23 years – was beginning to think that at last he would be able to play at Lord's. His family have been associated with *Linton Park* cricket for at least 100 years and the only one so far to appear at Lord's was his uncle, Alan Peach, who was a Surrey regular in the Twenties. Yet just when the 16-stone skipper's big hitting would have been most welcome for his side, Thirkell was 'leg before' for a duck. Bad luck, indeed.

LINTON PARK

P. Bowles, b Johns	48
A. Moss, b Thomas	25
J. Ames, st Rashleigh, b Johns	22
†C. Anscombe, b Dunstan	45
*J. Thirkell, lbw b Dunstan	0
M. Iliffe, b Dunstan	1
A. Cooper, not out	19
G. Mountford, b Dunstan	0
N. Thirkell, b Johns	2
R. Hickman, lbw b Johns	0
Extras (B 1, lb 3, nb 1)	5
40 overs. Total (9 wkts)	167

The Collingham team which played Astwood Bank in the semi-finals of the Haig. Seated, third from the left, is their captain Gordon Croft

The former Australian test batsman Ian Redpath makes the presentation to John Yoxall, captain of victorious Astwood Bank after their semi-final match with Collingham

A happy crowd at Collingham see a smart catch 'behind', in the semi-final between Collingham and Astwood Bank

The Kent champions Linton Park who were beaten by Cornwall's Troon in the Haig semi-final

Grandstand village style, at the semi-final played on Troon's ground against Linton Park – and very snug too!

Linton Park's captain, J. Thirkell, signs autographs for young enthusiasts during the semi-final

Troon's J. Spry chaired from the field after scoring 88 not out in his teams great nine wicket victory over Linton Park in the semi-final. With his partner B. Carter (74 n.o.) he took part in an unbroken stand of 146

Did not bat: T. Gauna.
Fall of wickets: 1–55, 2–88, 3–125, 4–126, 5–128, 6–162, 7–162, 8–167, 9–167.
Bowling: Dunstan 9–0–43–4; Johns 9–0–42–4; Thomas 9–1–24–1; Edwards 9–0–32–0; B. Carter 2–0–9–0; Moyle 2–0–12–0.

TROON

J. Spry, not out	88
T. Edwards, c and b Mountford	6
B. Carter, not out	74
Extras (Lb 3)	3
35.2 overs. Total (1 wkt)	171

Did not bat: T. Carter, J. Vincent, D. Rashleigh, P. Johns, B. Moyle, K. Lean, G. Dunstan, F. Thomas.
Bowling: Mountford 8–0–39–1; Cooper 8–2–35–0; Gauna 7–0–27–0; Hickman 7–0–38–0; Bowles 5–0–25–0; J. Thirkell 2–0–4–0.

Troon won by nine wickets.

CHAPTER SEVEN

The Lord's Taverners, and the Village Clubs

It was entirely fitting that The Lord's Taverners should have been invited to participate at the Haig final and once again to raise funds for the National Playing Fields Association – and through the N.P.F.A. to make further funds available as grants or loans to clubs for ground or amenities improvements.

Indeed, many of the clubs which took part in the Haig had received N.P.F.A. assistance in the past and the clubs' indebtedness to the Taverners is freely acknowledged – and can never be too often repeated. With the existing links between Taverners and the village clubs, there will be, I hope, future opportunities for even closer liaison between them. How pleasant it would be, for instance, for one of the Taverners' 1973 matches to be staged against a selected XI from the Haig sides of the previous season.

Ian Carmichael, although closely committed to his successful television series as the amiable Bertie Wooster and the ascetic sleuth Lord Peter Wimsey, crowned his term as chairman of the Taverners by being able proudly to announce in March 1972 that the Taverners' contributions to the N.P.F.A. – and thus to grass roots cricket – had passed the £250,000 mark.

Ian, himself no mean cricketer – he is 'in the book' with 5–27 against Egham – has recorded some of the Taverners' highlights and history. From here the stage belongs to him:

THE LORD'S TAVERNERS, AND THE VILLAGE CLUBS

'Given' – if I remember rightly, is how Euclid's Theorems always used to start. So—

GIVEN:
1. What you gain on the roundabouts, you lose on the swings.
2. Television is frequently blamed for the things that have changed for the worse in our society.

TO PROVE:
Both (1) and (2) above have a relevance to the Lord's Taverners. How? I will tell you.

I am an actor, and my mind travels back to those wonderful carefree days of comparative unemployment in the years after the war. (The LAST war, of course. I was once interviewed by a ten-year-old schoolboy for his school magazine. I got to the part of my life story when I said – 'Well, after the war, I was demobbed from the army—' and he said, 'Excuse me sir, which war was that?') To continue – yes, those wonderful carefree days of comparative unemployment. There was only one television station. Dear old Auntie B.B.C., with two small studios at Alexandra Palace. They only did about one play a week (twice) – one performance 'live' on the Sunday, and a repeat ditto on the Thursday. There was no such thing as a tele-recording in those days. This resulted in a lot of actors having time on their hands during the daytime hours. What did we do? Where did we go? I will tell you, dear reader, we went to Lord's.

For the princely sum of two shillings (for a county match), you could sit in the sun for seven hours and watch star players from all over the world playing the game of cricket. Those summers always seemed to be so full of sunshine. What else, when you had Compton and Edrich at the wicket for the majority of the season?

The Tavern was the great vantage point. There, you could quaff your ale, stand or sit for no extra charge beyond the two bob entrance fee to the ground, and in addition rub shoulders with other actors, and swap hop-vine chat about what new plays were being cast, who was casting them, and all the information requisite to finding future employment.

It was a grand coterie. If you were miserable, lonely, depressed, or if you had just landed a plum role and wanted to shout about it, you always knew (in those days) that you would find a mate to talk to outside The Tavern at Lord's.

I remember very vividly watching a game round about lunchtime on one Saturday, and amongst our group on that occasion was a very celebrated actor (though not then as celebrated as he is today) who was a member of The Old Vic Company. He was appearing in Othello, alternating the title role and that of Iago, with another actor – turn and turn about. On this particular morning we had all downed a considerable number of pints, and my turn had come round again. 'Same again?' I enquired to all concerned. I then said to this actor – 'Shall I skip you this time?' 'Certainly not,' he replied, 'Why?' 'You've got a matinée haven't you?' I said. 'Yes,' said Richard Burton, 'But it's only Iago this afternoon.' The Welsh have great constitutions.

Sadly, as the years rolled by, an irritating distraction came into being. Commercial Television! This, plus a second channel given to the B.B.C., put another ten stations on the air overnight. More and more employment was created for the poor actor/cricket-lover. Oh, happy wife! Oh, happy children! Oh, miserable father, who had to put down his pint pot, and go off and spend the glorious sunshine hours in dingy rehearsal rooms and artificially lit TV studios.

From that unfortunate day, our numbers outside The Tavern started to dwindle. Each season took a heavier toll. Not only plays and the like, but commercial advertisements now entered the arena. Fewer and fewer of our precious band had the time, the heart (or the courage) to continue living that gorgeous, irresponsible life of O'Reilly. Within a few years it was gone for ever.

So, as you can see:
1. What you gain on the roundabouts, you do lose on the swings; and
2. Television is (correctly in my view) frequently blamed for many things that have changed for the worse in our society, Q.E.D.

All, however, was not lost. Late in 1949, an enterprising actor by the name of Martin Boddey, an habitué of The Tavern, decided that a club, association, fellowship, call it what you like, should be formed to perpetuate this happy band of 'rogues and vagabonds'. It was to be called The Lord's Taverners. Its membership would be restricted to men connected with any of the Arts who loved cricket, and first-class cricketers with a similar affection for the Arts. Its object would be to raise money to be put back into the game that had given them all so much pleasure.

At this point let Martin Boddey, our Founder Member, take up the story.

Royal Twelfth Man

'Prince Philip, Duke of Edinburgh, is a man who likes to know what is going on – and why. It was, therefore, not surprising that, one day in the summer of 1950, I was told that His Royal Highness had heard rumours about some sort of lark to raise funds for The National Playing Fields Association, and would I please go along and tell him what it was all about.

'In fact, at this time the most there was to tell was of the hopes and ambition. It was true that we had already held our inaugural meeting – in the upstairs bar of the Comedy Theatre in London (a bronze plaque now marks the spot!). About twenty keen types attended, and we now boasted a Chairman and an Honorary Treasurer (I was both) and two Honorary Secretaries. Some minutes of this meeting had been taken, but were not yet written out. I did, however, have a list of exactly fifty-one names of prospective members, written on the back of a Watney's menu-card, and this rather bizarre document was then the only written evidence that The Lord's Taverners existed.

'I duly presented myself at Clarence House, Captain Jack Broome R.N., who was the moving spirit of this meeting, met me at the door, and together we went in to see Michael Parker. Meeting Mike Parker is always an occasion for laughter, and very soon, in an atmosphere of great good humour, we went along to the drawing-room on the south-west corner of the building. The air of good humour went with us, and soon I was sitting at ease in a comfortable chair telling His Royal Highness all about the aspirations of The Lord's Taverners.

'Prince Philip is the best listener I have ever met. He asks a question because he really wants to know the answer. And when you are giving the answer you have his undivided attention. This is a rare and courteous quality, which makes every conversation with him direct, enjoyable and uncomplicated.

'When I had finished my tale, His Royal Highness said that he thought it sounded like a spendid idea. He then went on to ask a number of pertinent questions. He was asking them, I felt, not only to assure himself that the idea was as splendid as it had at first seemed, but also to see if I had done my "prep". It appeared that I had.

' "And how many members have you got already?" I was asked. I said that there were exactly fifty-one, and proceeded proudly to name some of the more famous enthusiasts. To refresh my memory, I took my precious Watney's menu-card (with the little red barrel on it) from my pocket. Prince Philip reached out his hand. I gave the card to him with a muttered apology. Well, I mean, it did look a bit out of place in that drawing-room. But his Royal Highness handled it with the air of a connoisseur. Having studied the bill-of-fare with which the landlord of the *Gloucester Arms* daily teased the palates of his customers, he turned to the scribbled list on the back. "What are the question marks against some of the names?" he asked. "They are not question-marks, sir; that is my way of writing a 'p' and it stands for paid." "Do you really mean to say that some of them have already given you money?" "Oh yes, indeed, sir ... er, for subscriptions of course. It doesn't amount to much – as yet. But I've opened a banking account. I'm the Honorary Treasurer, you see, sir." "Ah, I see." He referred again to the menu-card ... "Then that means that Basil Radford and Naunton Wayne haven't paid yet." I agreed that this was so. "Well then – you tell them to pay up or else, will you." I promised to see that the command was delivered promptly to the proper quarter.

'A short while later, each of us with a little something in a glass held in the alert position, Prince Philip said "Well now, Boddey, what would you like me to do?" Just like that. Direct and unexpected. I mean, I knew that he was interested because of The National Playing Fields, and I also hoped that our intentions to try to help them would receive his approbation and his encouragement to carry on. But, until that very moment, it had never occurred to me that he might offer to *do* something to help *us*. It was the most exciting compliment to us, and I was fearful that I might make a mess of it. For I was completely taken aback. I stammered a bit, and then suggested that, perhaps, His Royal Highness might consent to be our President. His reply was typical – "No, Boddey, I can't do that," he said; "you see, if I were your President I should be expected, indeed I should wish, to attend your meetings, and I really haven't the time." I had to agree that this would be asking a bit too much. Before I could say any more Prince Philip went on "But I'll tell you what I will do; I'll be your Patron if you like."

'If we liked! If we liked! It is a wonder that the little red barrel in my pocket didn't burst. On looking back, I can only hope that I was sufficiently in control and well mannered to say "thank you" properly. I'm sure it must have been a near go.

'As I was doing my best to review these matters calmly I caught Jackie Broome's eye. It is a good, blue, mariner's eye, and conveys much, and it suddenly reminded me of a conversation which we had had some weeks before.

'Jackie had said that he thought we ought not have the usual titles for our officers, like "President" and that sort of thing, but something distinctive like "square leg" or "third man" – something of that sort. I had thought that any distinguished personage might not be exactly flattered and overjoyed to be invited to be our "square leg". As for "third man", I had appeared in the film with that title a year or so before, and the name still reeked a bit of dope-peddling and German spies and all that. On the other hand – "twelfth man" had a certain ring to it, and perhaps a certain reason ... and, all of a moment, I was telling Prince Philip all about it. I explained that we were all to be given membership numbers for life, which we would display on the backs of our ties, and would it be impertinent to invite

Astwood Bank, finalists at Lord's in the splendid match against Troon. Their skipper, John Yoxall, is seated centre. This picture was taken at Collingham during the semi-final

Before the title was theirs Troon posed for this 'historic' photograph against the backdrop of cricket's 'headquarters'

Terry Carter hooks Morrall in his 79 not out, an innings which brought him Troon's Man of the Match award in the final at Lord's

John Yoxall, the Astwood Bank captain, off-drives for 4 in the final. He made an attractive 36

Troon triumphant! Terry Carter, hoisted shoulder high by his team, displays the Haig Trophy to happy Cornish supporters

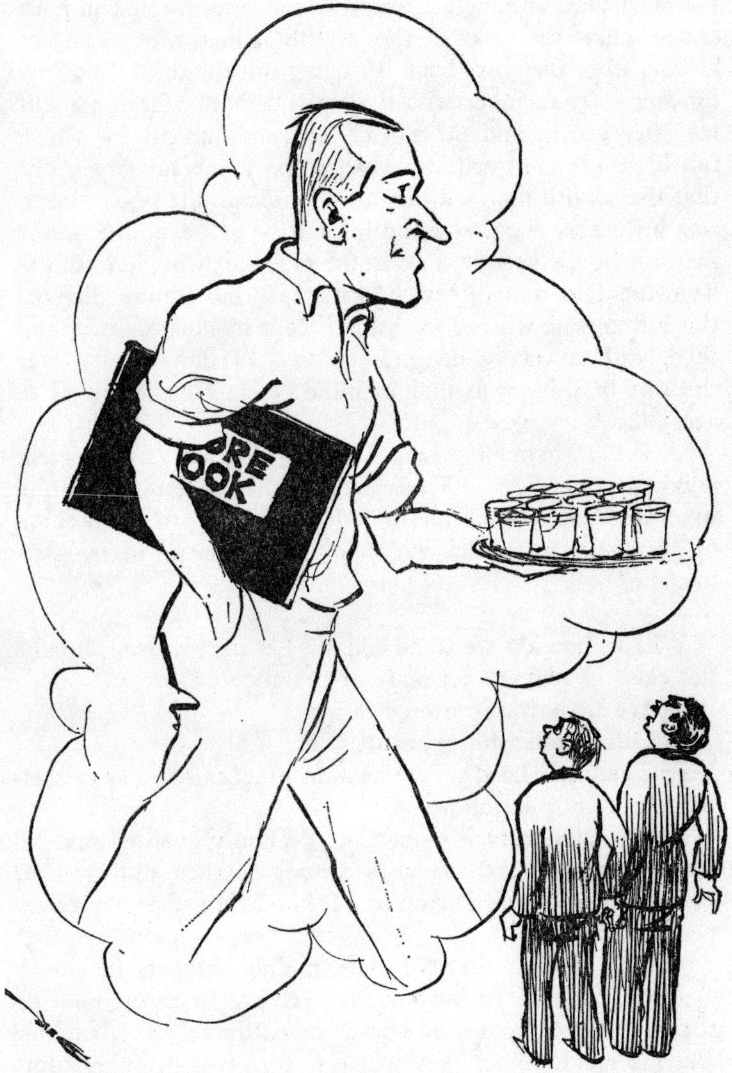

him to accept the position of our "twelfth man". It was an unusual request, to be sure, and Prince Philip savoured the idea for a moment. Then he asked, "Why the twelfth man?" I replied that, although it was reasonable to say that in most cricket clubs the tasks of the twelfth man consist mostly of looking after the score-book, bringing out the drinks, fielding for any older member who suddenly finds that he has a stiff leg after lunch, and other such accomplishments for which full Blues are not awarded, nevertheless it was my experience that the twelfth man, although by no means the finest player, was invariably the best informed on the game, and certainly he must be the keenest man in the club – or why, indeed, did he consent to remain "twelfth-man". Prince Philip digested this rather long-winded exposition for a moment or two, and then, with a very wide grin, he said "I thought that was the sort of thing you had in mind. I shall be delighted to accept".

'And thus, in one morning, Prince Philip not only did great honour to The Lord's Taverners, but he conferred a dignity upon all humble cricketers by adding a lustre to the position of "twelfth-man" which we hope will endure for many years to come.'

WELL, how do we stand today? Let me give you, briefly, the close of play at the start of the 1972 season.
1. We are now a registered charity.
2. Our membership numbers 580.
3. There are Lord's Taverners in practically every cricket-playing country in the world.
4. Our Honorary Membership (jealously guarded and infrequently awarded) includes amongst other distinguished persons, three Royal Dukes, one Prime Minister and three ex-prime ministers.
5. The revenue that we raise, mainly through an annual Ball at Grosvenor House and the twelve or so cricket matches that we play every season, goes in its entirety to The National Playing Fields Association, which in turn ploughs it back into the game of cricket. By the beginning of this season we had raised a grand total of £250,000 for our beneficiary.
6. This year saw the start of a knock-out competition for

THE LORD'S TAVERNERS, AND THE VILLAGE CLUBS

under thirteen-year-olds in four of the home counties. It was organised by the N.C.A. and sponsored by The Lord's Taverners. It is hoped that in subsequent seasons it will grow larger until it becomes a national competition.

Now, alas, the old Tavern, our spiritual home, is no longer standing. It was demolished in 1966 to make way for a new stand. On the last night of its existence ten Taverners (not a full XI regrettably) turned out as mourners to sink the last few pints to be drawn from its bar taps. The last round of all was purchased by Lord's Taverner No. 80, Mr Billy Griffith, the Secretary of M.C.C.

Our Patron and Twelfth Man once said that we, The Lord's Taverners, are 'unique in our aims', and the Rt. Hon.

Edward Heath referred to us as 'An Estate of The Realm'. We are proud of that, and quite immodestly believe it to be true. Cricket lovers everywhere may rest assured, that as long as there are Lord's Taverners, there will always be someone working to raise money to help the under-privileged and financially deprived Clubs that require assistance to enable them to play the game that we all love so much.

CHAPTER EIGHT
Results of County Group Matches

Note: in a few cases it has not proved possible to obtain match results and scores. The author very much regrets these omissions which, however, were beyond his control.

Group 1 – Scotland

FIRST ROUND: Rossie Priory 138–9 (M. Cormack 34), Luncarty 64 (I. McKenzie 3–13); Glendelvine – Bye; Stratheden – Bye; Craithie – Bye; Dunlop – Bye; Falkland – Bye; Yetholm – Bye; Crosshill 50 (A. Cameron 15, C. Scott 4–7), St Boswell's 51–8 (G. Smith 15); Freuchie 164, Fochabers 27; Meigle – Bye; Elton – Bye; Kintore – Bye; Lennox – Bye.

SECOND ROUND: St Boswell's 142–7 (G. Smith 45, P. Glover 33), Freuchie 141 (J. Christie 40, Glover 3–14); Kintore 189–5 (S. C. Martin 90), Lennox 128–8 (Martin 2–19); Meigle 77–3, Kintore 76; Dunlop 74, Falkland 48.

SEMI-FINALS: Meigle 45–3, St Boswell's 44; Glendelvine 144–7, Dunlop 36 (W. Reid 5–9).

FINAL: Meigle 108–4 (B. Reid 38 n.o.), Glendelvine 102.

Group 2 – Northumberland, Cumberland, Westmoreland and Durham

FIRST ROUND: Warenford – Bye; Belford 74, Kirkley 75; Newbrough 147 (R. Robson 3–17), Mitford 77; Medomsley 88 (S. Lancaster 46), Haydon Bridge 74 (Lancaster 2–7);

205

Felton 95 (P. Hall 25; J. Richardson 3-12), Stocksfield 116 (K. Fairness 36, W. Pile 3-12); Wylan 163-7, Wooler 48; Bomarsund 133-9, Blagdon Park 135; Belsay 72 (C. Shepherd 23), Scotby 77 (A. Ridley 17, J. B. Robson 6-7); Allendale 85-8 (A. White 27), Clara Vale 81; Cowpen Bewley 167 (K. Johnson 47), Coxhoe 225; Tudhoe 50, Wolviston 31; Burneside 88-6, Holme 87-9; Cleator beat Edenhall and Langworthy (no score supplied); Lanercost 194 (M. Richardson 91, G. Richardson 45, D. Lancaster 4-11), Lowther 57 (M. Hope 4-12); Plumbland – Bye.

SECOND ROUND: Warenford 57-5 (I. Patterson 25 n.o.), Kirkley 56; Medomsley 117-8 (Richardson 31), Newborough 116 (S. Lancaster 3-8); Wylam 141 (E. Whitfield 40), Stocksfield 24 (R. Helm 3-2); Blagdon Park 107-8, Scotby 106; Coxhoe 145-6 (S. Spinks 42 n.o.), Allendale 43-9 (S. Spinks 3-8); Burneside 121-9 (G. Scott 47), Tudhoe 100 (D. Scott 5-13); Lanercost 47-0, Plumbland 46-7.

THIRD ROUND: Warenford 82-6, Medomsley 80; Blagdon Park 201-5, Wylam 200-8; Burneside 123-8, Coxhoe 122; Lanercost walked over Cleator.
SEMI-FINALS: Warenford 178-6 (A. Patterson 88 n.o.), Blagdon Park 173; Burneside 202-8, Lanercost 136.
FINAL: Warenford 60-6, Burneside 59 (T. Thompson 5-20).

Group 3 – Yorkshire II

FIRST ROUND: Mountain – Bye; Upper Hopton 93 (B. Hart 4-23, K. Ramsden 3-26), Scholes 95-0 (E. H. Matthews 45 n.o.); Oakworth beat Totley Sports (no scores supplied); Whiteley – Bye; Harthill 58, Clayton West 189-9; Booth 134 (R. E. Oayes 4-19), Barkisland 135-6 (H. Whiteley 50); Great Preston – Bye; Thorpe Hesley 83 (I. Hardy 5-30), Wheldrake 86-6 (E. Gibson 52 n.o.); Bradfield beat Wortley Old; Lascelles Hall – Bye; Bradshaw 94, Everton 98-3; Colton beat Fishlake; East Bierley – Bye; Cookridge 49, Cawthorne 50-2; Cumberworth United – Bye; Tong – Bye.

SECOND ROUND: Scholes 107-5 (M. Roberts 41 n.o.), Mountain 106 (F. Mitchell 31); Oakworth 53-8, Whitley Hall 51 (R. Harris 5-13); Barkisland 119-3, Clayton West 118; Bradfield 86-6, Lascelles Hall 85 (J. Gott 3-9); Colton 199-4, Everton

RESULTS OF COUNTY GROUP MATCHES

162; Cawthorne beat East Bierley (202) on toss of coin in rain-wrecked game; Tong 260-8 (H. Cummings 76), Cumberworth United 107 (A. Pickersgill 4-22); Great Preston beat Wheldrake (no score supplied).

THIRD ROUND: Scholes beat Barkisland (no score supplied); Bradfield 67-1, Colton 66; Tong 99-3, Cawthorne 97; Great Preston beat Whitley Hall (no score supplied).

SEMI-FINALS: Great Preston 147-9, Scholes 105; Tong w.o. Bradfield (scratched).

FINAL: Tong 174, Great Preston 123.

Group 4 – Yorkshire I

FIRST ROUND: New Earswick 86 (M. Readman 4-15), Cloughton 87-5 (Readman 28); Aketon 173, Hawes 52; Folkton & Flixton beat Aldwick-on-Dearne (no score supplied); Sessay – Bye; Skelton Castle 83, Thorpe Arch & Boston Spa 84-6; Drax – Bye; Horbury Bridge 104, Bolton Abbey 105-8; Londesborough Park – Bye; Spofforth 176-7 beat Nostell St Oswalds (no score supplied); Glasshouses – Bye; Stamford Bridge beat Canwood (no score supplied); Little Ribston – Bye; Burnt Yates 62, Bubwith 64; Burton Leonard – Bye; Altofts 123-5 (B. Newby 39), Carlton 120-7 (W. Greatorex 3-16); Bradley 117-8; (G. Fryers 41, S. Ladle 2-7); Scarcroft 116 (Fryers 4-28).

SECOND ROUND: Cloghton 123-9, Aketon 122; Folkton & Flixton 166 (Stewart 64) Sessay 112 (Eldridge 4-7); Drax 101, Thorpe Arch 82-9; Londesborough Park 47-4, Bolton Abbey 44 (A. Thirsk 6-0); Spofforth 182 (D. Jackson 86), Glasshouses 116; Stamford Bridge 142-9, Little Ribston 141; Bubwith 143-4, Burton Leonard 140-8; Altofts 187 (D. Leek 58), Bradley 102 (Greatorex 3-16).

THIRD ROUND: Folkton & Flixton 68-4, Cloghton 66; Londesborough Park 169-5, Drax 86; Stamford Bridge beat Spofforth (no score supplied); Altofts 183-3, Bubwith 74 (P. Hayes 4-25).

SEMI-FINALS : Altofts bt Stamford Bridge; Folkton & Flixton 148–5, Londesborough Park (Baker 8–13).

FINAL : Folkton & Flixton 119 (Blackbarrow 43), Altofts 88 (Sellars 3–3).

Group 5 – Lancashire

FIRST ROUND : Bretherton 69 (H. Cox 4–13), Cherry Tree 72–3 (G. Eddleston 32 n.o.); Shireshead 27, Heyside 28–2; Lindal Moor 76–2 (E. Shuttleworth 37 n.o.), Caton 73–6; Moore & Daresbury 48, Salesbury 125–4; White Coppice – Bye; Thornham 150 (R. Peace 5–44), Alvanley 255–3 (K. Hinkley 144 n.o.); Warton 55, Newburgh 253–3; Ince Blundell 83 (L. Harrison 28, P. Whitehead 2–3), Delph & Dobcross 103–9; Croston 130–9 (N. Singleton 38), Brooks Bottom 117 (D. Alty 3–18, Singleton 3–27); Cartmel 104–4 (M. Davies 68 n.o.), Upper Mill 103 (D. Aires 4–24); Read 77–4 (J. Harwood 41 n.o.), Wrea Green 71 (J. Waddington 4–3); Winwik 67, Mawdesley 164–6 (K. Burton 62); Greenmount 174–9, Withnell Fold 153; Hoghton – Bye; Walshaw beat Arnside (G. Dearden 7–12).

SECOND ROUND : Cartmel 140–7 (M. Davies 39), Croston 122 (D. Birch 6–20); Heyside 214–5, Cherry Treee 98–4; Lindal Moor 77–3, Salesbury 75 (G. Greenwood 32, T. Gifford 5–21); Alvanley 174 (P. Griffiths 79), White Coppice 117 (W. Smethurst 46); Read 170–6, Pendle Forest 169–5; Greenmount 134–4, Mawdesley 131; Hoghton 68–2, Walshaw 66; Delph & Dobcross 96–2 (M. Richardson 60), Newburgh 94 (F. Bimpson 46, Richardson 4–27).

THIRD ROUND : Lindal Moor beat Heyside (toss of coin); Delph & Dobcross 33–1, Alvanley 31; Read 261–9, Cartmel 142; Hoghton 60–9, Greenmount 59.

SEMI-FINALS : Lindal Moor 91–2, (E. Shuttleworth 41), Delph & Dobcross 87; Read 95–5, Hoghton 91.

FINAL : Lindal Moor 125–5, Read 123–9 (Shuttleworth 3–13).

RESULTS OF COUNTY GROUP MATCHES

Group 6 – Cheshire and North Wales

FIRST ROUND: Marchwiel 112–7, Northop Hall 116–9 (H. Lloyd 34 n.o., S. Barrett 2–19); Hawarden Park – Bye; Bersham 89, Menai Bridge 195–6; Overton 86–5 (R. Williams 44 n.o.), Audlem 82 (I. Woollem 5–24); Charlesworth & Chisworth 187–8 (H. Hayes 64, P. Robinson 4–13), Oulton Park 63–4 (Charlesworth won on run-rate in 25 overs); Styal 134–8 (A Downes 40, A. Woodward 3–8), Woore 132 (J. Bailey 37); Rosherne 98 (D. Rushton 4–14), Pott Shrigley 101–5 (D. Brook 31 n.o.); Davenham 57–4, Arley 42; Buxworth 84 (D. Brown 3–11), Compstall 86–2; Mere – Bye; Chelford 65, Rushton Taveners 81; Toft 146 (P. Rafto 50, B. Manning 47, M. Gore 3–33), Oakmere 57 (A. Parker 3–4); Cholmondley 158–2, Ashton Hayes 157–4; Mellor – Bye; Bromborough Pool – Bye.

SECOND ROUND: Northop Hall 48–4, Hawarden Park 47; Overton 49–2 (M. Lawrence 32 n.o.), Menai Bridge 48 (M. Lawrenson 5–16); Charlesworth 198–7, Styal 72; Pott Shrigley 118–8, Davenham 80–8; Compstall 66–2, Mere 65; Toft 128–6, Rushton Taverners 126; Cholmondeley 121–8, Elworth 110 (A. Pennell 54); Mellor 80–9, Bromborough Pool 67.

THIRD ROUND: Northop Hall 164–9, Overton 155–9; Charlesworth 169–8, Pott Shrigley 87; Compstall 78–1, Toft 77; Cholmondeley 95–1, Mellor 89.

SEMI-FINAL: Compstall 198–6 (F. Wilson 84), Cholmondeley 99; Northop Hall 204–4, Charlesworth 160.

FINAL: Northop Hall 106–6, Compstall 105–8.

Group 7 – Derbyshire

FIRST ROUND: Clifton 92, Hilton 88–9 (B. Barley 2–17); Breadsall – Bye; Little Eaton – Bye; Netherseale St Peter's – Bye; Stanton-in-Peak – Bye; Holmsfield – Bye; Youlgrave – Bye; Openwoodgate – Bye; Risley – Bye; Sutton-on-the-Hill – Bye; Hathersage – Bye; Stainsby – Bye; Shipley Hall 176 (D. Stott 115), Lullington Park 74; Stanton-by-Dale – Bye; Kirk Langley 68–9, Dove Holes 32; Willington – Bye.

SECOND ROUND: Clifton 147–6, Breadsall 69 (S. Bryan 5–17); Netherseale 142–9 (L. Waring 59), Little Easton 65; Openwoodgate 68–2, Risley 64; Sutton 129–5 (J. Henderson 87 n.o.), Hathersage 123 (A. Barber 48); Shipley Hall 68–6, Stainsby 67; Kirk Langley 154–8, Stanton 86.

THIRD ROUND: Clifton 156–9, Netherseale St Peter's 79; Holmesfield beat Willington (toss of coin); Openwoodgate 39–5, Sutton 37; Shipley Hall 59–4, Kirk Langley 55.

SEMI-FINAL: Holmesfield 61–1, Clifton 60 (Guest 4–1); Shipley Hall 78–9, Openwoodgate 58.

FINAL: Holmesfield 139–9, Shipley Hall 111.

Group 8 – Nottinghamshire and Lincolnshire

FIRST ROUND: Messingham 191–7 (H. Birtwhistle 64, G. Hudson 3–45), Blyth 194–2 (B. Ginever 119 n.o.); Leverton – Bye; North Wheatley beat Alkborough (no score supplied); Welby – Bye; Farnsfield 122 (J. Franks 39, H. Ford 4–19), Gotham 125–7 (B. Head-Rapson 37 n.o.); Misson – Bye; Thoresby Park w.o. Castle Bytham; Collingham 65–3 (C. A. Watson 34 n.o.), Fiskerton 63 (B. Tomlinson 35, N. Thompson 4–3); Thrumpton – Bye; Thurgarton – Bye; Cuckney beat Clifton (no score supplied); Plumtree – Bye; Gedling 93 (D. G. Smith 51), Car Colston 60–8 (D. Wright 3–2, B. Harrison 3–25); East Bridgford 58–0, Kinoulton 57; Whatton & Aslockton – Bye; Fardon 70 (D. Storey 6–12), Firbeck 73–6.

SECOND ROUND: Blyth 106 (D. Wells 5–18); Leverton 82 (A. Samble 58); North Wheatley 197–4, Welby 95; Gotham 157–6, Misson 42; Collingham 140–8, Thoresby Park 135; Thrumpton 173–7; Thurgarton 170–8; Cuckney 123, Plumtree 100; East Bridgford 123–2 (M. Blagg 70 n.o.), Gedling 122–9; Whatton & Aslockton 89–6, Firbeck 88.

THIRD ROUND: Blyth 152–9, North Wheatley 64; Collingham 87–2, Gotham 86; Cuckney 81–3, Thrumpton 77; East Bridgford 70–4, Whatton & Aslockton 69.

SEMI-FINAL: Cuckney 148–7, East Bridgford 101; Collingham 98–7, Blyth 97.

RESULTS OF COUNTY GROUP MATCHES

FINAL : Collingham 98-9, Cuckney 97.

Group 9 – Shropshire and Staffordshire

FIRST ROUND : Ellesmere 181-3 (T. Wood 77, R. Bayling 52), Wroxeter & Uppington 131 (B. Roberts 4-26); Shawbury 47 (D. Gallagher 5-15, D. Raine 4-22), Fenns Bank & Iscoyd 195 (W. Griffiths 69, D. Gallagher 61); Quatt 116-7, Worfield 158-8; Alveley 83, Forton 87-7; St George's – Bye; Gnosall 62 (J. Lewis 30, B. Howe 4-17, K. Jones 3-9), King's Bromley 168 (M. Bell 40, M. Marsden 5-36); Lycett – Bye; Milford Hall 204-3 (D. J. Roberts 67 n.o., P. Allcock 58), Onneley 86 (M. Biggin 4-13); Rhode Park & Lawton – Bye; Hammerwich 66 (L. Bradbury 3-3), Enville 112 (J. Hards 31); Alrewas – Bye; Woodville beat Sandyford (no score supplied); Walton – Bye; Abbots Bromley beat Knypersley (no score supplied); Warslow 24, Old Netherseal Colliery 84 (B. Finch 32); Swynnerton Park beat Branston (no score supplied).

SECOND ROUND : Fenns Bank 135-9, Ellesmere 64; Worfield 145-2 (M. Seedhouse 40), Forton 74-8; St George's 52-1, King's Bromley 51-6; Milford Hall 112-2 (D. Roberts 55 n.o.), Lycett 109; Enville 61-4, Rhode Park 60; Alrewas 168-5, Woodville 101; Swynnerton Park 114-6 (R. Young 27), Netherseal 111 (C. B. Ellis 4-26).

THIRD ROUND : Fenns Bank 136-9, Worfield 126; St George's 168, Milford Hall 115-9; Enville 58-1, Alrewas 57; Swynnerton Park 192-8, Abbots Bromley 109-7.

SEMI-FINALS : Fenns Bank 169-8, St George's 153; Swynnerton Park 99-0, Enville 97-5.

FINAL : Swynnerton Park 91-3 (A. Giles 40 n.o.), Fenns Bank 87 (C. Ellis 5-23).

Group 10 – Leicestershire, Rutland and Lincolnshire

FIRST ROUND : Empingham 131-6, Ketton 130; Braunton – Bye; Great Ponton beat Buckminster (on toss of coin); Fulbeck – Bye; Ancaster – Bye; Walton-Le-Wolds 70-9, The Langtons 71-6; Medbourne 39 (A. Baker 3-4), Kirby Bellars

144–9 (A. Baker 50 n.o.); Billesdon – bye; Great Glen – Bye; Scraptoft – Bye; Newton Lindford – Bye; Queniborough – Bye; East Carlton – Bye; Hallaton – Bye; Sharnford – Bye; Hathern Old – Bye.

SECOND ROUND: Empingham 64–2, Braunton 63–7 (M. Pell 3–18) Fulbeck 67–2, Great Ponton 64–8; Ancaster 85–6, The Langtons 82; Billesdon 25–0, Kirby Bellars 24; Great Glen 40–2, Scraptoft 39; Newtown Linford 142–4, Queniborough 80 (S. Collington 3–6, M. Baskill 3–34); Hathern Old 162–9, Sharnford 81 (C. Burford 39, N. Bayly 3–10).

THIRD ROUND: Empingham 68–9, Fulbeck 66 (D. Want 5–24); Ancaster 165–8, Billesdon 135; Newton Linford beat Great Glen (no score supplied); Hathern Old 102, East Carlton 54.

SEMI-FINAL: Empingham 76–5, Ancaster 74 (Want 4–10); Newton Linford beat Hathern Old.

FINAL: Empingham 64–2 (D. Want 31 n.o.), Newton Linford 62.

Group 11 – Worcestershire

FIRST ROUND: Himbleton beat Birlingham (toss of coin); Hewell – Bye; Ombersley – Bye; Alveshurch lost to Sheppey; Hallow – Bye; Avoncroft – Bye; Belbroughton – Bye; Stoke Works 181–4 (W. Harrison 76 n.o.), Chaddesley Corbett 161–8 (A. Gould 58); Bredon – Bye; The Lenches beat Knighton-on-Teme (no score supplied); Oldswinford – Bye; Bringsty – Bye; Flyford Flavel – Bye; Willersley – Bye; Offenham 163–5 (M. Bell 50 n.o.), Cutnall Green 56 (P. Cresswell 3–9); Spetchley – Bye.

SECOND ROUND: Ombersley w.o. Sheppey; Avoncroft 18–0 Hallow 16 (G. Banner 3–9); Stoke Works 88, Belbroughton 66; The Lenches 139, Bredon 98; Offenham 100 (O. Wilson 35, D. Dance 6–28), Spetchley 20 (M. Gregory 4–3); Oldswinford beat Bringsty by default.

THIRD ROUND: Ombersley 102, Himbleton 98; Avoncroft 73–6,

RESULTS OF COUNTY GROUP MATCHES

Stoke Works 72; The Lenches 163-8, Oldswinford 155; Willersley 64-6, Offenham 63.

SEMI-FINAL: Avoncroft 154-7, Ombersley 125; Willersley (S. Lennox 107 n.o.) 203-8, The Lenches 200-8.

FINAL: Avoncroft beat Willersley (no score supplied).

Group 12 – Warwickshire

FIRST ROUND: Flecknoe 56 (G. Eathorne 7-20), Hockley Heath 112-9 (T. Wright 58 n.o.); Leek Wooton – Bye; Willoughby – Bye; Wishaw 113, Hampton-in-Arden 68 (T. Taylor 3-5, R. McDermott 3-9); Tanworth-in-Arden – Bye; Wolston 52-1, Great Alne 49; Farnbrough – Bye; Newbold-on-Avon beat Dunchurch (no score supplied); Nether Whitacre – Bye; Astwood Bank 43-1, (J. Poole 24 n.o.), Earlswood 42 (B. J. Spittle 5-13, C. Robinson 4-6); Claverdon – Bye; Catherine de Barnes beat Shipston-on-Stow (no score supplied); Offchurch beat Shilton; Rowington 94-8 (Higgerson 4-25), Berkswell 93 (Marlow 31); Dunton Bassett 92-2, Norton Lindsey & Wolverton 90; Fillongley 240-8, Bearley 37-9.

SECOND ROUND: Hockley Heath 155-9, Leek Wootton 74; Wishaw 168-8, (M. Trigger 47), Willoughby 103); Tanworth-in-Arden 106-7, Wolston 80-8; Newbold-on-Avon 126 (G. Fox 57), Farnborough 21 (T. Andrews 6-8); Astwood Bank 48-2, Nether Whitacre 47-7; Catherine de Barnes 60, Claverdon 34; Rowington 57-2, Offchurch 56 (G. Varney 4-15); Dunton Bassett beat Fillongley (no score supplied).

THIRD ROUND: Hockley Heath 102, Wishaw 65-4 (on faster scoring rate); Tanworth 139, Newbold 105; Astwood Bank 68-3, Catherine de Barnes 67-9; Rowington 88, Dunton Bassett 55-6.

SEMI-FINALS: Astwoood Bank 110-7, Rowington 51; Hockley Heath 148-7, Tanworth 102.

FINAL: Astwood Bank 209-7 (J. Yoxall 138 n.o.), Hockley Heath 136-5 (G. White 52 n.o., C. Robinson 4-9).

Group 13 – Northamptonshire

FIRST ROUND : Boddinton beat Castle Ashby 79 (D. Baldwin 35); Hinton-in-the-Hedges – Bye; Overstone Park – Bye; Thorpe beat Pytchley (no score supplied); Boughton – Bye; Billing – Bye; Charlton – Bye; Syresham 76, Rushton 80; Wesbury – Bye; Cogenhoe – Bye; Farthinghoe – Bye; Bugbrooke – Bye; Horton House beat Turweston (no score supplied); Little Harrowden 147–7, Titchmarsh 25 (D. Tapp 6–9).

SECOND ROUND : Boddington 57–3, Hinton 52; Overstone Park 80–6 (H. Moore 22 n.o., Thomas 3–26), Thorpe 78 (B. Freeman 5–27); Charlton 24–0, Guilsborough 23; Rushton 80, Syresham 76 (J. Neil 19); Westbury 127–5, Cogenhoe 126–7; Bugbrooke 11–0, Farthinghoe 10 (T. Fitzhugh 7–4); Horton House 88–7, Little Harrowden 87–6; Billing 88–5 (J. Malfait 36 n.o.), Boughton 66–2.

THIRD ROUND : Overstone Park 55–3, Boddington 54; Charlton (36–5) beat Billing (74) by toss of the coin after 14 overs; Rushton 109–7, Westbury 108; Horton House beat Bugbrooke (no score supplied).

SEMI-FINALS : Overstone Park 70–2, Charlton 69; Horton House 144–6, Rushton 105–5 (Spokes 3–33).

FINAL : Horton House 182 (J. Nutter 88), Overstone Park 132–6.

Group 14 – Cambridgeshire and Huntingdon

FIRST ROUND : Kimbolton beat Earith (no score supplied); Offord – Bye; Alconbury Weston 30, Houghton & Wyton 31; Fenstanton – Bye; Broughton – Bye; Stapleford beat Little Thetford; Abington 19, Fordham 20–1; Weston Colville 85, Bettisham 55; Isleham beat Little Shelford; Over – Bye; Sutton – Bye; Quy 124, Swaffham Bulbeck 132–8; Hoddenham w.o. Wilburton; Milton 45 (R. Arnold 7–14), Terrington St Clements 103 (R. Arnold 33); March St Mary's 82, Whittlesford 84–2; Horseheath 209–3, Barrington 133.

RESULTS OF COUNTY GROUP MATCHES

SECOND ROUND: Fenstanton 97-3 (S. Daniels 4-25), Houghton & Wyton 96; Stapleford 53-6, Broughton 52; Fordham 98, Weston Colville 60; Over 129-8, (M. Walker 27 n.o.), Isleham 101 (Walker 3-32); Swaffham Bulbeck 155-8 (P. Raby 82), Sutton 90; Terrington St Clement's 12-2, Haddenham 11 (R. Arnold 8-5); Whittlesford 92-4, Horseheath 90 (B. Polter 30, B. Gelder 3-9).

THIRD ROUND: Kimbolton beat Fenstanton (no score supplied); Fordham 149-8, Stapleford 144-9; Over 178-9, Swaffham Bulbeck 160-8; Terrington St Clement's w.o. Whittlesford.

SEMI-FINAL: Terrington St Clements 47-1, Over 46; Kimbolton 164, Fordham 63.

FINAL: Kimbolton 203-5 (G. Beeby 111 n.o.), Terrington St Clements 162-9.

Group 15 – Norfolk and Suffolk

FIRST ROUND: Yoxford 51, Burrough Green 170-5; Haughley 88, Southwold 120; Wetherden 112-6 (P. Carr 58 n.o.), Helions Bumpstead 109-9 (D. Lambert 3-10); Benhall beat Tattingstone (on toss of coin); Thorepness 90, Woolpit 118-8; East Bergholt 79, Coddenham 23; Bures & District beat Sutton (no score supplied); Bealings beat Nacton (no score supplied); Holkham – Bye; Swannington 39, Bradfield 203-5; Frettenham – Bye; Hales & District 66 (P. Baigent 5-16), Martham 78 (G. Nicholls 25); Mundford – Bye; South Walsham 124-7, Loddon 123 (P. Barton 34 n.o., R. Burdett 3-23); East Harling beat Harleston (no score supplied); Great Witchingham 42 (Bobbin 9-15), Mulbarton 43-1.

SECOND ROUND: Benhall 41-3, Wetherden 40 (A. Pinney 8-20); East Bergholt 81-6 (R. Smith 48), Woolpit 80 (G. Potter 4-3); Bures 57-6, Bealings 51; Bradfield 203-6 (C. Bidewell 87 n.o.), Holkham 60; Martham 187-8 (T. Dowe 80), Frettenham 60 (J. Whale 3-6); Mundiford 69-1, South Walsham 68 (T. Veal 5-12, G. Davies 3-13); East Harling 92-4, Mulbarton & Swardeston 90 (J. Bobbin 46, P. Rudd 6-14).

THIRD ROUND: Burrough Green 237-7, Benhall 100; East Bergholt 97-5, Bures 93; Bradfield 164-8, Martham 149; Mundford 66, East Harling 48.

SEMI-FINALS: Burrough Green 128, East Bergholt 64; Bradfield 119-4, Mundford 118.

FINAL: Bradfield beat Burrough Green.

Group 16 – Hereford and South Wales

FIRST ROUND: Crickhowell 109-6 (J. Devoy 60, S. Fisher 3-22) Tonmawr 108-7 (B. Davies 54); Whitland beat Builth Wells; Dafen Welfare – Bye; Hopkinstown – Bye; Llangwyn – Bye; Wicke District 12 (Capon 6-6, Griffiths 4-3), Rosemarket 15-0; Laugharne 34-4, Glansrwyney & Llangenny 29; Nantymoel 89-7 (D. Culliford 33), Presteigne 88 (M. Morgan 26, T. Amos 25); Newton – Bye; Bedwelty – Bye; Canon Frome & District – Bye; Kingsland – Bye; Bromyard 223, (A. Mills 109, R. Richardson 6-27), Kington 226-6 (R. Richardson 71); Hoarwithy 52, Brockhamton 65.

SECOND ROUND: Crickhowell 99-8, Whitland 96-9; Gowerton 123-6, Dafen Welfare 100; Nantymoel beat Pontyberem (toss of a coin); Newton 74-1, Bedwelty 38-9; Canon Frome 127-4 (B. Goode 42 n.o.), Kingsland 126 (J. Turner 51, B. Casselle 5-26); Kington 105-4, Brockhampton 104 (V. Hope 46, R. Richardson 3-25).

THIRD ROUND: Gowerton 131-8, Crickhowell 86-5 (on scoring rate); Llangwym 68-5, Rosemarket 64-7; Newton 75-8, Nantymoel 61; Kington 83-3, Canon Frome 80.

SEMI-FINALS: Gowerton 142-5, Llangwym 64 (W. Thomas 7-29); Kington 88-3, Newton 86-8.

FINAL: Gowerton 221 (R. Evans 80, J. Richards 65), Kington 149 (M. Gronin 63).

RESULTS OF COUNTY GROUP MATCHES

Group 17 – Gloucestershire

FIRST ROUND: Woodpeckers 98, Dowdeswell & Foxcote 149 (D. Parrott 44, T. Boore 4–28); Barnsley Beeches – Bye; Chalford 197–9 (G. Mayo 38 n.o., A. Bluett 3–29), Lechlade 235–3 (G. Cox 95 n.o., J. Deacon 81); South Cerney w.o. Poulton; South Hill 77 (J. Houghton 27, Redwood 5–29), Upton St Leonard's 43 (Leach 23, Houghton 4–9); Tormanton 107–7 (L. Walker 42), Woodchester 103 (R. Abbott 4–23); Andoversford Sports 42–3, Chedworth 41–9; Pilning – Bye; Speech House beat Daglingworth (no score supplied); Redmarley – Bye; Bibury beat Frampton-on-Severn (no score supplied); Cranham beat Down Hatherley (no score supplied); Whitcombe 119–6 (K. Putticj 53 n.o.), Slaughters United 59 (A. Fuller 5–11); Charfield v Hambrook (no score supplied); Stanway – Bye; Frocester 113, Dumbleton 58.

SECOND ROUND: Dowdeswell 105–5, Barnsley Beeches 37–9; Tormanton 138–6 (P. Hall 50), South Hill 78; Pilning 127, Andoversford 45; Speech House 37–3, Redmarley 36 (T. Jayne 5–2); Bibury 88–6, Cranham 87; Frocester 200–5 (G. Hudd 96 n.o.) Stanway 95 (F. Clifford 5–23); Lechlade 171–7 (J. Deacon 51), South Cerney 95 (R. May 5–14).

THIRD ROUND: Dowdeswell 123–8, Lechlade 122–9; Pilning 159–8, Tormanton 135; Speech House 130 (T. Day 5–10), Bibury 101; Frocester 109, Whitcombe 86.

SEMI-FINALS: Dowdeswell 57–2, Pilning 56; Frocester 118, Speech House 95.

FINAL: Dowdeswell & Foxcote 139–9, Frocester 134–8.

Group 18 – Oxfordshire

FIRST ROUND: Bledlow – Bye; Fingest 130, Garsington 56; Bletchington beat Warston St Lawrence; Combe 82 (C. Vere-Nicholl 4–16), Hambleden 85 (A. Wilson 23); Greys Green 91–7 (N. W. Dennis 29), North Leight 88 (B. Buckinham 20, I. Hutton-Penman 3–17); Shipton-under-Wychwood beat Warborough & Shillingford; Horspath beat Windrush Valley (no score supplied); Great & Little Tew 207–9 (G. J. Celland

82), Forest Hill 99 (R. Taylor 5-18); Great Milton beat Tetsworth; Wytham beat The Bladons (no score supplied); Burford beat Chearsley (no score supplied), Charlbury 99, Ardley 51; Ewelme 132 (D. Blakeley 37), Wolvercote 47-9; (S. Greenaway 5-15); Aston Rowant 304-4 (R. McQueen 77, W. Edward 61, G. Lindon 66 n.o.), Fleur de Lys (Dorchester) 78 (P. Lambourne 5-4); Broughton & North Newington – Bye.

SECOND ROUND: Bledlow 138-5, Fingest 132-7; Hambleden 200-9 (J. Pawson 129 n.o.), Bletchington 101; Greys Green 168-8, Warborough 110 (A. Crawshaw 3-19, A. Gibb 3-17); Great & Little Tew 95, Horspath 70; Wytham 114, Burford 77 (S. Neale 5-28); Ewelme 33-2, Charlbury 32; Aston Rowant 48-1 (P. Lambourne 35 n.o.), Broughton 47 Lambourne 4-10).

THIRD ROUND: Bledlow beat Hambleden (toss of a coin); Great & Little Tew 135, Greys Green 63; Milton-under-Wychwood 54-2, Wytham 53; Aston Rowant 157-5, Ewelme 48.

SEMI-FINALS: Bledlow beat Great & Little Tew (no score supplied); Aston Rowant 177-5, Milton 119

FINAL: Bledlow 127-5, Aston Rowant 126.

Group 19 – Buckinghamshire

FIRST ROUND: Booker beat Hanslope (no score supplied); Kimble – Bye; West Wycombe 63, Monks Risborough 76 (C. B. McQueen 26); Brill Sports – Bye; Maids Moreton 46-4, Hyde Heath 45-8; Knotty Green – Bye; Eversholt 168-8 (J. Inchbold 68, G. Garratt 32), Old Bradwell 141 (D. Bird 40, M. Anstree 3-6); Westcott – Bye; Milton Keynes beat Shabbington (no score supplied); Hughenden Valley – Bye; Great Kingshill – Bye; Lacey Green & Looseley Row – Bye; Stewkley Vicarage – Bye; Winchmore Hill 84, Holmer Green 54 (J. Morris 6-21); Chenies & Latimer – Bye; Apsley Guise – Bye.

SECOND ROUND: Booker 172-9, Kimble 92; Brill 111, Monks Risborough 91; Knotty Green 85-7, Maids Moreton 75-9;

RESULTS OF COUNTY GROUP MATCHES

Eversholt 184-7, Westcott 166-9; Milton Keynes 90-2, Hughenden 89; Great Kingshill 63-9, Lacey Green 62 (M. Nash 5-17); Winchmore Hill 113, Stewkley 98; Apsley Guise 150-7, Chenies & Latimer 107.

THIRD ROUND: Booker beat Brill (no score supplied); Eversholt 192-6, Knotty Green 88; Milton Keynes 161-2, Great Kingshill 157; Winchmore Hill 130, Apsley Guise 65.

SEMI-FINALS: Eversholt 166-4, Booker 137-5; Winchmore Hill 121-9, Milton Keynes 121.

FINAL: Eversholt 105-6, Winchmore Hill 104.

Group 20 – Bedfordshire and Hertfordshire

FIRST ROUND: Dean 29, Roxton 35-2; Silsoe beat Eggington (no score supplied); Bayford & Hertford Nondescripts 91, Cople 148-7; Blunham – Bye; Great Barford 56-3, Southill Park 55; Oakley – Bye; Henlow 65-9, Biddenham Esquires 48-6; Studham 117-7 (B. Austin 35 n.o.) Ickfield Green 108 (J. Ibbitt 25, A. Foskett 3-10); East Hanningfield 75 (D. Neal 5-19), Widford 76-2; Aspenden beat Gaddesden Row (no score supplied); Knebworth Park beat Little Gaddesden (no score supplied);Boreham 72, Datchworth 73-2; Langleybury 166, Audley End 134-9; Whitwell 71 (M. Bailey 26, R. Bennett 3-7), Stansted Hall 122; Howlell 106, High Easter 107-9; Essendon 54, Wilstone 24.

SECOND ROUND: Essendon 89 (K. Venables 49), High Easter 49 (K. Venables 4-11) Langleybury 212-7 (G. Riddick 76), Stansted Hall 92 (B. Davey 3-18); Roxton 84-7 (E. Grimshaw 5-30), Silsoe 83; Aspenden 126-9 (W. Wallace 45, A. Bird 4-18), Widford 89; Blunham 108-1 (P. Ranson 55 n.o.), Cople 107-7 (C. Minney 52); Great Barford 69, Oakley 33 (B. Odell 5-7, T. John 4-4); Studham w.o. Henlow (scr).

THIRD ROUND: Blunham 151-8, Roxton 147; Studham 58-1, Great Barford 57; Aspenden 134, Datchworth 63; Langleybury 249-6 (D. Davey 128), Essendon 70-9 (Davey 4-8).

SEMI-FINALS : Blunham 62-0, Studham 58; Aspenden 180-8, Langleybury 179.

FINAL : Blunham beat Aspenden.

Group 21 – Essex

FIRST ROUND : Blackmore End *v.* Tendring; Tillingham 58, Tendring Park, 49; Weeley *v.* Dedham; Tolleshunt D'Arcy 99, Elmstead Market 100-2; Woodham Mortimer 127, South Weald 131-6; Willingale 78, Rettendon 79-3; Sandon 133, Copford 78; Fyfield 68, Manuden 112; Little Waltham 65-1, High Roding 61 (P. Arnold 23 n.o.); Stock 34-2, Henham 33; Gosfield 41, Roxwell 109; Lindsell 21, Great Bentley 123; Cressing 100 (A. Watson 29), Abberton 102-5; Wormingford 48, Little Bardfield 49-2; Havering beat Abridge (no score supplied); Roydon 65-3, Sampfords 64.

THIRD ROUND : Tillingham 102-6, Elmstead 101; Rettendon 189-8, Sandon 113-9; Little Waltham 37-4, Roxwell 36; Abberton 142-5, Havering 90.

SEMI-FINALS : Tillingham beat Rettendon (no scores supplied); Abberton 96, Little Waltham 88.

FINAL : Abberton beat Tillingham.

Group 22 – Berkshire

FIRST ROUND : Cookham Dean 63-6, Hurst 67-7; White Waltham 86-3, East Garston 46-7; Welford Park – Bye; Ardington & Lockinge 198-5, Blewbury 84; Letcombe Regis – Bye; Buscot Park – Bye; Sonning 102-7 (R. Sheridan 36 n.o.), Littlewick Green 101 (K. Horcutt 21, P. Kay 4-6); Mapledurham – Bye; Pinkneys Green 162 (T. Gough 34, A. Walker 27), Spencers Wood 48 (D. North 5-8); Burghclere – Bye; Braywood – Bye; Kidmore End beat Moreton (no score supplied); Hurley – Bye; Buckland & District 56, Sulhamstead & Upton 92 (K. Dade 28 n.o., R. Hughes 6-13); Sunningwell – Bye; Taplow – Bye.

RESULTS OF COUNTY GROUP MATCHES

SECOND ROUND: Braywood 77-4 (B. Bowditch 30, J. Graveson 3-21), Kidmore End 74 (S. Langley 5-19); Mapledurham 47-7 (N. Bentley 4-6), Sonning 43; Buscot Park 172 (D. Williams 51), Letcombe Regis 78 (B. Talbot 4-21); Welford Park 137-8 (G. Sampson 35), Ardington & Lockinge 57 (D. Uzzell 4-5); Pinkneys Green 92-3 (D. Jinman 44, L. Timms 33); Burghclere 91 (Timms 4-30, W. Miles 3-16); Hurst 110-6, White Waltham 107-5; Taplow 87-7, Sunningwell 33; Sulhamstead & Upton beat Hurley (no scores supplied)

THIRD ROUND: Welford Park 146-8, Hurst 126; Buscot Park 77, Mapledurham 24-3 (on toss of a coin); Braywood 74-8, Pinkneys Green 73; Sulhamstead & Upton 71, Taplow 67.

SEMI-FINALS: Welford 136-9, Buscot Park 65; Braywood 175 Sulhamstead & Upton 121.

FINAL: Welford Park 161-8, Braywood 160-7.

Group 23 – Devon and Cornwall

FIRST ROUND: Troon 119-4 (T. Carter 37), Bosconnoc 115-6 (J. Key 41); Grampound Road 87, Perranarworthal 129-8; Paul – Bye; Werrington 132-9, Roseudgeon & Kennegy 64; Gorran – Bye; Whitestone 96, Stoke Gabriel 108; Halberton beat Bishopsteighnton (no score supplied); Lustleigh beat Kentisbeare (no score supplied); Thorverton – Bye; Wimple & Whiteways 143-4, Stoke-in-Teignhead 141-8; Bradnich – Bye; Filleigh beat Chagford (no score supplied); Chardstock – Bye; Feniton 116, Cornwood 151-9; Clyst St George – Bye; Kilmington – Bye.

SECOND ROUND: Werrington 76-0 (M. Martyn 38 n.o., T. Redman 38 n.o.), Paul 75 (M. Densford 5-11); Gorran 28-2, Stoke Gabriel 26 (R. Bunney 7-17, R. Daniel 3-8); Chardstock 177-6, Cornwood 177 (D. Palmer 87, R. Parris 3-18) by losing fewer wickets in a tied match; Lustleigh 152-9, Halberton 151 (A. Deary 91, D. Germon 4-23); Troon 85-3, Perranaworthal 84-9; Thorverton 105-8, Whimple & Whiteways 35; Filleigh beat Bradnich (no score supplied); Clyst St George 88-6, Kilmington 54-6.

THIRD ROUND : Troon beat Werrington (15 overs only); Gorran 196–6, Lustleigh 50; Thorverton 59–0, Filleigh 57; Chardstock 183, Clyst St George 119.

SEMI-FINALS : Troon beat Gorran (no score supplied); Thorverton 193–6, Chardstock 71.

FINAL : Troon beat Thorverton

Group 24 – Somerset

FIRST ROUND : Evercreech 91, Ruishton 32 (G. Wood 5–15); Whitchurch 47, Bathford 49–4; Wembdon beat Chilton Crickets (no scores supplied); Cranmore 61–3 (T. Barker 32 n.o.), Chew Magna 60 (A. G. Mason 5–9); Dulverton 49 (N. Harding 4–16), Temple Cloud 303–5 (A. Dyer 122 n.o.); Merriott – Bye; Lydford beat Blagdon (no score supplied); Leigh-on-Mendip 83–5, Horsington 77; Wedmore 64–4, North Newton 62–4; Tintinhull beat Ascott & Shapwick (no score supplied); Brent Knoll 40–7, Mells 38 (R. Saviour 4–2); Timsbury 20–1, Buckland St Mary 19; Dinder & Croscombe – Bye; Hinton Charterhouse 28 (B. Keates 6–14), Milverton 29–3; Barrington 80, Butleigh 80–4; Over Stowey 57, Stogumber 47.

SECOND ROUND : Milverton 43–1 (A. Hannaford 36), Dinder & Croscombe 42 (R. Cornish 4–4); Evercreech 59–2 (Jacobs 23 n.o.), Bathford 56 (Mann 26, Percra 4–13, Maher 3–12); Leigh on Mendip 151–4 (F. Tucker 64 n.o.), Lydford 50 (A. Jelly 4–17, F. Stock 4–20); Tintinhull 100 (B. Walsh 35), Wedmore 96 (D. Maidment 6–34, M. Hayne 3–11); Butleigh 40–0, Over Stowey 39 (A. Guyver 8–17); Temple Cloud 264–6 (A. Corner 86, R. Appleyard 49), Merriott 45 (N. Harding 5–9); Timsbury 105 (M. Gregory 30 n.o.), Brent Knoll 51 (G. Parfitt 4–5); Wembledon beat Cranmore (no score supplied).

THIRD ROUND : Evercreech 148–8, Wembledon 61; Temple Cloud 80–9, Leigh-on-Mendip 55; Timsbury 155–8, Tintinhull 118; Milverton 148–8, Butleigh ?.

RESULTS OF COUNTY GROUP MATCHES

SEMI-FINALS: Evercreech beat Temple Cloud (no score supplied); Milverton 89–3, Timsbury 88.

FINAL: Milverton 148, Evercreech 149–4.

Group 25 – Dorset

FIRST ROUND: Byes – Abbotsbury; Shillingstone; Cattistock; Milton Abbas; Marnhull; Stratton; Beaminster; Melplash; St Giles; Compton House; Hinton St Mary; Ashmore; Kingston Lacy; Stalbridge; Whitchampton. Studland beat Thornford (no score supplied).

SECOND ROUND: Witchampton 123–9 (P. Downton 36, P. Moore 5–16), Stalbridge 53; Wimborne St Giles 56–7 (P. Robinson 23), Studland 55 (M. Andrews 3–4); Marnhull 101 (R. Dye 36), Straton 68 (W. Woodrow 4–17); Milton Abbas 94–7 (M. Holiday 41), Cattistock 47–6 (M. Holiday 3–11); Shillingstone 62–7, Abbotsbury 58 (D. Willy 23, D. Crane 6–20); St Giles 56–7, Studland 55; Beaminster 106 (H. Davis 36, R. Wyatt 4–17), Melplash 60; Compton House 131 (E. Young 45), Hinton St Mary 56 (G. Hooper 4–13).

THIRD ROUND: Shillingstone 129–9, Milton Abbas 128–9; Beaminster 78–9, Marnhull 76; St Giles beat Compton House (on toss of coin); Whitchampton 75–2, Kingston Lacy 74.

SEMI-FINALS: St Giles 74–8, Witchampton 73; Shillingstone 100, Beaminster 99.

FINAL: Shillingstone 152–2 (D. Mace 62 n.o.), St Giles 138 (G. Redout 5–22).

Group 26 – Wiltshire

FIRST ROUND: North Bradley 76, Compton Chamberlayne 29. All other 15 teams had first-round byes.

SECOND ROUND: Shrivenham 158–5 (F. Hambridge 62, G. Pratt 59, T. Maslen 5–38), All Cannings 19–9; Seagry 67–9, Biddestone 65 (K. Mitchell 30, D. Stoneham 5–15); Goatacre

92–0 (D. Westrup 58 n.o.), Bishopstone 91 (G. Newman 34, K. Butler 3–7); North Bradley 100 (D. Spong 49, J. Powell 4–15), Great Durnford 57 (B. Cole 6–27); Mere 79 (G. Lush 21, E. Woods 5–19), Beanacre 59 (G. Thomas 3–9); Little Durnford 68–3 (M. Combes 32 n.o.), Corsely 67 (P. Rowlands 33, D. Wilkins 3–9, C. Biddle 3–16); Shrewton 86 (G. Hackett 3–6), Nettleton 59 (G. Hackett 25); Potterne 71–8, Winsley 70 (Sinburn 25 n.o., Woolford 4–22).

THIRD ROUND: Shrivenham 130, Mere 100; North Bradley 118, Goatacre 102; Little Durnford 95, Potterne 41; Seargry won on toss from Shrewton.

SEMI-FINALS: Shrivenham 82–2, North Bradley 81; Little Durnford 62–9, Seagry 59–9 (R. Reeves 4–12).

FINAL: Shrivenham 164, Little Durnford 150–9.

Group 27 – Hampshire

FIRST ROUND: Lindford won on toss from Chute Casuals; Hambledon 33–0 (D. Dunham 23 n.o.), Preshaw & Holt 32 (L. Marchant 6–10); Hursley Park beat Linkenholt (no score supplied); Longparish beat Highclere (no score supplied); Sarisbury Athletic 127–7 (M. Brogan 52 n.o.), Wherwell 125–9 (C. Hitching 60). All other 11 teams had first-round byes.

SECOND ROUND: Compton & Shawford 42–2 (M. Richardson 29 n.o.), Damerham 41 (N. Chalke 3–2); Steep 73–4, East Tisted 72–9; Sarisbury Athletic 75–3 (C. Budden 50 n.o.), Ellingham 73 (B. Rose 5–8); Hambledon 107–3 (R. Miller 45), East Tytherley 106; Bramshaw 143, Lindford 35 (S. Smithson 5–9, Haydon 3–9); Easton & Martyr Worthy 139, Godshill 37; Crown Taverners beat Hursley Park (no score supplied); Longparish beat Worthies (no score supplied).

THIRD ROUND: Steep 174, Bramshaw 117; Hambledon 99–7, Easton & Martyr Worthy 98; Crown Taverners 142–9, Longparish 117; Compton beat Sarisbury (no score supplied).

SEMI-FINALS: Steep 123–7, Hambledon 20 (J. Balstone 4–11, M. Clements 3–2) Crown Taverners 107–7, Compton 105–9.

FINAL: Steep 106–3, Crown Taverners 105–9 (Clements 4–10).

RESULTS OF COUNTY GROUP MATCHES

Group 28 – Surrey

FIRST ROUND: Ockley 154–5, Weston Green 45; Whiteley beat Hambledon (no score supplied); Peper Harrow 26, Brook 89–2; Bisley w.o. Chiddingfold; South Nutfield 78 (D. Wilderspin 34), Shamley Green 235–8; Churt beat Holmbury St Mary (no score supplied); Chaldon 121, Salfords 78. All other 9 teams had first-round byes.

SECOND ROUND: Bisley 121 (C. Renahan 25), Newdigate 68; Churt beat Ockham (scr.); Shamley Green 91 (M. Watkinson 40), Chipstead 66 (M. Glew 6–6); Brook 94–7, Outwood 90–9 (N. Parker 36, A. Hart 3–36); Stoke D'Abernon 91–7, Ockley 88; Blackheath 117–0, Newchapel & Horne 115; Effingham Crickets 87–3, Chaldon 86; Whiteley beat Limpsfield Chart.

THIRD ROUND: Stoke D'Abernon 142–9, Blackheath 93; Brook beat Whiteley (no score supplied); Shamley Green 50, Bisley 47–5; Effingham beat Churt (by default).

SEMI-FINALS: Brook 116–5 (R. Scott 61 n.o.), Stoke D'Abernon 115; Shamley Green beat Effingham (no score supplied).

FINAL: Shamley Green beat Brook.

Group 29 – Sussex I

FIRST ROUND: Eastergate 145–7, Fernhurst 141–6; Anstye 94 (R. Mill 32, K. Mitchell 4–13), Balcombe 95–8 (Mitchell 19); Watersfield 34 (R. Fisher 4–7, R. McCormick 3–1), Barns Green 136–9 (R. Parker 37 n.o.); Clymping 121–5, North Bersted 118–9; Slinfold 112, Findon 114–3. All other 10 teams had first-round byes.

SECOND ROUND: Findon 26–0, Linchmere 25 (R. Walker 6–13); Wisborough Green 110–7 (J. Pegley 39), Scaynes Hill 109–8 (L. Cheeseman 5–24); Lurgashall 113 (F. Thiselton 55, K. Walters 5–24), Barcombe 112 (B. Horsecroft 43, P. King 27, G. Court 5–30, I. Taylor 3–4); Harting 131–6 (D. Daniels 57 n.o.), Warnham 130 (D. Daniels 5–39); Lower Beeding 149 (J. Kirkham 44, D. Read 43), Barns Green 143–4 (R. Nunn 48, R. Fisher 42 n.o.); Rudgwick 110–2 (J. Randel

61 n.o.), Clymping 108–8 (R. Wells 3–24); Rudgwick 189–3 (J. Randel 112, R. Wells 42), Wisborough Green 185–9 (L. Cheesman 62); Eastergate beat Balcombe (no score supplied).

THIRD ROUND: Eastergate beat Lower Beeding (no score supplied); Rudgwick 189–3, Wisborough Green 185–9; Findon 70–2, Lurgashall 66; West Chiltington beat Hartington (no score supplied).

SEMI-FINALS: Eastergate 102, Rudgwick 57 (A. Cockburn 4–17); Findon 57–1, West Chiltington 56.

FINAL: Eastergate 193–7 (Cockburn 68); Findon 39–1 (on toss of coin).

Group 30 – Kent I

FIRST ROUND: Bredgar 71–3, Southfleet 70; Hollingbourne 75, High Halstow 131; Leeds & Broomfield 81–8, Linton Park 88–8; Stoke & District beat Teston (no score supplied); Loose Amenities 80–4 (R. Sharp 29 n.o.), Ash (Dartfod) 78 (R. Merton 5–27); Stansted Invicta 105, Detling 46; Marden beat Hempstead (no score supplied); Wrotham St George's 78–6, Shoreham 75; West Farleigh 169–6 (M. Back 49, C. Clark 34), Falconhurst 72 (J. Underdown 3–7, M. Back 2–8); Betsham 158–9, Cudham 83; Shipbourne 46–6, Borden 45 (J. Wakeman 4–14); Cowden ?, Luddesdown ?; Nurstead 85 (R. Beecham 41, V. Kohler 5–13), Boughton 86–4; Farningham beat Upchurch (no score supplied); Iwade 25, Boughton Monchelsea 73–7; Harvel 105, Offham 149–7.

SECOND ROUND: West Farleigh 214–5 (M. Back 82), Betsham 142 (D. Day 55); Linton Park 141–7 (M. Iliffe 44), Stoke & District 63 (P. Bowles 5–14); Farningham 95–7 (R. Scott 28 n.o., J. Bailey 4–18), Boughton 91 (D. Vincent 3–24); Stansted Invicta 38, Loose Amenities 26 (A. Whatman 6–10, Clarke 3–6); Shipbourne 27–2, Luddesdown 26 (P. Buss 5–3); High Halston 85–9 (D. Lapthorn 33, J. Button 3–18, G. Dutnall 3–21), Bredgar 84 (D. Lapthorn 4–22); Marden 206–4 (J. Sunnulks 61), Wrotham St Georges 83 (D. Neve 4–11).

THIRD ROUND: Linton Park 138–8, High Halston 68; Stansted

RESULTS OF COUNTY GROUP MATCHES

Invicta 63-7, Marden 62-9; Shipbourne beat West Farleigh (no score supplied); Offham 143-4, Farningham 142.

SEMI-FINALS: Linton Park 80-2, Stansted Invicta 78; Shipbourne beat Offham (no score supplied).

FINAL: Linton Park 148-6, Shipbourne 145-8.

Group 31 – Sussex II

FIRST ROUND: Catfield 27-3, Blackboys 30; Burwash Common 52, Withyham 176-9; Poynings beat Stapleford (no score supplied); Chiddingly 154, Hartfield 55; Rotherfield 140-9 (W. Jopson 64), Stonegate 101 (Jopson 3-23); Glynde & Beddingham 164-8, Hurst Green 77; Ditchling 50-5, East Hoathly 49. All other 9 teams had first-round byes.

SECOND ROUND: Bolney 95-6 (T. Acus 3-42), Nutley 93-6 (W. Scott 56 n.o.); Poynings 61-9, Albourne & Sayers Common 60 (C. Hollebon 5-13); Crowhurst Park 107-8, Ditchling 86 (D. Griffith 4-12); Withyham 134-9 (Standing 64, Dixon 3-10), Peasmarsh 64; Rotherfield 171-9 (J. Hilton 56), Warninglid 119 (A. Blackman 4-23); Chiddingly 77-6 (P. Carr 30), Maresfield 76-7 (B. Salvage 3-26); Catsfield 86-7, Hooe 49; Glynde & Beddingham 93-0, Newick 89.

THIRD ROUND: Withyham 71-8, Catsfield 59; Chiddingly 49-6, Poynings 48; Glynde & Beddingham 226-4, Rotherfield 66-3; Bolney 144-9, Crowhurst Park 143-9.

SEMI-FINALS: Glynde & Beddingham 114-7, Bolney 107-9; Withyham 81, Chiddingly 77.

FINAL: Glynde & Beddingham 150, Withyham 110-9.

Group 32 – Kent II

FIRST ROUND: Marfield Green 96 (L. Linin 3-14), Great Chart 145-9 (C. Mercer 57, G. Lee 45); Saltwood 134-7, Ash (Canterbury) 133-8; East Langdon 71, Benenden 75-1; Nonington beat Tilmanstone Ravens (no score supplied);

Selsted – Bye; Langdon Green 48, Horsmonden 52–5; Ashurst 94 (R. Ashby 41, M. Betts 6–16), Castle Hill 180–8 (P. Beale 44 n.o., M. Hammond 6–19); Leigh – Bye; Selling 48, Sissinghurst 52–1; Groombridge 77, Stowting 100–6 (J. Jamieson 47); Bidborough 77–7, Yalding 78–7; Fordcombe 45, Little Chart 47–3; High Halden 26, Biddenden 114–9; Speldhurst – Bye; Sheldwich beat Smarden (no score supplied).

SECOND ROUND: Horsmonden 93–3 (S. Knight 32 n.o.), Castle Hill 92 (Parke 29, Bateup 3–27); Biddenden 91 (B. Watts 27, F. Lillicrap 5–29), Little Chart 73; Benenden 135, Stanford & Sellindge 58; Sheldwich 76–6, Speldhurst 75 (A. Creed 3–10); Saltwood 142–9 (B. Uden 40), Great Chart 110 (D. Plumb 4–9); Nonington 94–9, Selsted 93 (N. Medgett 5–10); Sissinghurst 68–6 (M. Burgess 36), Leigh 67 (D. Knowler 3–8); Yalding 133–8, Stowting 128–7.

THIRD ROUND: Benenden 217–5, Saltwood 169; Horsmonden 107–9, Nonington 105; Sissinghurst 246–3, Yalding 205–8; Sheldwich 74, Biddenden 67–7.

SEMI-FINALS: Horsmonden 99, Benenden 38–3 (Horsmonden won on faster over-rate for 15 overs); Sheldwich beat Sissinghurst on toss of coin.

FINAL: Sheldwich beat Horsmonden.

APPENDIX

The Rules of The Haig National Village Cricket Championship

To organise a national competition comprising nearly 800 village clubs drawn from all parts of the country was never envisaged by the organisers as a simple task in any of its aspects, and one of the more difficult items was the formulation of a set of rules which would be fair and straightforward to all teams involved. Fortunately, once again, club officials were quick and helpful in raising points of possible anomaly.

The Committee, with Aidan Crawley, President-designate of M.C.C. and chairman of the National Cricket Association at its head, and Michael B. Henderson, managing director of John Haig & Co. Ltd., B. G. Brocklehurst, owner of *The Cricketer* and a former captain of Somerset, and J. G. Dunbar, secretary of the N.C.A. and an assistant secretary of M.C.C., as members, got its collective head down and drew up the rules under which the 1972 Haig National Village Cricket Championship would be played. I feel that the results of their deliberations, suitable adapted, could well be of guideline value to other organisations desirous of running knockout championships at local levels. The rules of The Haig are reprinted here in full as they applied in 1972.

1. The Competition shall be called The Haig National Village Cricket Championship.
2. The Competition shall be organised by *The Cricketer*

APPENDIX

in conjunction with the National Cricket Association and John Haig & Company Limited.

3. The object of the Competition shall be to promote the best in village cricket and give an opportunity to village cricketers to compete in a national event.
4. The Competition shall be controlled by a committee consisting of one N.C.A. member, one *Cricketer* member, and one member from John Haig & Co. Ltd. The Chairman of the N.C.A. will preside.
5. Each member of the committee present shall have the right to vote. A quorum shall consist of not less than three persons. There shall be not voting by proxy.
6. All clubs entering must be affiliated to their County Cricket Association, providing one exists.
7. A village shall be deemed a rural community of not more than 2,500 inhabitants.
8. Teams entering will be required to fill in a special subscription form to *The Cricketer* thereby ensuring a continuous means of communication between organisers and competitors.
9. Players shall be eligible to compete for their village under the following conditions:
   (a) If they are a paid-up member of the club and have played an aggregate of eight games in less than three years.
   (b) Players need not live in the village.
   (c) Players will not be eligible if they have ever played first-class cricket, unless they are over 60, nor if they are competing in the National Club Knock-Out during the same year, nor if they receive a fee for playing cricket.
   (d) The Committee reserves the right to decide the eligibility of any team or player.
10. The Laws of Cricket shall apply, plus the following special conditions as laid down by N.C.A. for 1972:
    (a) Each side shall bat for forty overs unless their innings is completed earlier, or unless the captains agree to a lesser number of overs before the start of the match.
    (b) No bowler may bowl more than nine overs. In the

APPENDIX

event of a bowler breaking down and being unable to complete an over, the remaining balls will be bowled by another bowler. Such part of an over will count as a full over only in so far as each bowler's limit is concerned.

(c) The side which scores the more runs shall be the winner.

(d) If scores are level, the side which has lost least wickets shall be the winner.

(e) If still equal, the side which has scored most runs at the end of fifteen overs shall be the winner.

(f) If still equal, the side which has lost least wickets at the end of fifteen overs shall be the winner. If still level, that is to say, both sides having scored equal number of runs and having lost equal number of wickets at the end of fifteen overs, a spin of a coin shall decide.

(g) If rain or bad light curtails play before the completion of the match, the winner shall be the side which has scored more runs per over throughout its innings providing the side batting second has received at least fifteen overs.

(h) If the start of a match is delayed by the weather or there is a subsequent interruption, the captains may agree to a lesser number of overs, the minimum being fifteen.

(i) If the match is abandoned after each side has played fifteen overs, Rule 10(f) applies.

11. Replays:
If rain prevents a decision the match can be replayed on a mutuall agreed date. Captains may, on the other hand, if they agree, decide the result by the spin of a coin.

12. Umpires:
In rounds 1 to 4 teams will arrange their own umpires. In round 5 (the Group Finals) County Association Secretaries will arrange for neutral umpires.
In round 6 onwards the committee will arrange all umpiring appointments.

APPENDIX

13. Scorers:
   Teams will provide their own scorers.
14. Cricket Balls:
   In rounds 1 to 4 teams will provide their own cricket balls. Umpires must agree that the conditions of the cricket balls is similar.
   In round 5 cricket balls will be sent to the organisers of the Group Finals.
   From round 6 onwards cricket balls will be brought by umpires appointed by the committee.
15. Travel:
   Teams are divided into 32 Groups to avoid unnecessary travel in the early rounds. If a village has to travel more than 100 miles there and back in any round they can apply to the organisers for a contribution towards travel expenses after, and within 30 days of, the event.